Teenage Mothers

Decisions and Outcomes

**Isobel Allen and Shirley Bourke Dowling
with Heather Rolfe**

UNIVERSITY OF WESTMINSTER

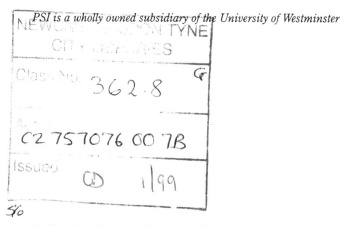

PSI is a wholly owned subsidiary of the University of Westminster

A CIP catalogue of this book is available from the British Library.

ISBN 0 85374 751 2
Report No. 856

Printed in Great Britain

Policy Studies Institute is one of Europe's leading research organisations undertaking studies of economic, industrial and social policy and the workings of political institutions. The Institute is a registered charity and is not associated with any political party, pressure group or commercial interest.

For further information contact
Policy Studies Institute
100 Park Village East, London NW1 3SR
Tel. 0171 468 0468   Fax. 0171 388 0914
Email: pubs@psi.org.uk

Contents

Acknowledgements

This study was one of 17 projects funded by the Economic and Social Research Council (ESRC) in the *Population and Household Change* programme.

We would like to thank the consultant obstetricians and gynae-cologists in the three areas in which we conducted the study for their great help in arranging access to the women who had had first babies when aged 16–19 in their hospitals. Particular thanks are due to Mr Marcus Setchell, Dr Mary Macintosh, Mrs Susan Blunt and Mr Ralph Settatree. We are also grateful to the hospital staff who compiled the appropriate lists and dealt with our enquiries.

The study was designed and directed by Isobel Allen. Shirley Bourke Dowling carried out the analysis of the data and was the co-author of the report. Heather Rolfe was closely involved in the initial stages of the study in questionnaire design, setting up the sampling frame, contacting the respondents and conducting some of the interviews. She also drew together the material for the first chapter of the report. Lynda Clarke acted as a consultant in the early stages of the research and also conducted interviews. Other interviews were carried out by Hilary Gellman, Mary Ruth Haydon, Marion Kumar and Alison Rolfe.

Penny Swann was responsible for the administration of the fieldwork. Karen MacKinnon was responsible for the computing and computer analysis. Mary Ruth Haydon coded and selected material from the questionnaires.

Finally, our greatest debt is to the young women whom we inter-viewed, and to the babies' fathers and grandparents who also took part in the research. We are most grateful for the time they gave us and the interesting accounts they gave of such an important period in their lives.

Chapter 1

Introduction

This study was one of 17 projects funded by the Economic and Social Research Council (ESRC) in the *Population and Household Change* programme which was set up to explore how recent changes in the population structure have affected household and living arrangements. The study was designed to provide an understanding of the processes by which teenage mothers make decisions about their housing, household changes and living arrangements after they decide to continue with their pregnancy, during the latter stages of their pregnancies and after the birth of their babies. The research was based on in-depth interviews with 84 women who had their first babies when aged 16–19. The interviews took place when the babies were just over a year old on average. Twenty-four fathers of the babies and 41 grandparents of the babies were interviewed separately.

The objectives of the study were:

a   to examine the factors surrounding the women's decision to continue with the pregnancy;

b   to identify the women's individual housing careers;

c   to examine the women's reasons for staying put or moving;

d   to explore the women's perceptions of their housing options during pregnancy and after the birth;

e   to explore the women's perceptions of the role and support of the father of the baby, their own parents and others in their decisions about the pregnancy and their housing and living arrangements; and

f   to examine the women's awareness and utilisation of benefits before and during pregnancy and after the birth.

The study was conducted in three areas: Hackney, Leeds and Solihull, which were selected to represent three different types of area, with high, medium and relatively low teenage pregnancy rates (see below for details of numbers of teenage conceptions and conception rates).The sample of women was drawn from hospital records of all women having a first baby when aged 16–19 during specific periods in 1995. The fathers and grandparents were approached through the teenage mothers interviewed. Details of the methods of sampling and approach are given later in this chapter and in the Appendix to this report.

The social and political context

The research was started at a time when there was considerable public discussion about the perception that teenage mothers were becoming a burden on the state by choosing to have a baby while single, living on benefits in local authority housing, and receiving housing priority over married couples with children. Increasing attention was being paid to the costs of supporting lone mothers, whether they were teenagers or not, and the Child Support Agency had been charged from 1993 with the task of requiring lone parents who claim means-tested benefits to identify the father of their children (Marsh, Ford and Finlayson, 1997).

The widely held view of teenage mothers described above is not supported by research,which shows that most young women do not make a positive choice to become pregnant (Bury, 1984; Hudson and Ineichen, 1991). They do not become pregnant in order to receive benefits or in order to receive priority in housing over other families (Hopkinson, 1976; Clark, 1989). In any case, they know very little about housing and benefits before they become pregnant (Clark, 1989). They would not receive housing priority if they did become pregnant (Institute of Housing, 1993) and mothers under 18 are not usually allowed to put their names on local authority housing lists (Burghes and Brown, 1995). Although early motherhood substantially increases the chances that young women's first major tenure is social housing, they usually enter social housing with a partner (Ermisch, 1996).

According to previous research, half of teenage mothers experience a number of different housing arrangements in the first year (Clark and Coleman, 1991; Simms and Smith, 1986). They also have to stay in poor quality accommodation for many months before receiving more appropriate accommodation (Institute of Housing, 1993). Although local authorities are required to house mothers with children who are homeless or fleeing from violence, they do not offer priority to single parents in this respect (Institute of Housing, 1993).

Teenage mothers and household change

Although there is some evidence to suggest that many teenage mothers move during their pregnancy or in the first year after the birth of their babies (Hopkinson, 1976; Clark, 1989), the relationship between pregnancy and moving has not been explored in much detail. Simms and Smith (1986) reported that 45 per cent of the teenage mothers in their sample were still living with their parents 15 months after the birth of their babies. Two-thirds of these were in overcrowded conditions (defined as an average of more than one person per room). Those who had moved were in better accommodation but financially less well off. 38 per cent of their sample had moved once only, 10 per cent had moved twice and 6 per cent had moved three times. The main reasons for young mothers moving include insecurity, overcrowding, lack of privacy and family tension (Clark, 1989; Simms and Smith, 1986). Little has been written about teenage mothers who do not move.

Few studies have examined young mothers' decisions about household change or the factors affecting these decisions. Some research studies have identified patterns of household composition and the support available to young mothers (Hopkinson, 1976; Hudson and Ineichen, 1991; Clark and Coleman, 1991). The options include: living at home with their parents with or without the father of the baby, living with the father of the baby, living with a friend or relative, in mother and baby accommodation or bed and breakfast accommodation, or living alone. The amount of support available from parents, partners, friends, relations and professionals varies widely, often related to the living arrangements of the young women. Family support has been noted as of paramount importance to young mothers leaving the parental home, and Speak et al (1995) found that some mothers in their study spent a considerable amount of time at their parents' home in their first year of independence, using their own homes simply to sleep in.

There has been surprisingly little research on the fathers of babies born to teenage mothers. It is clear that the role of the father of the baby is important both in the decision to continue with the pregnancy and in household formation and change, although there have been indications that it has become relatively less important in recent years with the steady change in attitudes towards single mothers, the increase in the number of births outside marriage and the decline in 'shotgun marriages'. Simms and Smith (1986) explored in some depth the relationships between teenage mothers and their partners. Hudson and Ineichen (1991) noted that any initial enthusiasm about the pregnancy and birth noticeably tailed off with the realisation of the hard work and commitment required by a growing baby. There is a high rate of breakdown in teenage marriages and cohabiting relationships (McRae, 1993).

We were particularly interested in this research in exploring the role of the fathers in the decisions made by the teenage mothers and to examine the processes through which relationships change after a teenage woman becomes pregnant. The implications of the breakdown of relationships for changes in housing and living arrangements, as well as for increasing dependence on benefits, are clearly of vital importance in the debate about the future of welfare.

Methods

The main evidence collected in this study came from interviews conducted in three areas in 1996 with 84 women who had had a baby in 1995 when aged between 16 and 19: Hackney, Leeds and Solihull. We interviewed 27 women in Hackney, 34 in Leeds and 23 in Solihull. Our aim had been to interview 100 women, but we experienced difficulty in achieving sufficient responses within a reasonable time from the available sampling frames in Solihull and Hackney. As we note in the Appendix, it was clear that there was considerable movement after the birth in both areas, but especially in Hackney, so that we were not able to make contact with the numbers we had hoped for.

We also interviewed 24 fathers of the babies: 20 in Leeds, 2 in Hackney and 2 in Solihull. We interviewed 41 grandparents of 39 babies (both maternal grandparents were interviewed in two cases): 8 grandparents in Hackney, 13 in Solihull and 20 in Leeds. Most of the grandparents interviewed were maternal grandmothers (35), but we also interviewed 2 paternal grandmothers in Solihull and 4 maternal grandfathers (one in Hackney, one in Leeds and two in Solihull).

Access to the fathers and the grandparents was achieved through asking the women interviewed whether we could approach them. It will be shown in this report that only half the women were still in a relationship with the father of the baby, and that a relatively high proportion of those who were not had no contact at all with him. In other cases the women were reluctant for us to approach the fathers, while in other cases the fathers were reluctant to be approached, in some instances, we suspected, because of our interest in housing and benefits. Women did not always have close relationships with the grandparents of the baby, and, in addition, not surprisingly, we were unable to interview those who lived some distance away.

We discuss in the Appendix and in Chapters 6 and 7 the reasons for the relative over-representation of both fathers and grandparents in Leeds. The fathers interviewed were mostly married or cohabiting with the women interviewed, which was more common in Leeds than in the other areas. The greater closeness of family ties in Leeds may well have resulted in easier access to grandparents.

The babies were born between March and November 1995 and interviewing took place between June and November 1996 when the babies were on average 13 months old.

The questionnaires were developed drawing on previous work conducted by one of the authors (Allen, 1985) on counselling services for women seeking a termination of pregnancy. Many similar issues arose in the present study, including information on conversations with key people involved in the decisions made by the young women about their pregnancies. We also drew on other studies we have carried out where teenagers were interviewed about sexual health and fertility issues (Allen, 1987; Allen, 1991).

The questionnaires were fully structured, in that the exact wording of each question was specified and the questions were in a predetermined sequence. A fairly high proportion of questions allowed for an open-ended response and the interviewers were expected to record the answers verbatim. The interviews were carried out by a team of experienced interviewers and PSI staff.

Data analysis

The analysis of the type of data generated in a study of this kind is multi-faceted, combining both quantitative and qualitative methods. The questionnaires were analysed with the software package Quantum, using the predetermined codes on the questionnaires, as well as coding frames developed from detailed textual analysis of the open-ended questions. Verbatim quotes were extracted from the questionnaires and selected for inclusion in a rigorous manner in proportion to the numbers making such comments. We aimed to draw on the strengths of both quantitative and qualitative approaches.

The study was essentially qualitative in design, but we considered it important to establish a firm quantitative framework for the analysis. The report draws on the quantitative data to illustrate the wide variety of characteristics and experience of the teenage mothers from the time that they became pregnant to the time of the interview. The extent to which the quantitative data can be regarded as a basis for generalisation to a wider population must be treated with some caution, but it is fair to say that the data are much in line with other recent research and provide a firm basis for the qualitative analysis presented in this report.

Teenage pregnancies in England and Wales

The women in this study gave birth to their babies in the period between March and November 1995 when they were aged between 16 and 19. Their babies were among the 41,900 born to teenage women in that year, which represents only 6.5 per cent of the 648,100 babies born in 1995. The fertility rate (births per thousand women in the age group) of women aged 15–19 in 1995 was 28.5. This was considerably lower than the fertility rate for women of all ages, which in 1995 was 60.4 per thousand. The peak fertility rate is found among women aged 25–29, with a rate of 109 in 1995, more than three times that of teenage women. Women aged 20–24 had a rate of 77 per thousand. Therefore, in comparison with older women, teenage motherhood is less common, and, as Table 1.1 shows, it has become more uncommon both in relative and absolute terms over the last twenty years. In 1975, 63,500 babies were born to teenage women, representing 10.5 per cent of all babies born in that year, compared with 8.5 per cent in 1985 and only 6.5 per cent in 1995, when only 41,900 babies were born to teenage women.

Table 1.1   Births to teenage women and women aged 20–34, 1975–1995 (numbers and percentage of all births)

Age of mother at birth	All ages	Under 20	20–24	25–29	30–34
1975	603,445	63,507	190,198	225,990	88,379
	(100%)	(10.5%)	(31%)	(37%)	(15%)
1985	656,417	56,929	193,955	227,486	126,185
	(100%)	(8.5%)	(29.5%)	(34%)	(19%)
1995	648,100	41,900	130,700	217,400	181,200
	(100%)	(6.5%)	(20%)	(33.5%)	(28%)

Source: Population Trends, England and Wales

However, although both the number and proportion of teenage births has fallen steadily, the teenage fertility rate has fluctuated. Rates among teenage women declined throughout the 1970s, increased during the 1980s, largely as a result of an increase in births among 18 and 19 year olds, and then declined. Consequently, by 1995 the fertility rate among teenage women was similar to that in 1981 (ONS, 1996). Therefore, although the recent trend has been generally downwards, the teenage fertility rate would seem to be subject to short-term variations. In comparison, the fertility rate of women only just out of their teens, aged 20–24, has undergone a more steady decline, while that of women aged over 30 has increased. Nevertheless, England and Wales still have the highest teenage fertility rate in Europe and compare unfavourably with other European countries, where teenage fertility rates have fallen sharply (Babb, 1993). Many European countries have rates less than half those of England and Wales.

The reasons for the fluctuation in teenage birth rates are by no means clear. A recent report based on analysis of data from the National Survey of Sexual Attitudes aims to explain these and other trends in teenage birth (Wellings et al, 1996). The survey found a progressive increase in the proportion of young people who have had sexual intercourse in their teenage years, but that the teenage birth rate has risen more slowly, and has at times fallen. This is explained with reference to the take-up of contraception and also by increasing access to abortion since the passing of the1967 Abortion Act. The report suggests that fluctuations in teenage birth rates since the 1960s reflect the extent and effectiveness of public awareness campaigns on contraception. Other data from the same study draw a strong association between knowledge and information about sexual matters and rate of teenage pregnancy and births.

Other researchers have also drawn attention to the downward trend in teenage birth rates. From their analysis of birth statistics, Burghes and Brown conclude: 'Taken overall, the statistical evidence does not support the popular notion that we are in a period of unprecedented teenage sexual activity and childbearing...' (1995:15)

Conceptions

The fertility rate is a measure of births rather than of pregnancies, which are measured by the conception rate (conceptions per 1,000 women). In 1995 the conception rate for women of all ages was 73.7 per thousand, while for teenage women it was 58.7 (ONS, 1997b). While this does show a clear difference, it is much smaller than the difference in the fertility rate which was 60.4 for all women and 28.5 for teenage women (ONS, 1996). This is because a considerably higher proportion of pregnancies among teenage women are terminated, compared with older women.

Conceptions in the three areas compared with England and Wales

There were 86,000 teenage conceptions in England and Wales in 1995, with a teenage conception rate of 58.7 per thousand women. In Leeds, there were 1,300 teenage conceptions, with a conception rate of 59.0, almost the same as the national average. In East London and City (including Hackney) there were 1,900 teenage conceptions, with a conception rate of 100.5, the highest in the country. In Solihull, there were 300 teenage conceptions, with a conception rate of 48.8, which was relatively low (ONS, 1997b).

Abortions

Official statistics on abortion show a steady increase over the last 20 years. In 1995, 162,400 abortions were performed, compared with 142,900 in 1985 and 106,400 in 1975. Although the total number of abortions increased during the 1970s and 1980s, there has been a decline in the1990s with a slight upturn in 1995. The abortion rate (the number of abortions performed per thousand women) increased in the 1970s and 1980s and, after a peak in the early 1990s, has levelled off to around 12.5. This pattern has been broadly similar for teenage women, although the rate of abortion is higher: for women aged 16–19 it was 22.3 per thousand in 1995, compared with 19.1 for women aged 20–34 and 5.9 for women aged 35–44 and an average of 12.7 for women of all ages. This is a consequence of the higher termination rate for teenage pregnancies: in 1995 over a third of pregnancies to teenagers were terminated, and the rate was very similar in 1994, the year in which many of the women in our study made the decision to continue with their pregnancies.

Table 1.2   **Percentage of conceptions resulting in termination of pregnancy, 1975–1995, all women and women under 20**

	Women of all ages	Women aged under 20
1975	15	26.5
1980	16.5	31
1985	18	34
1990	18	36
1995	20	35

Source: Birth Statistics for England and Wales

As Table 1.2 shows, the proportion of teenage pregnancies which result in termination has changed very little since the 1980s. Table 1.3 shows interesting differences within the teenage age group: the abortion rate among 16 and 17 year olds has changed little since the 1970s, but it has increased dramatically among 18 and 19 year olds.

Table 1.3   **Percentage of conceptions resulting in termination of pregnancy, 1975, 1985 and 1995, women aged 16–19**

	16 years	17 years	18 years	19 years
1975	38	28	21	18
1985	44	35	30	26
1995	39	35	33	30

Source: Birth Statistics for England and Wales

Marriage and teenage motherhood

During the last 20 years there has been a big increase in the proportion of births outside marriage and by 1995 over a third of all births were outside marriage. However, among teenagers the rate of births outside marriage was as high as 86 per cent in 1995 and continued to rise in 1996. As Table 1.4 shows, the increase in births outside marriage has been far more marked among teenagers than among other age groups. In 1975, 68 per cent of births to teenage mothers were within marriage, compared with only 35 per cent in 1985 and only 14 per cent today. The dramatic decline in births to married teenage mothers, from 43,000 in 1975 to only 5,600 in1995, a fall of 87 per cent, is probably the greatest of all the changes in teenage motherhood. Burghes and Brown call this the 'decline of the shotgun marriage' (1995:19).

Table 1.4 **Percentage of births outside marriage 1975–1995, by age of mother**

	All age groups	Under 20	20–24	25–29	30–34
1975	9	32	9	4	5
1985	19	65	25	11	9
1995	34	86	53	27	20

Source: Population Trends

Structure and presentation of the report

We begin the report with a description in Chapter 2 of the main characteristics of the women interviewed and the fathers of the baby as described by the women, in terms of their personal and family circumstances and educational and employment status. We examine the changing relationships between the women and the fathers of the baby over the time from the start of the pregnancy to the time of the interview. The chapter gives an essential framework to the ensuing chapters which present and analyse the views and experience of the women on a variety of issues. Although the study is essentially a qualitative piece of research, we have considered it important to give detailed quantitative data where appropriate in order to put the findings into perspective and to highlight patterns which might be replicated in larger surveys.

In Chapter 3 we examine the ways in which the women made their decisions about whether to continue with their pregnancies and about their housing and living arrangements during pregnancy and after the birth. We look at their perceptions of the support they received in making these decisions from the father of the baby, their parents and other key people. Chapter 4 looks at the characteristics and composition of women's households when they became pregnant and at the time of the interview. We conduct a detailed analysis of the moves they made before and after the birth and their plans for future housing. In Chapter 5 we look at the women's knowledge and use of social security benefits before they became pregnant, during pregnancy and after the birth of their babies.

In Chapter 6 we turn to the fathers we interviewed. They were different from the fathers as a whole in that most of them were co-habiting with or married to the women interviewed. However, they shed interesting perspectives on the decisions made by the women and give an insight into the views of the fathers of babies born to teenage mothers on a number of key issues. Chapter 7 discusses the interviews with the grandparents of the babies, looking at their views on the pregnancy and living arrangements of the women and giving their assessment of how things have worked out. We covered the same topics in interviews with the grandparents, fathers and the women themselves.

In Chapter 8 we examine the perceptions of the women, the fathers and the grandparents on three key issues concerning teenage mothers and housing and benefits. We were interested in establishing to what extent those who had been closely involved in teenage motherhood shared the views of many of those in the media and general public on the motivation of teenage mothers.

Chapter 9 looks in detail at twelve case histories representing the wide variety of teenage mothers whom we interviewed, in terms of their relationship with the father, housing careers, use of benefits and educational and employment history and status. Chapter 10 summarises the report and presents an overall discussion of the findings of the research.

Chapter 2

Characteristics of the Women and the Fathers of the Babies

In this study we set out to investigate the ways in which teenage pregnant women and young mothers made decisions about their housing and household circumstances and whether or not to continue with their pregnancies. We were clear from the start of our research that the teenagers we were interviewing did not represent a homogeneous group of women. We considered it important to present their characteristics at the beginning of the report, in order to show the diversity of background, family structure, achievement and aspirations found among a group of women whose common characteristic was the fact that they had become pregnant as teenagers and had continued with their pregnancies, unlike a substantial proportion of teenagers who become pregnant.

We have observed that many teenage mothers move during pregnancy or in the first year of parenthood (Hopkinson, 1976; Clark, 1989) and that the main reasons for moving identified by previous research have included insecurity, overcrowding, lack of privacy and family tension. But we considered that one of the key factors in determining the extent and nature of moves made by teenagers during pregnancy and after the birth of their babies was their relationship with the father of the baby and its development over this time. Therefore one of the aims of the current study was to investigate the ways in which changing relationships with the father of the baby played a role in decisions about housing and household change.

In addition, we wished to examine the important characteristics of the women which might have had an effect on their decisions to continue with the pregnancy or their decisions about housing and household circumstances, such as their age, ethnic group, country of birth, religion, first language, educational achievements, employment history and housing history. We were interested in their own family structure and whether their mothers had also been teenage mothers.

In this chapter we present the main characteristics of the women and of the fathers of the babies. We examine the changing relationship between the women and the fathers of the babies in detail since this had considerable impact not only on the women's decisions about housing and household composition but also on the extent to which they had come to be dependent on social security benefits by the time we interviewed them.

Much of the information in this chapter is presented in tabular form, mostly using percentages so that comparisons across the three areas, Hackney, Solihull and Leeds, can easily be made. We use numbers in the text and tables where it is more appropriate to do so. We are aware that the bases for the sub-samples in the areas are small, but we felt it useful to present the main characteristics of the women in this way in this chapter. In later chapters we concentrate more on the numbers of women in our tabular presentation.

Table 2.1   Age of women when they had their baby

				column percentages
	Total	Hackney	Solihull	Leeds
16	8	7	13	6
17	24	19	30	24
18	33	26	52	26
19	35	48	4	44
Mean age	*17.9*	*18.2*	*17.5*	*18.0*
Base: all women	*(84)*	*(27)*	*(23)*	*(34)*

Age of women at the birth of their baby

Table 2.1 shows that the average age of the women at the time of the birth of their baby was 17.9 years, with women in Solihull rather younger on average (17.5 years) than those in the other two areas. Just over two-thirds of the women were aged 18 or 19 when their babies were born. One third were 19 (29), one third were 18 (28), a quarter were 17 (20) and 8 per cent were 16 (7). Nearly half of those interviewed in Hackney and Leeds were 19 when their babies were born compared with only one woman in Solihull, where over half the women were aged 18 at the birth.

Marital status and relationship changes

We were particularly interested in looking at the way in which relationships had changed from the time that the women became pregnant to the time of the interview when the majority of babies were more than 12 months old. The mean age of babies when the study was carried out was 13 months, with a broad age range from 4 to 21 months, but most clustering around the mean. The average time between women having first suspected their pregnancy to the time of the interview was 20 months. During this period many relationships experienced considerable pressures which resulted in their breakdown, while other relationships survived and some became more stable.

Many factors influenced the shaping of relationships and their final outcome, not least the different starting points from which couples had embarked on both pregnancy and parenthood. Table 2.2 shows the women's marital status at three different stages: when they became pregnant, at the time of the birth and at the time of the interview. It is important to note that this table merely represents snapshots in the lives of the women but does not give the full picture in that it does not capture changes in relationships between each of the stages. The categories themselves also mask certain complexities. For example, the category 'single' includes women with no relationship as well as those in steady or casual non-cohabiting relationships with the father of the baby and those in non-cohabiting relationships with new partners.

Table 2.2   **Marital status of women when they became pregnant, at the time of birth and at the time of interview**

column percentages

	At time of pregnancy Total	At time of birth Total	At time of interview Total
Single	58	64	50
Married	11	14	18
Cohabiting with baby's father	31	23	27
Cohabiting with new partner	0	0	5
Base: all women	*(84)*	*(84)*	*(84)*

At first sight, the table suggests relatively small movements in the proportions of women who were single, married or cohabiting at each point in time. However, looking at each of the categories in more detail, there was cross flow, particularly from cohabiting to single relationships and from single to cohabiting relationships. Between the time they became pregnant and the birth there was an increase in the proportion of single women, a decline in the proportion of cohabiting women and a slight increase in the proportion of married women. Between the time of the birth and the time of the interview there was a decline in the proportion of single women, an increase in the proportion of cohabiting women and a slight rise in the number of married women.

But when we came to examine these movements in more detail we found a much more complex picture of changing relationships which we summarise in the next section and in Table 2.3. It is clear that a simple description of marital status by single, cohabiting or married at three points in time is by no means sufficient to show what had happened in the relationships of the women.

Mapping changes in relationships

We look first at how the status of relationships with the father of the baby changed for the 84 women from the time that they became pregnant to the time of the interview. We will map those changes for the different groups of women separately: women who were married, cohabiting, in steady relationships or in casual relationships with the father of the baby when they became pregnant.

Married relationships at the time of the pregnancy

9 women were married to the father of the baby when they became pregnant and remained married throughout.

Cohabiting relationships at the time of the pregnancy

26 women were living with the father of the baby when they became pregnant:
- 4 subsequently married the father of the baby
- 11 continued to live with the father of the baby
- 11 of the relationships split up:
    - 1 before the pregnancy was confirmed
    - 5 between the confirmation of the pregnancy and the birth
    - 5 between the birth and the time of the interview (1 of these continued to have a non-cohabiting relationship with the father of the baby).

Steady relationships at the time of the pregnancy

Over half the women (43) said that the father of the baby was a steady boyfriend when they became pregnant:

- 2 married the father of the baby (1 before and 1 after the birth)
- 11 went on to live with the father of the baby (1 before and 10 after the birth)
- 21 split up with the father of the baby and were alone at the time of the interview:
    - 5 split up at the time the pregnancy was confirmed
    - 4 between the confirmation of pregnancy and the birth
    - 10 after the birth

- 2 women had a steady relationship until the birth, lived together after the birth but had split up at the time of the interview
- 5 women split up with the baby's father but had met new partners at the time of the interview:
  - 2 women had split up with the father before the birth and both were in new cohabiting relationships at the time of the interview
  - 3 women had split up with the father after the birth
  - 1 had a new cohabiting relationship
  - 1 had a new non-cohabiting relationship
  - 1 cohabited with the father of the baby after the birth – split up with him and had a new non-cohabiting relationship at the time of the interview
- 4 of the women continued to have a steady relationship with the father of the baby. 1 had lived with him before the birth, stopped cohabiting after the birth but continued to have a steady relationship.

Casual relationships at the time of the pregnancy

Six women described their relationship with the father of the baby as casual at the time they became pregnant:
- 1 woman started living with a new partner after the birth, having been single throughout her pregnancy
- 1 woman lived with the baby's father after the birth
- 4 women had no relationship with the father after the pregnancy was confirmed.

Patterns of change

Many relationships underwent significant changes after the women became pregnant. The 9 women who were married at the time they became pregnant all remained married. By the time of the interview, the number of married women had increased to 15. A similar number of women were recorded as cohabiting with the baby's father both at the time of becoming pregnant (26) and at the time of the interview (23).

However, this masks the changes that had occurred in both cohabiting and steady relationships. We found that nearly half (11) of the original cohabiting relationships had broken up at the time of the interview. But this number was the same as the number of steady relationships which resulted in cohabitation with the father of the baby (11).

However, it was not only cohabiting relationships which were vulnerable, since nearly two-thirds (26) of the steady relationships (43) had broken up, although a few of the women did have new partners. For both groups – cohabiting and steady relationships – relationship failure was equally likely to occur during pregnancy and after the birth.

Table 2.3 Status of women's relationships at start of pregnancy and time of interview

	Nos	Married to baby's father (9)	Cohabiting with baby's father (26)	Non-cohabiting relationship with baby's father (43)	Single/casual relationship with baby's father (6)
Status at interview					
Married to baby's father	(15)	9	4	2	0
Cohabiting with baby's father	(23)	0	11	11	1
Non-cohabiting relationship with baby's father	(5)	0	1	4	0
Cohabiting with new partner	(4)	0	0	3	1
Non-cohabiting relationship with new partner	(2)	0	0	2	0
Single alone	(35)	0	10	21	4
Still with baby's father	(43)	9	16	17	1
Not with baby's father	(41)	0	10	26	5

The overall picture

In Table 2.3 we present a summary of the change in relationships between the time that the women became pregnant and the time of the interview. We can see that at the time of the interview, of the 84 women:

* 15 were married to the father of the baby
* 23 were cohabiting with the father of the baby
* 5 had a steady relationship with the father of the baby but were not living with him
* 4 were cohabiting with a new partner
* 2 had a steady relationship with a new partner but were not living with him
* 35 women were single and alone.

We compared the status of the women's relationships at the time of the interview with the status of their relationships with the father of the baby at the time they became pregnant.

* *Of the 15 women who were married to the father of the baby at the time of the interview:* 9 were married to him, 4 were cohabiting and 2 were in a steady non-cohabiting relationship with him at the time they became pregnant.
* *Of the 23 women who were cohabiting with the father of the baby at the time of the interview:* 11 were cohabiting with him, 11 were in a steady non-cohabiting relationship and 1 was in a casual relationship with him at the time they became pregnant.
* *Of the 5 women who had a steady non-cohabiting relationship with the father of the baby at the time of the interview:* 4 were in a steady non-cohabiting relationship and 1 was in a cohabiting relationship with him at the time they became pregnant.
* *Of the 4 women who were cohabiting with a new partner at the time of the interview:* 3 were in a steady non-cohabiting relationship and 1 was in a casual relationship with the father of the baby at the time they became pregnant.
* *Of the 2 women who had a steady non-cohabiting relationship with a new partner at the time of the interview:* both had had a steady non-cohabiting relationship with the father of the baby at the time they became pregnant.
* *Of the 35 women who were single and alone at the time of the interview:* 10 were in a cohabiting relationship, 21 were in a steady non-cohabiting relationship and 4 in a casual relationship with the father of the baby at the time they became pregnant.

Ethnic group

Table 2.4 shows that the majority (83 per cent) of women interviewed
were of white ethnic origin although there was more ethnic diversity in
Hackney and Solihull than in Leeds. All the women in Leeds were of
white ethnic origin (34). 67 per cent of women interviewed in Hackney
were of white ethnic origin (18), 11 per cent were from black minority
groups (2 women were Black Caribbean and 1 was Black African), and
the remaining 21 per cent were equally divided between Indian,
Bangladeshi and women of mixed race. 78 per cent of women in Solihull
were of white ethnic origin (18), 4 were Pakistani and 1 woman was
Black Caribbean.

Table 2.4   Ethnic group of women

column percentages

	Total	Hackney	Solihull	Leeds
White	83	67	78	100
Black Caribbean	4	7	4	0
Black African	1	4	0	0
Indian	2	7	0	0
Pakistani	5	0	17	0
Bangladeshi	2	7	0	0
Mixed race	2	7	0	0
Base: all women	*(84)*	*(27)*	*(23)*	*(34)*

Country of birth

The overwhelming majority of women in all three areas (77 of the 84)
were born in the United Kingdom – 81 per cent in Hackney, 96 per cent
in Solihull and 97 per cent in Leeds. 1 woman in Solihull was born in
Pakistan and 1 woman in Leeds was born in Ireland. In Hackney, 2 of the
women were born in European countries and the remaining 3 were born
in India, Bangladesh and Africa respectively.

Religion

43 per cent of the women (36) said that they had no religion: over half of
the women in Hackney (14), compared with over a third in Solihull (9)
and Leeds (13). Just under a third of the women (26) were Church of
England (13 in Leeds, 8 in Solihull, 5 in Hackney), just under a sixth (12)
were Roman Catholics and just under a sixth were Muslim (4 in Solihull,
5 in Hackney and 1 in Leeds).

First language

English was the first language of the majority of women (77), including all the women in Leeds, all but 5 women in Hackney and all but 2 women in Solihull.

Age of respondent's mother when she had her first baby

A particular group of teenage women which have been identified from previous studies as being at increased risk of pregnancy are the daughters of teenage mothers themselves (NHS CRD, 1997). We were interested to know when the respondent's mother and siblings had had their first baby in order to establish a picture of the incidence of teenage pregnancy in their households, and to examine whether there were recurring patterns both within and between generations.

Table 2.5 shows how common teenage pregnancy was among the mothers of the respondents, with just under half of the women interviewed (40) saying that their mothers were aged between 15 and 19 when they had had their first baby. However, the distribution was slightly skewed, with 60 per cent of the respondents' mothers in Solihull having had their first baby as teenagers compared with 42 per cent in Leeds and 45 per cent in Hackney. The average age of the respondent's mother at the birth of their first child was 19.9 years with little difference between the areas.

Table 2.5   **Age of women's mother when she had her first baby**

column percentages

	Total	Hackney	Solihull	Leeds
15	2	4	4	0
16	6	4	13	3
17	7	7	4	9
18	17	11	22	18
19	15	19	17	12
20–24	39	56	22	38
25–29	10	0	17	12
Don't know	4	0	0	9
Mean age	*19.9*	*19.7*	*19.9*	*20.2*
Base: all women	*(84)*	*(27)*	*(23)*	*(34)*

Over a quarter of the women (22) had siblings who were also teenage parents. It is possible that this figure could increase as some of the younger siblings become teenagers themselves. 19 of the women (7 in Hackney, 3 in Solihull and 9 in Leeds) had a sister who was a teenage parent and one woman in Hackney had 2 sisters who were teenage parents. In addition, one woman in Leeds had a brother who was a teenage parent and a woman in Solihull had 2 brothers who were teenage parents.

Number of siblings and size of women's family

The women had an average number of 3.1 siblings (3.5 in Solihull, 3.1 in Hackney and 2.8 in Leeds). The average number of children in families (including the respondent) was 3.9, well above the national average in all areas (4.0 in Hackney, 4.4 in Solihull and 3.7 in Leeds).

Marital status of women's parents

A number of studies have found a link between sexual activity and parenthood in teenagers and factors such as the size and the structure of families and the relationships within them. Women from larger than average families, and those who lived with only one of their parents during their childhood, were found more likely to become parents themselves at an early age. This was also found for women whose parents had been divorced, or separated or who had died (Simms and Smith, 1986; Russell, 1988). A more recent study has found that women who lived with one parent because of divorce or separation appeared more likely to be teenage parents than those who had suffered the death of a parent (Wellings et al, 1996 and see Kiernan, 1995).

Table 2.6   Marital status of women's parents at the time of interview

column percentages

	Total	Hackney	Solihull	Leeds
Married to each other	55	48	70	50
Mother with different husband/partner	17	15	9	24
Father with different wife/partner	7	11	0	9
Both with different spouses/partners	14	11	13	18
Apart but neither with different spouses/partners	4	7	4	0
One/both parents dead	4	7	4	0
Base: all women	*(84)*	*(27)*	*(23)*	*(34)*

We asked women about the marital status of their parents and whether they had entered new relationships if they had separated or divorced. Table 2.6 shows that only just over half of respondents' parents (55 per cent) were still married to each other at the time of the interview.

However, the distribution across the areas varied, with nearly three-quarters (70 per cent) of parents in Solihull still married compared with around a half in Leeds and Hackney.

Table 2.6 also shows the proportion of parents who had entered new relationships. 38 per cent of women (32) had at least one parent in a new relationship: 17 per cent of their mothers, 7 per cent of their fathers and 14 per cent of both parents were with different partners. 4 per cent of the parents were apart but alone, and in 4 per cent of cases one or both parents had died.

Age of women when parents separated

We found that nearly half the women whose parents had separated were aged 5 or under at the time, just over 10 per cent were aged between 6 and 10, nearly a quarter were between 11 and 15 and the rest were 16 or over.

Age of women when they first left home

73 of the women were either currently living away from home or had lived away from home at some point. The average age of women when they left home was 17 in all areas, but Table 2.7 shows some area differences. Independence from parents for some women began at a remarkably young age, most notably in Leeds where one fifth of the women (6) had left home at 15 years or under, compared with only 3 in Hackney and 1 in Solihull. Around 40 per cent of those who had left home in both Solihull and Leeds had done so at 16 or under, while the Hackney women tended to be older.

Table 2.7   Age of women when they first left home

column percentages

	Total	Hackney	Solihull	Leeds
Under 15	4	8	0	3
15	10	4	5	17
16	22	17	35	17
17	23	25	25	21
18	26	33	25	21
19	11	13	10	10
20 or over	4	0	0	10
Mean age when first left home	*17.1*	*17.0*	*17.0*	*17.1*
Base: all women living or ever lived away from home	*(73)*	*(24)*	*(20)*	*(29)*

Leaving home was usually preceded by leaving school, and if women left home at 15 or younger they were unlikely to have obtained any educational qualifications at all. Indeed, their youth might have put some of them at an immediate risk because of their vulnerability, and their lack of educational qualifications undoubtedly made it more difficult for them to enter employment. The older the woman when she left home the more likely she was to have educational qualifications. For instance, only 2 of the 10 who were 15 or under when they left home had educational qualifications, compared with 22 of the 33 women who left home at 16 or 17 and 26 of the 30 women who left at 18 or over.

Why did women leave home? A relatively common reason was relationship problems with other household members – noted by a third of women in Hackney and Leeds and a fifth of those in Solihull. Relationship problems were a prominent feature of family life, often accompanied by family breakdown and much personal upheaval. One woman in Leeds who was 17 when she had her baby and was living with a new partner at the time of the interview described how history had repeated itself and noted how acrimonious family relationships were a relatively constant feature throughout her childhood and into her teenage years: 'Neither of my parents wanted us when I was about 8, so my dad's brother's wife took us in and later adopted us. But I didn't get on with my stepfather and they didn't like my boyfriend, so I went to live with my adopted parents' daughter.' Another woman said simply: 'My parents got divorced and I didn't like my mum's other half.' Some existing relationship problems were often exacerbated by the respondent's pregnancy.

For other women, however, leaving home was part of growing up and making a life for themselves independent of their parents and family. Many of these moved in with a boyfriend and some had married. This was more common in Solihull where half of the women who moved away did so to be with their partner or husband, compared with a third of the women in Hackney and Leeds. The need for independence also prompted women to leave home, as did the need for physical space and a place of their own. Given the size of some families, and the number of siblings in some of these households, it is hardly surprising that overcrowding was mentioned by women as a reason for wanting to leave the family home.

A few women said that they moved out because they became pregnant. One woman in Hackney who left home at 17 described why she moved away: 'Because I was pregnant and I thought it would be better to start my own life, or it would turn into my mother's baby. But now I'm away from home, I'm down at my mum's all the time.'

Regular contact with either or both parents

All the women who were not currently living with their parent(s) at the time of the interview (62) had regular contact with one or both parents, apart from three women – one in each area – who had no regular contact with either parent. Despite the fact that only half the women in Leeds said that their parents were still married to each other, the vast majority of those who had moved still had regular contact with both parents. Close family ties were just as evident in Solihull, with three-quarters of women reporting regular contact with both parents compared with only half the women in Hackney. 7 of the 20 women who were not living with their parents in Hackney, 3 of the 16 in Solihull and only 2 of the 26 in Leeds said that they had contact with their mother only. Another 2 women in Hackney said that they had contact with their father only.

Whether living with their parents at the time of the interview

We asked women where and with whom they were living at the time of the interview. Table 2.8 shows that a surprisingly high number: 22 (26 per cent) were living with one or both parents. We asked the 22 women who were currently living with their parents if they had ever lived away. 11 of the 22 (a similar proportion in each area) had lived away from home at some point. Overall, the vast majority of women were currently living away from their parents (74 per cent) or had lived away at some point (13 per cent). Only 11 women (13 per cent) had never lived away from their parents.

Table 2.8   **Women living with one or both parents at time of interview**
numbers and column percentages

| | Total | | Hackney | Solihull | Leeds |
	Nos	%	%	%	%
Living with both parents	15	18	19	22	15
Living with mother only	7	8	7	9	9
Living with father only	0	0	0	0	0
Not living with parents	62	74	74	70	76
Base: all women	*(84)*		*(27)*	*(23)*	*(34)*

Education and vocational attainment

We looked at the educational background of women, the age at which they had left school and the qualifications they had obtained. Previous research has demonstrated that a good general education is strongly associated with deferring pregnancy in girls and young women, and that a lack of academic attainment and educational goals has been associated with teenage pregnancy (NHS CRD, 1997). Of course, the relationship between education and teenage pregnancy is even more far-reaching because of the limiting effects of pregnancy on the future realisation of academic and vocational goals. Recent research demonstrated different strategies for coping with conception according to scholastic achievement (Wellings et al, 1996). The frequency of teenage motherhood declined with increasing educational level and the educational gradient was reversed for abortion. Graduates who conceived were more likely than women with no educational qualifications to terminate a pregnancy than to have a baby.

Age of women on completion of full-time education

Table 2.9 shows the age of women when they completed their education. Nearly one fifth (16 women) said that they had left school before the statutory school-leaving age and 46 per cent had left at 16 (39). Just under a sixth (10) had left at 17 and 10 per cent at 18 or 19 (8). Just under a sixth were still in education (10) and 1 had had no education.

Table 2.9   Age of women on completion of education

column percentages

	Total	Hackney	Solihull	Leeds
14 or under	5	11	0	3
15	14	15	9	18
16	46	37	57	47
17	12	19	0	15
18	6	0	4	12
19	4	4	0	6
Still in full-time education	5	7	9	0
Still in part-time education	7	7	17	0
No school	1	0	4	0
Base: all women	*(84)*	*(27)*	*(23)*	*(34)*

A quarter of the women in Hackney and a fifth in Leeds said they had finished their full-time education at 15 years or less compared with less than one tenth in Solihull. Solihull women were more likely to leave at 16 than those in the other areas.

Overall, 13 per cent (10) women were still in full-time or part-time education at the time of interview: 25 per cent in Solihull, 14 per cent in Hackney but none in Leeds. This, of course, was related to their age at the time of the interview. 18 per cent of the women in Leeds had completed their education at 18 or 19 compared with one in Hackney and one in Solihull.

Educational qualifications

Two-thirds of the women (56) reported having educational qualifications (over three-quarters in Solihull but less than two-thirds in Hackney and Leeds). We found that those without educational qualifications were almost all women who had left school at 14, 15 and 16 years. Only 1 of the 16 women who had left school at 15 or under had qualifications, compared with 29 of the 39 who had left school at 16, and 16 of the 18 women who had left school aged 17 or over. All those still in full-time or part-time education at the time of the interview had educational qualifications. One woman who was born in Pakistan said that she had not attended school at all.

Although two-thirds of all women had some qualifications, Table 2.10 shows that the overwhelming majority had no qualifications above GCSE/O-level. A third of the women in Solihull and a quarter in Hackney reported having GCSEs but did not say how many or at what grade. Table 2.10 shows that a similar proportion of women in all areas had between 1 and 8 GCSEs but more women in Leeds obtained high numbers of GCSEs (9 or more) than elsewhere. One woman in Leeds had A-levels and one in Hackney had A-levels and was studying for a degree.

Table 2.10   Educational qualifications of women

column percentages

	Total	Hackney	Solihull	Leeds
1–2 GCSEs	10	7	13	9
3–4 GCSEs	5	4	4	6
5–6 GCSEs	11	11	9	12
7–8 GCSEs	12	11	13	12
9–10 GCSEs	7	0	0	18
Over 10 GCSEs	2	0	4	3
GCSE number not stated	18	26	35	0
GCE A-level	2	4	0	3
No qualifications	33	37	22	38
Base: all women	*(84)*	*(27)*	*(23)*	*(34)*

Vocational qualifications

Even if women had planned to do further studies and obtain vocational qualifications, becoming pregnant had either completely dashed those plans or had precluded them from starting or completing college courses until after they had had their babies, by which time their earlier ambitions were more difficult to achieve because of competing pressures, such as the lack of time and absence of suitable and affordable childcare arrangements.

Against this background, it is perhaps surprising that so many women
had vocational qualifications (30). Just under half the women in Hackney
(11) and Leeds (16) and a third of women in Solihull (8) reported having
or studying for a vocational qualification. For those women with
qualifications, a wide range were mentioned including: NVQ Level 1, 2
and 3, BTEC (OND) and (HND), RSA, City and Guilds and YTS.

The effects of teenage motherhood on employment

There is evidence that the rate of teenage conceptions is higher in areas
with low scores on a range of socio-economic indicators (Wilson, 1980;
Wilson et al, 1992; Smith, 1993). In addition, a higher proportion of the
conceptions in more affluent areas are terminated (Smith, 1993).
Explanations for the differences in the rates of teenage births have
turned from 'fecklessness' to life expectations and the absence of
positive alternatives to motherhood for supplying status (Phoenix, 1991).
In addition, Joshi (1990) argues that women who have poor earning
potential have less reason to defer motherhood. In comparing the
characteristics of men and women aged 29 to 59 who had had a teenage
birth with those who had not, Wellings et al (1996) found a strong social
class gradient for teenage birth among both men and women. Women
who had had a child when they were teenagers were more likely to be
currently in manual rather than non-manual occupations, and this was
even more striking for men who became parents when teenagers. Early
fatherhood was rare among men in professional and managerial
occupations.

Women's occupation when they became pregnant and at the time of the interview

Table 2.11 shows that nearly 40 per cent of the women in this study (32)
had been in some form of paid employment when they became pregnant
compared with one sixth (13) at the time of the interview. Over a quarter
of the women (24) were in full or part-time education when they became
pregnant compared with less than one sixth (10) at the time of the
interview. Nearly one third of the women (26) were unemployed when
they became pregnant compared with 71 per cent (60) at the time of the
interview.

There were some area differences. Two-thirds of the women in Leeds
were in paid employment when they became pregnant compared with
only one third in Solihull and Hackney. Over half of the Solihull women
were in either full-time or part-time education when they became
pregnant, compared with 40 per cent in Hackney and only 18 per cent in
Leeds. This is not surprising since the Solihull women were rather

younger at the birth of the baby than those in other areas. 35 per cent of the women in Leeds, 30 per cent in Hackney and 26 per cent in Solihull were unemployed when they became pregnant.

Table 2.11   **Employment status of women when they became pregnant and at the time of interview**

numbers and column percentages

	At pregnancy		At interview	
	Nos	%	Nos	%
Full-time paid employment	17	20	4	5
Part-time paid employment	15	18	9	10
Full-time/part-time education	24	29	10	13
Government training scheme	2	2	1	1
Unemployed	26	31	60	71
Base: all women	*(84)*		*(84)*	

We looked more closely at the current employment status of the women. We have already seen that the overwhelming majority of women (60) were unemployed at the time of the interview. The women were more likely to be in part-time rather than full-time employment. 8 of the 13 women in employment were married or cohabiting and 10 had educational qualifications.

We examined the women's current employment status across the three areas:

- Of the 27 Hackney women: 20 were unemployed/not in paid work; 3 were in part-time employment; 4 were in full or part-time education.
- Of the 23 Solihull women: 12 were unemployed/not in paid work; 2 were in full-time and 3 in part-time employment; 6 were in full or part-time education.
- Of the 34 Leeds women: 28 were unemployed/not in paid work; 2 were in full-time and 3 in part-time employment; 1 was on a government training scheme.

Of the 60 women who were unemployed or not in paid work at the time of the interview, 39 had been in paid employment at some point. Most of these had only worked for less than six months.

Current social class and occupation

Given the high proportion of women who were unemployed or in full-time or part-time education, only a few women in each area could be assigned a social class status on the basis of their own occupation (see Babb, 1993). In Hackney, 3 women were in non-manual occupations and one woman in a manual occupation. In Solihull, 2 women were in non-manual and 3 in manual occupations. In Leeds, 3 women were in non-manual and 3 in manual occupations.

Changes in women's work, study or training plans as a result of the pregnancy

A high proportion of pregnancies were unplanned (three-quarters), so that it is not surprising that around two-thirds of the women felt that becoming pregnant had changed their work, study and training plans. Women in Leeds were more likely to note that their plans for further studies had either been completely ruined or had had to be put on hold, as this woman's comments illustrate: 'I wanted to go into Art and Design (BTEC) and I lost incentive. I was hoping to go on to university.' Another woman in Leeds was more optimistic about her future and felt that while her immediate plans would not be realised, she could still pursue her study at a later stage: 'I had a place at university for a teaching course. Then I had (the baby), but I may go back and do it.' Another woman in Leeds said: 'My life's on hold until he's older, but I'm planning to do an OU course when he's older.'

Some women could not finish school because of the pregnancy. A woman in Hackney explained: 'I stopped home tuition because of morning sickness and my mum said I'd have to pay a £10 entry fee for each exam, so I said – forget it.' Another woman in Solihull had had to postpone taking her examinations and said: 'I had to put them off for a bit, and now it's more difficult to study.'

For other women the pregnancy itself heralded many changes which affected their lives. Some women were faced with unpalatable choices. One woman in Leeds described the domino effect of her changing circumstances: 'I was doing A-levels at college because I wanted to go to university, but then I had to choose between college and work when (partner) left me, so I gave up college. My mum isn't very well off and she couldn't help me.' Another woman in Solihull also recognised just how much everything had changed: 'I couldn't do my GCSEs. I was planning to be a hairdresser. I think it changed just about everything really.'

Some women had to stop working when they were pregnant and others after the baby was born, often because of difficulties in arranging suitable and affordable childcare. A woman in Solihull explained why she had stopped working: 'Because it was too much to pay for a child-minder and there was no-one else who could look after him. So it was a dead end.' Another woman in Leeds had had the same experience: 'I loved the job but it was impossible for me to stay on. I can't work because I've got no-one to look after (the baby), and if I got a child-minder, I'd be working for nothing.'

Frequency of contact with the baby's father

We asked women how often they and their baby saw the baby's father. Just under half (38) were married to (15) or living with (23) the father of the baby. Just under a fifth (16) said that they and the baby never saw the father. One woman in Solihull (who was 18 when the baby was born) said that the father of the baby was a steady boyfriend until their relationship split up after the birth and she described his lack of interest in keeping contact with her and the baby: 'I don't see him (boyfriend) at all. The baby was in hospital, and he just slapped me in the face and said, "I don't want to see him, even if he dies".'

A small proportion saw the father every day (7) or several times a week (6) but were not living together. A slightly higher proportion of babies (12) than women (10) saw the father once a week, possibly due to the fact that where some relationships had broken up, the baby still continued to see the father. The rest of the women and their babies saw the father less often – twice a month (2) or less than once a month (5).

One woman in Leeds described what happened when her relationship broke up: 'He went to court and now he sees the baby once a week for an hour. He makes no financial contribution. When we split up he was seeing someone else. He attempted suicide, smashed up her home and he's married since.' This reflects not only the level of acrimony in some relationships, but also gives some insight into the violent nature of some of the relationships described by other women.

The crucial nature of the relationship with the father of the baby has been clearly illustrated in this description of the characteristics of the women interviewed. We asked them to give us similar information about the fathers so that we could put together a picture of the families into which the babies had been born.

Characteristics of the father of the baby

We asked women about the age of the father of the baby, their current marital status, ethnic origin and place of birth, religion, their first language, when they had finished their full-time education, their educational and/or vocational qualifications, and details of their current employment and employment history. A few women could not supply some of the information, but most women gave detailed information on the father's characteristics.

Age profile of the fathers

Table 2.12 shows that the average age of the fathers at the time of the birth was 23.0, with little difference between the three areas. Just over one fifth (18) were teenagers themselves, aged between 16 and 19 when the baby was born, and over two-thirds were under 25 at the birth of the baby.

Table 2.12　Age of baby's father at the time of the birth

column percentages

	Total	Hackney	Solihull	Leeds
Under 20	22	11	22	29
20–24	46	52	48	41
25–29	24	30	22	21
30 and over	7	7	9	6
Don't know	1	0	0	3
Mean age	*23.0*	*23.3*	*23.1*	*22.7*
Base: all fathers of the baby	*(84)*	*(27)*	*(23)*	*(34)*

Current marital status of the father

We have already looked in detail in this chapter at the changing relationships between the women and the fathers of the baby from the time that women became pregnant to the time of the interview. We saw in Table 2.3 that, at the time of the interview, just over half the fathers were married (15) or cohabiting (23) with the mother of the baby and 5 had a steady relationship but were not cohabiting.

Of the fathers who no longer had a relationship with the women (41), 7 were living with a new partner and 1 was married to a new partner. One man was already married to another partner when he had had an extra-marital relationship with the mother of the baby and was still married at the time of the interview. Three women (1 in each area) had lost contact with the baby's father and did not know their marital status at the time of the interview.

Ethnic origin of the baby's father

Table 2.13 indicates more ethnic diversity among fathers than among the women. Men of white ethnic origin accounted for 69 per cent of fathers. In Hackney just over half of fathers were of white ethnic origin, while a quarter were from black minority groups (6 Black Caribbean and 1 Black African), and the rest were Indian, Bangladeshi and mixed race. In Solihull nearly two-thirds were of white ethnic origin, 2 were Black Caribbean, 4 were Pakistani, 1 was mixed race and 1 Middle Eastern. In

Leeds, 85 per cent of fathers were of white ethnic origin, 2 were Pakistani, 1 was mixed race, 1 was Middle Eastern and 1 was Mexican.

The majority of fathers (80 per cent) were born in the United Kingdom (74 per cent in both Hackney and Solihull and 88 per cent in Leeds).

Table 2.13   Ethnic group of baby's father

column percentages

	Total	Hackney	Solihull	Leeds
White	69	52	65	85
Black Caribbean	10	22	9	0
Black African	1	4	0	0
Indian	2	7	0	0
Pakistani	7	0	17	6
Bangladeshi	2	7	0	0
Mixed race	5	7	4	3
Middle Eastern	2	0	4	3
Mexican	1	0	0	3
Base: all fathers of the baby (84)		*(27)*	*(23)*	*(34)*

Religion of the baby's father

43 per cent of fathers (36) were reported to have no religion, the same proportion as the mothers. A quarter of the fathers (20) were Church of England (12 in Leeds, 4 in Solihull and 4 in Hackney). Just under a sixth (14) were Muslim (5 in Solihull, 4 in Hackney and 3 in Leeds). 10 per cent (8) were Roman Catholic and 1 was Greek Orthodox. In 7 cases the father's religion was unknown.

First language

In Leeds English was the first language of 91 per cent of fathers compared with 78 per cent in Solihull and 81 per cent in Hackney.

Age of father on completion of full-time education

We have already seen how important a good general education is in deferring pregnancy in young women (NHS CRD, 1997) and the potential adverse social and economic outcomes for teenage mothers and their children at a later stage. The educational attainment and economic prospects of the father of the baby also play an important part in family welfare.

Like the women, the fathers had a broad range of educational achievements. Table 2.14 shows that 16 per cent of the men had left school at 14 or 15 compared with 19 per cent of the women. 42 per cent of the men had left school at 16. Fathers in Leeds were more likely to have left school earlier than fathers elsewhere, reflecting the picture among the Leeds women.

Table 2.14   Age of baby's father on completion of education

column percentages

	Total	Hackney	Solihull	Leeds
14 and under	6	7	0	9
15	10	4	9	15
16	42	44	39	41
17	5	4	4	6
18	10	15	4	9
19	4	4	0	6
20 and over	2	0	9	0
Still in full/part-time education	8	11	13	3
No school	4	4	4	3
Don't know	10	7	17	9
Base: all fathers of the baby	*(84)*	*(27)*	*(23)*	*(34)*

Two-thirds of the fathers had completed their full-time education by 16 in Leeds compared with over half in Hackney (55 per cent) and less than half in Solihull. 3 fathers in Hackney, 3 in Solihull and 1 in Leeds were still in full-time education, usually studying for their first degree. One father in each area was thought not to have attended school, while 10 per cent of respondents had no information on the schooling of the father.

Educational qualifications of fathers

We found a picture of low educational attainment for the fathers, a third of whom were reported to have no educational qualifications at all (30), while another quarter (23) had GCSE or O-level qualifications. Indeed, very few of the fathers were reported to have higher status educational qualifications such as GCE A-levels (4) or a first degree (5). A small proportion of women said that the father did have educational qualifications but they did not know what they were (6), and a further 23 per cent of women (19) said that they did not know whether they had any educational qualifications.

Fathers in Hackney were almost twice as likely to have GCSE or O-level qualifications as fathers in Solihull and Leeds. There were no area differences in the proportion with GCE A-level qualifications. Three fathers in Solihull were studying for or had obtained a first degree.

Looking at age and educational attainment together showed a similar pattern to that found among the young mothers: the younger the father the less likely he was to have educational qualifications. For example, less than a third of the 10 fathers who were teenagers themselves when the research was conducted had educational qualifications, compared with just under half of the fathers aged between 20 and 25. The differences between fathers was greater when educational attainment and marital status were looked at in conjunction. Married fathers were far more likely to have educational qualifications than any other group:

- 11 of the 15 fathers who were married at the time of the research had educational qualifications, including 4 with a first degree
- 11 of the 23 fathers who were living with the baby's mother had educational qualifications, of whom 3 had GCE A-levels and 1 also had a first degree
- None of the 4 fathers whose partners were cohabiting with a new partner had any educational qualifications
- Only 13 of the 42 fathers whose partners were single had any educational qualifications.

Father's vocational qualifications

Only around a third of fathers had any vocational qualifications. Some of the women who said that the father had vocational qualifications did not know what they were, and indeed, only 23 women could identify the type of qualification. Single men were least likely to have vocational qualifications. A wide range of vocational qualifications were mentioned, including NVQ Level 1, 2 and 3, City and Guild qualifications, BTEC ordinary level and higher levels, London Chamber of Commerce certificates and trade apprenticeship qualifications.

Employment status of fathers

We asked respondents if the father of the baby was in paid employment at the time of the interview so that we could build a picture of family welfare, income and economic prospects for couples, and identify possible sources of support for women who were not living with but were in some way dependent on the father of the baby.

Table 2.15 shows that over a third of fathers (35 per cent) were unemployed, but the distribution varied across the three areas: 48 per cent in Solihull, 32 per cent in Leeds and 26 per cent in Hackney. The proportion of unemployed fathers was fairly equally distributed according to marital status.

Table 2.15   Employment status of baby's father at the time of
             interview

column percentages

	Total	Hackney	Solihull	Leeds
Full-time paid employment	45	44	30	56
Part-time paid employment	7	11	4	6
Self-employed	1	4	0	0
Full/part-time education	8	11	13	3
Unemployed	35	26	48	32
Don't know	4	4	4	3
Base: all fathers of the baby	*(84)*	*(27)*	*(23)*	*(34)*

53 per cent of fathers were employed or self-employed, the majority in full-time paid work, mainly in manual occupations. Fathers in full-time paid work were equally distributed according to marital status. However, over half the fathers in Leeds were in full-time paid employment compared with 44 per cent in Hackney and only 30 per cent in Solihull. 7 fathers were still in full-time or part-time education.

20 per cent of all fathers were in skilled manual occupations while another 22 per cent were in semi-skilled or unskilled occupations – all equally distributed according to marital status. None were in professional occupations and only 5 (2 married, 2 cohabiting and 1 single) were in managerial occupations. A very small proportion (3 single fathers) were in skilled non-manual occupations.

Conclusions

This chapter has shown the wide diversity of background and characteristics of the women we interviewed and of the fathers of the baby. We have stressed the importance of mapping the changing relationships over the period between the start of the pregnancy and the time of the interview. The fact that half of these teenage mothers were no longer in a relationship with the father of the baby approximately a year after the birth may not be surprising but is of considerable significance in determining a number of outcomes of teenage pregnancy. Most of the women were not in employment or education and most of them were claiming income support and were dependent on benefits, whether they were still with the father of the baby or not. The consequences of teenage motherhood were by no means what many of these women had anticipated when they became pregnant.

In the next chapter we examine the way in which the teenage women reached their decisions on whether to continue with the pregnancy and where and with whom they should live during the pregnancy and after the birth.

Chapter 3

Decision-making about the Pregnancy and Living Arrangements

This chapter looks at how the women made decisions about their pregnancies and about their housing and living arrangements. We will examine the reasons why they chose to continue with their pregnancy. We will explore their perceptions of the support available from the father of the baby, their parents and other key people in making their decisions about the pregnancy and their living arrangements during pregnancy and after the birth.

In the first part of the chapter we examine the reactions of women when they first suspected they might be pregnant and when they confirmed the pregnancy. Over a third of teenage pregnancies end in termination of pregnancy, so that we felt it important to establish what was different about the women we interviewed who had all continued with their pregnancy. Women were asked a number of key questions: whether they had planned to become pregnant when they did; what they had wanted to do about the pregnancy when they suspected it and when it was confirmed; whether they had considered the possibility of having a termination of pregnancy; and whether they had considered the possibility of having the baby adopted.

Planned and unplanned pregnancies

Only just over a quarter (23) of the women had planned to become pregnant. Most of these were older teenagers (18 and 19 year olds), and the more committed the relationship the more likely women were to plan their pregnancy. Seven of the 9 married women, 9 of the 26 cohabiting women, 6 of the 43 in steady non-cohabiting relationships and 1 of the 6 in casual relationships had planned their pregnancy.

We asked the 23 women who had planned to become pregnant (7 in Hackney, 6 in Solihull and 10 in Leeds) for their reasons. Nearly half of them said that they had just decided to have a baby at that particular time, but some said they had always wanted a baby.

It was by no means always a joint decision: less than half of the 23 women said they had planned the pregnancy with their partners. Indeed, one Hackney woman's comments reflect the findings of other studies: that some teenage women become pregnant because they perceive an absence of positive alternatives to motherhood (Joshi, 1990): 'I just wanted a baby since I was 15 or 16. I've always had kids around me and I didn't have anything else to do at the time.'

Even for women in steady relationships, the decision was not necessarily joint. A woman in Leeds seemed determined to become pregnant against the wishes of her partner: 'I wanted to have a baby but he didn't. I just wanted one. I'd had tablets to make me ovulate.' Half the women in Solihull and Leeds who had planned their pregnancy said that it was a joint decision, as one explained: 'We just sat down one night and said we'd like to have a baby. It was (baby's) dad who suggested it actually. We both love kids, me especially.' Another woman said: 'The pill was making me very poorly so we talked it over and decided I'd come off it and we'd have a baby.'

Suspecting and confirming pregnancy

Women first suspected that they were pregnant when they were on average 6.3 weeks pregnant (5.0 weeks in Leeds, Solihull 6.1 weeks and Hackney 8.1 weeks). Table 3.1 shows that over half the women had suspected that they were pregnant by the time they were 5 weeks pregnant – when they had just missed a period. By the time they were 10 weeks pregnant 89 per cent had suspected it, although the proportion was lower in Hackney. Four women did not suspect it until they were between 11 and 15 weeks pregnant, and five not until they were over 16 weeks pregnant.

Table 3.1   **Number of weeks gestation when women first suspected their pregnancy**

column percentages

	Total	Hackney	Solihull	Leeds
5 weeks or less	53	44	52	62
6–10 weeks	36	33	39	35
11–15 weeks	5	7	4	3
16–20 weeks	6	15	4	0
Mean number of weeks	*6.3*	*8.1*	*6.1*	*5.0*
Base: all women	*(84)*	*(27)*	*(23)*	*(34)*

Many women sought confirmation of their pregnancy almost immediately. Half of them had confirmed their pregnancy within a week and over two-thirds within two weeks of first suspecting it. A fifth waited for 3 to 6 weeks, five women waited for 7 to 10 weeks, while one woman waited for 10 weeks after she had first suspected it.

Table 3.2 illustrates further that women in Leeds suspected and confirmed their pregnancy much earlier than the others. The average number of weeks gestation at confirmation of pregnancy was 8.3 weeks (6.8 in Leeds, 8.8 in Solihull and 9.7 in Hackney). A quarter had confirmed their pregnancy by the time they were 5 weeks pregnant, but again, there were area differences, with half the Leeds women confirming their pregnancy by 6 weeks.

Table 3.2   **Number of weeks gestation when pregnancy was confirmed**
column percentages

	Total	Hackney	Solihull	Leeds
5 weeks or less	23	22	22	24
6–10 weeks	55	44	48	68
11–15 weeks	11	15	13	9
16–20 weeks	10	19	13	0
Don't know	1	0	4	0
Mean number of weeks	*8.3*	*9.7*	*8.8*	*6.8*
Base: all women	*(84)*	*(27)*	*(23)*	*(34)*

While 90 per cent of women had confirmed their pregnancy by 14 weeks and all had confirmed it by 20 weeks gestation, late confirmation was more common in Hackney, with a fifth of the women not confirming their pregnancy until they were more than 16 weeks pregnant.

Women's reactions at first suspicion of pregnancy

Women's reactions when they first suspected they were pregnant differed considerably and, not surprisingly, were influenced by a number of factors, such as whether the pregnancy had been planned or not, the woman's relationship with the baby's father, and where or with whom she was living. Although a few of the women who were not in steady relationships had planned their pregnancies, women in stable relationships were happier about the pregnancy.

Although only a quarter of women had planned to become pregnant, a much higher proportion reacted positively to the suspicion that they were pregnant. 40 per cent of women said that they were delighted and overjoyed or happy, pleased and excited, with women in Leeds more positive than those in the other areas.

A quarter of the women said they were shocked and surprised. One woman described her feelings of shock and disbelief: 'Really shocked. I couldn't believe it. I didn't think it would happen. I took the morning-after pill and it didn't work.'

A quarter of the women said that they had felt scared, panicked and horrified. One woman said: 'Oh God, what have I done?' Those who felt scared were often looking ahead, some with fear and trepidation about telling parents and how they would react. In contrast, the task of telling the father of the baby was rarely mentioned. A woman in Hackney said that her first thought was: 'What are my parents going to say? That's what I thought of first, not about what am I going to do.' Another woman thought: 'Oh my God! What am I going to tell my mum? What am I going to do? My mum's quite strict, and I thought, "She's going to go off her head." '

Others felt more frightened about being pregnant and having to decide what to do than the prospect of telling others about it. A woman described how she had felt: 'I was shocked. Shocked and scared. Very scared actually.' Those who had planned their pregnancy were often as confused as those who had not, often because they had become pregnant more quickly than expected. Some women who had not planned to become pregnant often felt confused about what to do next and whether to have the baby or not. One woman described both the urgency and confusion that she felt: 'I wasn't sure whether I was going to keep him or whether to have an abortion, and I didn't have much time to think about it.'

Some women described mixed emotions such as a woman (who was 18 when the baby was born) for whom history had repeated itself: 'In a way I was glad because I had had a termination when I was 16, so I was quite happy really. Just scared of what my mum was going to say.'

What happened after women first suspected they were pregnant?

Although 73 per cent of these young women had not planned to become pregnant, all of them went on to have their babies. We were interested to know what happened after they suspected they might be pregnant, to whom they talked and their main sources of support, whether they had considered having an abortion or having the baby adopted, and what they did about it. If they had not considered options other than having and keeping the baby, we wanted to know why. Our main aim was to find out how these young mothers arrived at their decision to have and keep their baby, when many teenagers opt for termination of pregnancy.

Considering a termination of pregnancy before the pregnancy was confirmed

Overall, a quarter of the women (21) said that they had considered having a termination of pregnancy before the pregnancy was confirmed. The younger teenagers – 16 and 17 year olds (11 of the 27) – were rather more likely to have considered it than 18 and 19 year olds (10 of the 57), and single women were more likely than cohabiting women to have considered it. None of the married women had considered it.

But even if women had not personally considered termination of pregnancy it still arose in conversations about what to do about the pregnancy and where and with whom they might live. Table 3.3 shows that as many as 18 women who had *not* themselves considered having a termination of pregnancy said that the possibility was discussed in conversations with partners, relatives, friends and professionals. Some of these women were advised to have a termination of pregnancy or to consider it as an option.

Table 3.3   **Number of women who had considered or discussed the possibility of having a termination of pregnancy**

		numbers and column percentages
	Nos	%
Considered having a TOP	22	26
Did not consider a TOP but option mentioned/discussed	18	22
Did not consider or discuss a TOP	44	52
Base: all women	*(84)*	

However, most of those who had considered a termination of pregnancy did nothing about it. Only a third of them (7 of the 21) went on to seek professional advice from pregnancy advisers or counsellors. Four of these women made appointments but did not keep them. One explained what had happened: 'I phoned up a place and made an appointment to see a counsellor, but I didn't have the guts to go.' A Hackney woman described what happened on the morning of her appointment: 'When the day came I just couldn't get out of bed – my whole body wouldn't move, I was literally stuck to the bed. My legs just went.'

The other three women spoke to an adviser or counsellor before deciding not to go ahead with a termination of pregnancy for a variety of reasons. One said: 'I made an appointment at the hospital but I walked out when they told me how I would have to push the baby out. I couldn't go through with that.' Another who went with her mother for counselling decided not to go ahead because of her concern about future complications: 'My mother asked the nurse – if I had an abortion would I be able to have children later on. The nurse said I'd have a 50:50 chance. I didn't want to have an abortion. I thought, "If my friend can do it (have a baby), why can't I?" '

The remaining two-thirds (14 of the 21) who had considered the possibility of having a termination of pregnancy said that they did nothing about it, mostly because they felt they could not go through with it. A woman in Leeds explained: 'I thought, "How could you do that? It's a little life in there." ' Five women said they realised they did not agree with abortions, while some said that they just decided not to have an abortion. One said that she was afraid that she might never have a chance to have a baby again, while two women said that they did not pursue it because they knew that they would get support from family and friends.

Support for women at this early stage amounted to words of encouragement and empathy rather than concrete actions. A woman in Leeds mentioned how her father's advice had influenced her: 'At the time I felt very confused, but I didn't really agree with abortion. And my dad really surprised me. He said, "You can cope with the baby – Your life doesn't really have to change that much," and that I'm young enough to be able to carry on with whatever I want to do when she (the baby) is older.' Another woman described her own and her partner's confusion: 'I spoke to the baby's father and he was just as confused as me, and he said he'd support me if I did decide to have him.'

Most women who did not consider having a termination of pregnancy said that they did not agree with or believe in abortion, although women in Leeds were much more likely to say this than women in Hackney or Solihull. Some felt that they had been irresponsible in becoming pregnant and that they had to take responsibility for their actions. A woman in Solihull said: 'I don't agree with abortions unless there is a really good reason for it. I can look after the baby. I brought it into the world so it is my duty to look after it.' Another woman in Leeds said of abortion: 'No way. I don't agree with them. When you do something wrong you have to pay for it. I agree with abortion if you get raped, or if there is something very wrong with them. But other than that, no way.'

Women in Hackney were much more likely than those in other areas to say that they did not consider having an abortion because their pregnancy was planned. But planning a pregnancy did not always guarantee a long-term commitment to parenthood, reflected in comments from a woman in Hackney who said: 'I suppose I was feeling broody and (the father) was saying that he wanted another one. When she was little he was interested in her, but now the novelty's worn off.' Women in Solihull were more likely to say that abortion was against their religion than women in Hackney and Leeds. Five women (2 in Hackney and 3 in Solihull) said that they had not considered having an abortion because they had already had one. Three women had not considered it because of the experience of friends or relatives who had had an abortion, as this woman in Hackney described: 'I've seen a close friend of mine have one and it all went wrong. She had a double wound and lost a lot of blood and had a lot of grief afterwards.'

How was the pregnancy confirmed?

Around half the women had their pregnancy confirmed by their GP, while a few had it confirmed by a practice nurse. Confirmation at a family planning clinic was much more common in Hackney (22 per cent) than in Solihull (13 per cent) or Leeds (6 per cent). 35 per cent of women in Leeds, 22 per cent in Hackney but only 9 per cent in Solihull used a home test kit. Five women had a pharmacy test and 4 had a hospital confirmation. One woman in Hackney and another in Leeds had their pregnancy confirmed at LIFE.

Having confirmed their pregnancy, 88 per cent of the women said that they wanted to have the baby: all the women in Leeds, 87 per cent in Solihull and 74 per cent in Hackney. Three women in Hackney were then still considering a termination of pregnancy and another woman in Hackney said that she wanted to have the baby and then have it adopted. The remaining six women were still undecided.

Considering a termination of pregnancy after the pregnancy was confirmed

Although 21 women had considered having a termination when the pregnancy was first suspected, only 12 had considered it after the pregnancy was confirmed, of whom 11 had also considered it when they first suspected they were pregnant. Only one woman, who was 19 when the baby was born, did not consider it until the pregnancy was confirmed. Overall 22 of the 84 women had considered having a termination of pregnancy at some stage.

Of the 12 women who had considered it after confirming their pregnancies, only six did something about it. One woman who had spoken to a counsellor could not explain her final decision: 'I decided not to have the abortion but I'm not sure why. I don't think it was talking to the hospital that decided me.' Another woman recalled how she had been influenced by her father: 'When my dad found out he just turned round and said, "It's against your religion." '

The lapse of time between first suspecting and confirming the pregnancy was critical to the decision-making process for some women. One woman had suspected that she was pregnant when she had just missed a period but admitted: 'I didn't want to believe it.' By the time she had confirmed the pregnancy she was 20 weeks pregnant and she explained: 'Once I knew it was there I wouldn't dare get rid of it.'

Considering adoption

Another option was the possibility of continuing with the pregnancy and then having the baby adopted. However, the overwhelming majority said that they had not considered adoption at all, and the only woman who had considered it subsequently decided against it. None of the other women had considered it, mainly because they felt that once they had had the baby they would not be able to give it up. A woman in Hackney described why: 'Because going through the pain and then giving it away, and then knowing I've got a baby somewhere. No.' Another woman agreed: 'I wouldn't be able to live with myself knowing that someone else had my baby.' Another felt that the thought of someone else having her baby was so intolerable that a termination was a more acceptable option: 'I wouldn't do it. I'd rather have a termination than have it adopted.'

Sources of support for women during pregnancy

Previous research has shown how important friends and relatives can be in helping women come to terms with the news of their pregnancy and in acting as a confidante in the early days and weeks of pregnancy (Allen, 1985). We asked women to whom they had spoken during their pregnancy and how influential these discussions had been in helping them decide whether or not they should continue with their pregnancy. We looked in detail at the conversations women had had with their partners, relatives, friends, colleagues and professionals, and particularly at their advice on whether the women should have the baby and where and with whom they might live during their pregnancy and after the birth. Women's accounts of their discussions suggest that they referred to the most significant ones rather than giving details of brief conversations in which the pregnancy was spoken about in passing.

Total number of people spoken to about the pregnancy

Table 3.4 shows the total number of people including partners, family members, friends, other relatives and professionals to whom women had spoken about the pregnancy. It shows that very few women had spoken to a large number of people, while most had only spoken to two or three key people.

Table 3.4   **Total number of people spoken to by women about the pregnancy**

numbers and column percentages

	Nos	%
No. of people spoken to		
None	9	11
One	9	11
Two	15	18
Three	14	17
Four	7	8
Five	14	17
Six	6	7
Seven	3	4
Eight	3	4
Nine	4	5
Mean number of people spoken to	*4*	
Base: all women	*(84)*	

Nine of the women said that they had not had discussions with anyone at all about their pregnancy. They were a rather diverse little group: 3 were married and 4 were cohabiting, while the remaining 2 were living at home with their parents and said that the father of the baby was a steady boyfriend at the time. Five of the women had planned the pregnancy and 4 had not. Four were 16 or 17 and five were 18 or 19.

Number of conversations with partners, relations and friends

We were interested first in the conversations women had with informal, rather than professional, contacts. Table 3.5 shows the number of partners, relatives, friends and colleagues to whom women had spoken. A sixth (13 women) spoke to one person only and a quarter (19 women) spoke to two. Over a third (29 women) spoke to 3 or 4 people while just over a sixth spoke to 5 or more people. Older teenagers (11 of the 57) were more likely to speak to five or more informal contacts than younger teenagers (2 of the 27).

Married or cohabiting women spoke to fewer people than the single women, a quarter of whom had spoken to 5 or more informal contacts about their pregnancy compared with none of the married women and only one cohabiting woman.

Table 3.5   **Number of partners, relatives and friends spoken to by women about the pregnancy**

column percentages

No. of partners/relatives/ friends	Total	Hackney	Solihull	Leeds
None	11	4	4	21
One	15	11	17	18
Two	23	26	22	21
Three	23	30	22	18
Four	12	11	13	12
Five	12	15	13	9
Six	0	0	0	0
Seven	4	4	4	3
Eight	1	0	4	0
Base: all women	*(84)*	*(27)*	*(23)*	*(34)*

It was clear that women were not only selective about whom they spoke to but were also selective about what they discussed with whom. They often commented that it had not been appropriate or necessary to talk about some issues with particular people. For some women, the decision to talk about the pregnancy was a practical one, especially in relation to their discussions with professionals.

However, there was ample evidence to suggest that discussions with partners, relatives and friends were not always open and honest. Some women were left wondering what people really thought, particularly about whether they should continue with the pregnancy. One woman said that her mother never gave her a straight answer about what she should do, but felt that she had tried to influence her to have a termination of pregnancy: 'I think she tried to convince me really to have an abortion. She tried to put me off. But I think she would have stood by me whatever.'

One factor which appeared to have influenced the stage at which women spoke with people was how quickly they suspected they were pregnant. The majority of women had not planned their pregnancies and some just hoped they were not pregnant, while others knew they were but could not accept it. This woman explained why she did not discuss having the baby or having an abortion: 'I did not think about having an abortion or having the baby because I just hoped that I wasn't pregnant. Anything but being pregnant.' Another woman recalled that her mother's observations prompted her recognition of the pregnancy and said: 'It was my mum who thought I was pregnant. I think I denied it for quite a long time.' Some did nothing out of fear of having to reveal the pregnancy to other people: 'I think I was more scared than anything about how to tell people. I think that's the worst thing.'

Table 3.6   Partners, relatives and friends spoken to by women about the pregnancy

numbers and column percentages

	Nos	%
None	9	11
Husband	6	7
Partner/boyfriend	53	63
Mother	48	57
Father	16	19
Sister	10	12
Brother	4	5
Other female relative	16	19
Friend (1)	30	36
Friend (2)	6	7
Friend (3)	1	1
Woman at work	3	4
Husband/boyfriend's mother	13	15
Husband/boyfriend's father	3	4
Husband/boyfriend's sister	7	8
Husband/boyfriend's other relative	4	5
Base: all women	(84)	

Table 3.6 shows the number of women who spoke to partners, relatives and friends.

- Most women (70 per cent) spoke to their partner about the pregnancy and about where and with whom they might live during the pregnancy and after the birth. More women with a steady boyfriend spoke to their partner about the pregnancy (33 of the 43 women) than married women (6 of the 9) or cohabiting women (17 of the 26). This seems remarkably low and one possible explanation could have been that women in settled relationships, and particularly those who had planned the pregnancy, felt they had nothing detailed to discuss.
- The respondents' mothers were the second most common group of people spoken to (57 per cent), but women in Solihull were twice as likely to talk to their mother (74 per cent) as women in Hackney (37 per cent). A higher proportion of women in Leeds spoke to their mothers (62 per cent) than to their partners. We found that cohabiting or married women were less likely to talk to their mother than those in less settled relationships. Only 1 of the 9 married women and less than half of the cohabiting women spoke to their mother, possibly

because most of them had already 'flown the nest' and were independent (although a few were still living with their parents or their partner's parents).

- The third most common group of people spoken to was a key friend. Over a third of the women spoke to at least one friend and some spoke to three or more.
- A much smaller proportion of women spoke to their father than their mother, often because women thought that if they told their mother they might have some moral support when broaching the subject with their father. Indeed, some mothers decided that it would be better if they broke the news themselves. Overall, a fifth of women spoke to their father but women in Solihull were more likely to do so than those in the other areas.
- We have already seen that a quarter of the women said that another sibling had also been a teenage parent. 17 per cent of the women had spoken to a sister and/or a brother, some of whom were teenage parents themselves.
- Just under a fifth of women had spoken to another female relative (usually an aunt or grandparent).

Discussions with partners

70 per cent of women spoke to their partner about their pregnancy, mostly by the time they were 10 weeks pregnant.

All the husbands were pleased or happy when they heard of the pregnancy although one was also surprised. Reactions varied among the boyfriends, and often depended on whether the pregnancy had been planned. Half the boyfriends spoken to (26 of the 53) were pleased or happy about the pregnancy especially if the pregnancy had been planned: 'He was looking forward to it. He'd just lost his dad, and he was looking forward to having a boy so he could name it after him.'

Over a third of the women who had spoken to their boyfriend said that he was surprised or shocked. A woman in Hackney explained that although her pregnancy had been planned, she and her partner were surprised: 'He was actually very shocked. We had stopped using things once or twice and hadn't expected anything to happen quite so quickly.' Another woman's partner seemed equally shocked to hear of the unplanned pregnancy despite the fact that the couple had not been using any form of contraception: 'He didn't seem as happy as I was. He wanted to know how it had come about.'

Although a relatively small number of women described negative reactions to the news of the pregnancy such as anger and disappointment, there was a striking lack of communication and consensus between some couples about whether they both wanted to have a family

and about the timing of pregnancy and parenthood.   Serious
misunderstandings between couples sometimes only became apparent
when the woman announced her pregnancy, resulting in reactions of
shock and anger from the father of the baby.

One woman (who said that the father was a steady boyfriend when
she became pregnant and was 19 when the baby was born) described how
her boyfriend had tried to blame her for the pregnancy: 'He lost his
temper and walked away. He said, "We're not having any children yet,"
and he blamed me. He told me I should have been on the pill and that I
should have an abortion.'

We have already seen that some women knew before they became
pregnant that their partner either did not want to have children at all or
did not want a child at the time. A number of women appeared to have
decided not to use contraceptives and had knowingly run the risk of
becoming pregnant, while others who had not used contraceptives had
not even thought of the consequences.

Partners expressed a wide variety of opinions about the pregnancy
and what to do about it. If the pregnancy had been planned, husbands and
boyfriends usually just discussed the pregnancy itself. Suggestions that
women should talk to their parents and family were more about sharing
their news, and suggestions to consult professionals such as GPs often
related to organising maternity care and preparing for the baby. Some
couples who had not planned the pregnancy but were in stable
relationships still wanted the baby so that the discussion of what to do
about the pregnancy never arose. One woman who said that she had
planned to marry the baby's father brought her wedding forward when
she became pregnant unexpectedly, and explained that she and her
boyfriend had shared the news with their relatives and their plans to
move away: 'He told his parents. He had a really good job and we were
going to stay there. And he bought some wallpaper for the nursery.'

Some boyfriends did not want to discuss the pregnancy at all, let alone
give advice about it. A third (19) of the women who had spoken to their
boyfriends said that the possibility of having a termination was discussed
but none of the 6 married women who had spoken to their husbands
discussed it. Six women said that their boyfriends advised or simply told
them to have an abortion. A Leeds woman (who said that the father was
a steady boyfriend and who was 18 when the baby was born) described
what her boyfriend had said: 'The first thing he said to me on the phone
was, "Get an abortion".'

Other women said that their boyfriends felt strongly against abortion.
A woman in Hackney (who was living with the father of the baby when
she became pregnant and was 16 when the baby was born) said that her
boyfriend issued her an ultimatum: 'Don't have an abortion. If you do I'll

leave.' Eight of the women who had spoken to their boyfriend said that they were advised to have the baby and others said that their boyfriend told them to consider their options: 'He was a bit worried and said, "Think about what you're doing." '

A quarter of the women who had spoken to their boyfriend said that he had left it to them to decide what they should do next. However, some appeared to have had very little opportunity to talk over their options and a few women had only brief, unhelpful and unpleasant discussions: 'He was really horrible. He said, "I don't want the baby. I can't afford one. I want to go on holiday this year and I want a new car".' Others were unsure about whether their boyfriend wanted the baby and whether they still had a relationship, as this woman explained: 'He didn't say anything. I said, "Do you want me to get rid of it or what?" He didn't talk to me for a while. But he did want it at the end of the day.'

Discussions with mothers and fathers

Well over half the women spoke to their mother and a fifth spoke to their father about the pregnancy, usually by the time they were 10 weeks pregnant.

Parents were less likely than partners to be pleased about the pregnancy. Just over a sixth of the women who had spoken to their mother said she was happy or pleased and only 2 of the 16 women who had spoken to their father said he was. A woman in Hackney described her mother's reaction to the news: 'She was all excited. She opened a bottle of wine. She nearly had a heart attack with excitement.'

Although fathers and mothers often reacted differently to the news, their reactions were generally negative. Most mothers were shocked and surprised. A woman in Solihull described what happened when she broke the news to her mother: 'She didn't speak for ages, she was like in shock. She had to go to the doctor's for some tablets.'

Not all mothers were surprised to hear their daughter was pregnant, and indeed, a few mothers had already suspected, sometimes before their daughter did. A woman in Leeds recalled her mother's reaction: 'She burst out crying and said, "I'll be here for you." She knew before me. She asked me the week before if I was.' Another woman in Leeds explained that her mother had also suspected that she was pregnant: 'She gave me a hug and produced a small baby hat she'd bought the day before. She said, "I had a feeling." '

In contrast, the most common reaction expressed by fathers was one of anger (7 of the 16 fathers), illustrated in this woman's description of her father's reaction: 'He was screaming and shouting, telling me how stupid I was. He was really strict so I was really scared at the time.'

Mothers expressed disappointment more than anyone else. Some of the women said their mother was disappointed with the news because of the effect it would have on their future. For instance, some parents felt that the pregnancy had ruined or severely limited their daughter's chances of a career or further studies. Some mothers were clearly already anxious about their daughter's relationship and some had disapproved of their daughter's boyfriend even before the pregnancy, like this woman in Leeds whose mother had foreseen problems: 'She was disappointed. I've done well at school and she felt I'd gone downhill since I met (boyfriend).' Other parents were worried that their daughter was too young for both the pregnancy and parenthood: 'I think she (mother) was a bit worried because she feels I'm a bit young. I think my mum and dad think I've a lot of ability and could do something.' Some parents, such as one father in Leeds, were quite clear that having the baby was not the right thing for their daughter: 'He said I was too young and I had too much of my life ahead and it would ruin everything.'

Women's accounts of their conversations with parents suggested that they were concerned not only that their daughters should make the right decision, but also a decision that they could live with. Nearly a quarter of the women who had spoken to their mother about the pregnancy and 6 of the 16 who had spoken to their father said that they had been assured of their support. Parents often made it clear that their support was unconditional, and that they would stand by their daughter whatever she decided to do. This support was not just extended to the baby's mother, but in some cases, to the baby's father as well, as this woman's account of a conversation with her father shows: 'He was brilliant really. He just said whatever we wanted to do, he'd help. He said he'd pay for an abortion if that's what I wanted to do. If not, he'd stand by me whatever I wanted.'

Parents and partners were equally likely to advise women that they should decide themselves what to do next, but parents were less likely to be as directive about having the baby or having a termination of pregnancy as partners were. However, it was clear from some of the women's comments that their mother had cast the role of motherhood as one fraught with difficulties. These mothers were determined to ensure that women who wanted to continue with the pregnancy understood the consequences.

One woman in Solihull who was living with the father of the baby when she became pregnant and was 17 when the baby was born recalled conversations with her mother: 'She just used to tell me how difficult it was – that I wouldn't be able to go out. She never said not to keep him, but I know that's what she thought.' Another woman who said that the father of the baby was a steady boyfriend and was 18 when the baby was born had a similar experience with her mother: 'She said it was up to me. It was not easy bringing up a child but it was up to me.'

A higher proportion of mothers than partners encouraged women to consider their options before deciding what to do and a few accompanied women to their GP or a pregnancy counsellor to seek advice. It was clear that women valued the opportunity to talk through their options and receive advice. They especially valued their parents' support in whatever they decided. One woman described how helpful she had found her mother throughout: 'She was completely supportive and she didn't try to force her opinions on me and she helped me through them, whether she thought it right or wrong.'

A third of the women who had spoken to their mothers about the pregnancy discussed the possibility of having a termination of pregnancy (16 of the 48 women). However, mothers rarely advised women categorically either way. Few mothers reacted like this mother who told her daughter (who became pregnant with a casual partner and was 17 when the baby was born): 'Keep the baby. No other opinion. If I didn't want it, she would have it.'

Mothers tended to advise or warn women to think carefully about what they wanted. A woman in Hackney described what her mother had to say: 'If you have a termination, make sure you know what you're doing – you might regret it.' Another woman (who said the father was a steady boyfriend when she became pregnant and who was 19 when the baby was born) said that she had hoped her mother would give her firm advice, but her mother's response was: 'I can't tell you what to do. It must be your own decision. I wanted her to tell me what I should do, but she wouldn't. I wanted her either to say, "It'll be bloody hard, have an abortion" or "You're doing the right thing in keeping it." ' Mothers were clearly reluctant to be too directive with their daughters.

Mothers were more likely than anyone else to encourage women to continue with their plans for education or to complete their schooling. A few advised women to make enquiries about housing and accommodation immediately. One mother said: 'Just sort yourself out, your benefits, your house.' Other women said that their mother started to organise and plan for the pregnancy and the baby. A woman (who was cohabiting when she became pregnant and 17 when the baby was born) said of her mother: 'She wanted to start planning and wanted to go out and buy things. The first thing she did was go out and buy me a big bunch of flowers.'

Discussions with friends and other relations

Over a third of the women (30) turned to their friends for advice. Again, it was clear that women referred to their most significant discussions rather than giving details of all the friends they had spoken to about their pregnancy. Some had spoken to a friend as soon as they had suspected they were pregnant and most had spoken to a friend by the time they were 10 weeks pregnant.

Friends were more likely to be surprised and shocked to hear the news of the pregnancy than anyone else and some women could not understand why: 'She was just shocked really. I don't know why. She was more pregnant than I was.' Many women also said that their friends were pleased or happy to hear about the pregnancy, but it was clear from their comments that some friends were glad to have mutual support, particularly those who had also had a baby or were pregnant at the same time. A woman in Solihull recalled her friend's reaction and remarked: 'I think she was pleased because she was pregnant as well, but she wasn't going to keep her baby.'

The pregnancy may have tested, strained and even ruined some women's relationships with partners, parents and other relations, but it had also brought people together, particularly those who had had a similar experience. A Leeds woman described the friendship that had developed with another pregnant woman who was sharing the same hostel accommodation: 'I'd only known her for two days. We were both in the hostel. We just gelled and hit it off straight away. We were both nervous and scared, both in the same situation.'

Friends often expressed concern that the women were too young to take on parental responsibilities. Some were speaking from personal experience, like a friend in Solihull talking to a 19 year old who became pregnant in a casual relationship: 'She said I'd get tied down, won't be able to go out. She just thinks I'm too young.'

Comments from the women themselves suggested that some had a romantic and a rather naive impression of motherhood. However, not all of them did and, indeed, some women whose siblings or friends had been teenage parents were under no illusions about the difficult times ahead. One woman recalled her friend's reaction to the news, and how she had pointed out that as a teenage parent herself, she had had to make sacrifices: 'She was happy. She was pleased. She was 15 when she had a baby, but she said that she missed out on a lot.' The thought of the changes that pregnancy and parenthood would bring was too much for some friends, as one woman observed: 'She thought I wouldn't be able to do what I wanted, go to college. My life was over!'

Some women had confided in friends before talking to their parents or partner. A few were encouraged to talk about the pregnancy with their parents and partner before making any decision. Friends also advised women to consider their options carefully. Five women said that their friends had encouraged them to have the baby, such as one woman whose friend simply said: ' "Keep it." We were both in childcare and fond of little ones.'

A few women felt that people had judged their ability and suitability for motherhood only on their age – and felt that there was an implicit assumption that they would not be able to take care of a child. A Leeds woman (who was 19 when the baby was born) described how she and her friend who was also pregnant were determined to continue with their pregnancies and prove that this was not the case: 'We both discussed it and the more we discussed it, the more we decided we wouldn't have a termination because there was nothing wrong with our babies or with us. It was like an admission of failure to have a termination. People expect you not to be able to cope because we're young, single and homeless and all the odds are against us. We both wanted to keep our babies and it was a hard decision to make, but we knew we could do it. It was a challenge to prove that I could cope against all the odds.'

Around a third of the women who had spoken to a friend said that they discussed the possibility of having a termination of pregnancy and a few friends suggested termination as an option, but rarely said that women should go ahead and have one.

A relatively small number of women spoke to a sister (10) or brother (4) about the pregnancy. Four of the women said that their sister was pleased but negative reactions from siblings were not uncommon, although some said that they would support or stand by their sister. They often said that their sister should make her own decision about the pregnancy. Relatively few spoke about the possibility of having a termination of pregnancy and only one sister and one brother recommended a termination.

Women also turned to other female relatives such as aunts and grandmothers. The possibility of having a termination was discussed with 3 of these 16 female relatives. None of the women were advised to have a termination of pregnancy.

Women spoke to 27 of their partner's relatives including their partner's sisters and mothers. Half of these relatives were happy to hear the news of the pregnancy but some, like one partner's mother, had mixed feelings about it and shared her own experience of teenage parenthood: 'She was happy for me, but because she been through the same situation she told me how she felt, what she had missed out on.'

Other relatives were angry and annoyed to hear the news of the pregnancy and made their feelings perfectly clear to the women. One partner's mother thought that having the baby was out of the question and that the woman (who said that the father was a steady boyfriend and was 18 when the baby was born) should have a termination of pregnancy: 'She was really annoyed. She thought I'd done it on purpose so he'd never leave me. She was exactly the same as (boyfriend) and wanted me to get rid of it. She said I was too young and immature and couldn't afford to have a baby.' One woman recalled how her partner's sister raised many searching questions about how she would cope: 'She told me I was stupid. I wanted to get a job. She said, "It will be hard. Where's the money going to come from? Where are you going to live?" She raised all the questions.'

Some women spoke to their partner's relatives before they spoke to their partner and their own parents. Some advised women to continue with the pregnancy and organise their maternity care and a place to live, while others advised them to consider termination or to have one. One woman said that her partner's mother thought that the issue was clearcut and said: 'Get an abortion and stop being silly and feeling guilty.' Overall a third of the women who spoke to their partner's relatives discussed the possibility of having a termination of pregnancy.

Number of conversations with professionals

Table 3.7 shows that nearly half the women had not spoken to any professionals and we have already seen that 9 of the women had spoken to no-one at all about their pregnancy. However, nearly three-quarters of the women who had not spoken to any professionals had spoken to informal contacts. A third of all women had spoken to one professional, while around a fifth had spoken to 2 or 3 and one woman had spoken to 4 professionals. There was little age or marital status difference among women in the number of professionals consulted.

Table 3.7   **Number of professionals spoken to by women about the pregnancy**

				column percentages
	Total	Hackney	Solihull	Leeds
No. of professionals				
None	46	30	35	68
One	33	37	43	24
Two	12	19	9	9
Three	7	15	9	0
Four	1	0	4	0
Base: all women	*(84)*	*(27)*	*(23)*	*(34)*

Table 3.8 shows that a quarter of all women (21) spoke to a GP about the pregnancy and the options available to them. Midwives, family planning nurses and pregnancy advisory staff were less often consulted. Social workers and teachers were approached for general advice and support but also for specific guidance on how study, examinations and courses might fit in with their new circumstances. The issue of where and with

whom women might live was also discussed with some professionals, but many women did not think that it was necessary or appropriate to do so. Discussions with housing officers, benefits officers and welfare rights officers concentrated mainly on where women might live and their eligibility for social security benefits and housing. We will discuss the issue of housing in more detail in Chapter 4 and social security benefits will be discussed fully in Chapter 5.

Table 3.8   Professionals spoken to by women about the pregnancy

number of respondents and column percentages

	Nos	%
None	39	46
GP	21	25
Midwife	9	11
Health visitor	4	5
Family planning nurse	1	1
Pregnancy advisory service staff	1	1
LIFE	1	1
Social worker	3	4
Teacher	5	6
Youth worker	3	4
Housing officer	6	7
Benefits officer	1	1
Welfare information officer	1	1
Base: all women	*(84)*	

Discussions with doctors

Half of the women went to their GP to confirm they were pregnant, but Table 3.8 shows that a quarter spoke to their GP about the pregnancy and what they were going to do about it. GPs discussed what options were open to them and advised them to consider their circumstances carefully before making a decision. One woman was surprised and disappointed with her GP's reaction when she said she was pregnant: 'He wasn't shocked. He seemed more disgusted than anything. I didn't think a doctor could be like that, but he was.' But not all women had the same experience, as a Leeds woman's comments illustrate: 'He was really lovely. He never suggested I should get rid of it. He said it was my choice, but he did point out I was at college and had a job.'

Some women described how they had been taken through all the options: 'He told me to get a piece of paper and write down all the things I wanted to do in life and then in the next column all the things I'd be able to do in life if I had the baby, and then decide. He said have a week or so to think about it before I had the counselling and then another week before I went into hospital, and that I should have a really good think before deciding what to do. He also told me all the ins and outs of having an abortion because I was really worried that I might be killing something.'

Only a third of the women who had spoken to their GP said that they discussed the possibility of having a termination of pregnancy. There was very little evidence to suggest that GPs were trying to influence women either way. This woman recalled how her GP had just presented her with options: 'He said, "As it's a teenage pregnancy, there's an option for adoption or abortion," and I says, "No. It's not what I want." ' A Solihull woman felt that her GP was trying to convince her to have an abortion: 'He just went on about having an abortion, and how having a baby ruins your life. He was horrible. He just rambled on for about half an hour.'

Discussions with other professionals

Nine women spoke to a midwife about what to do about the pregnancy and a few women spoke to a health visitor and a family planning nurse. Three women discussed the possibility of having a termination of pregnancy but one woman was told by her midwife that her pregnancy was too advanced and that a termination of pregnancy was not an option: 'She asked me what I wanted to do, but she told me it was too late to have an abortion even if I did want one.'

Six women spoke to a social worker or youth worker, two of whom advised the women to continue with their studies. Three of the women said that the possibility of having a termination of pregnancy was discussed and one of them was advised to have one.

Five women had spoken to a tutor or teacher about the pregnancy. Women appeared to have valued the chance to discuss their pregnancy and most said that their teachers had assured them of their help and support and urged them to finish their studies. One woman said that her teacher had been the most sympathetic. None of the women discussed having a termination.

However, some women felt that they were treated in an inflexible and uncaring manner by professionals. A woman who spoke to her teacher about continuing with her studies described what happened: 'I was offered a place at a unit for pregnant girls to continue my education, but I decided it wasn't for me. I'd have preferred to stay at school but my teacher said it wasn't appropriate.'

Discussions which influenced the decision about the pregnancy

We asked women if their discussions with people had made any difference to their decision to continue with their pregnancy. Most felt that their discussions had not made any difference but just under a fifth (15 women) singled out one or two people with whom they had had influential discussions.

Eight of these women had considered having a termination of pregnancy but all but one of these had been influenced by their discussion with their partner to continue with the pregnancy. Some women also referred to a second person such as a friend, parent, other relative or professional as having influenced their decision to continue with their pregnancies. Two women singled out their GP, another two their midwife and one a youth counsellor.

A few women were aware from the outset that even if they did decide to keep the baby, they might still have to cope with parenthood on their own. One woman who was living alone when she became pregnant said that the baby's father was a steady boyfriend. She recalled his response when she discussed the pregnancy with him: 'He wanted me to have an abortion and suggested it. He said he couldn't guarantee he would stay with me.' She had not considered having a termination and said that her mother had been particularly unhelpful: 'Because she tried to force me into having an abortion.' She felt that her GP and the youth counsellor with whom she had spoken had been influential and she explained why the youth counsellor had influenced her decision: 'She encouraged me to feel that I could cope on my own.' In the event, she lived temporarily with her boyfriend after the birth but when their relationship broke up she moved into a flat on her own with the baby.

Other women had been given a clear signal of support and assistance from their boyfriend at the outset. A woman who was living with her partner when she became pregnant had considered a termination of pregnancy when she first suspected the pregnancy. She said that her discussions with her boyfriend, his mother and sister had influenced her decision to continue with the pregnancy and she recalled what her boyfriend had said: 'He asked me if I wanted to give it up or to keep it, and at the end of the day, he said, "It's your decision. I'll be behind you all the way".' She had had a poor relationship with her mother for a long time and had left home when she was 13 to live with a friend. Although she had had regular contact with her mother they had not discussed the pregnancy and she relied almost entirely on her partner's family for assistance and support.

Initial support and assistance from partners was sometimes short lived and two-thirds of the women said that their relationship with the baby's father had broken up by the time of the interview (10 of the 15). Only five women reported that their relationship had remained stable throughout. Two said that their relationship with the baby's father had ended before they realised they were pregnant, but one of these said that her boyfriend had been very supportive throughout and influenced her to continue with the pregnancy. Although he was eager to re-establish the relationship when he learned of the pregnancy, she said that she did not want this: 'He wanted us to get back together but I didn't want to.'

Women who had little family support or poor family relationships often singled out professionals as influential and supportive. Some women noted that their parents had reacted negatively to the news of the pregnancy and they appreciated the advice of professionals who were neutral, like this woman speaking about a youth worker: 'She was outside the situation and was supportive.'

Decision-making: where and with whom to live

After deciding to continue with the pregnancy women had to decide where and with whom they would live during their pregnancy and after the birth. There was a marked difference in the range of options available to women. The issue of where they would live was closely linked to the status and stability of their relationship with the baby's father and, to a lesser extent, their relationship with their parents. It was clear that some women in stable relationships would continue to live with the baby's father, but for many women pregnancy had preceded any decision or discussion about the future of their relationship with their partner.

There was considerable evidence to suggest that couples had different expectations and preferences about where and with whom they would live, and some women said that the pregnancy was not a reason for moving in with the baby's father. Parents and partners often had different views on what women should do and offered very different advice. In some cases, parents were uneasy about the prospect of any continued relationship with the baby's father and, as a result, their discussions with the women concentrated more on options such as staying at home than options for joint living arrangements.

Discussions with partners about where and with whom to live

Around half of the women who had discussed their pregnancy with their partners also discussed where and with whom they might live during their pregnancy (26 of the 53 women). 19 of the 26 discussed living with their boyfriend but, not surprisingly, most of these had been living at home with their parents when they became pregnant. Some of the cohabiting women discussed where they might live with their partner, but most of these women saw no reason, at least at the time, to discuss their future living arrangements. Another option discussed with partners was staying at home with parents.

Four of the 6 women who had spoken to their husbands had talked about where they might live during pregnancy. Living together with relatives was the main option discussed but two women said that they discussed living alone with their husband and applying for council accommodation.

It was clear that women often received conflicting advice from their partners, parents and others about their future living arrangements. For example, one woman who was 17 when she had her baby described the different options she had discussed with her parents and boyfriend. She had become pregnant unexpectedly and recalled that her mother was keen for her to have a termination of pregnancy and accompanied her to the consultation. However, her boyfriend advised her to take her own decision and said that he would stand by her. They talked about living together: 'We were planning to live together. He was all right about that... He said he'd get in touch with housing and see what they had to say.' Although her mother advised her to apply for housing, she described how she also tried to convince her to continue to live at home and said: 'I should try for a house but I could stay here. She (mother) said, "I'd prefer you to stay at home"... if anything goes wrong with the baby she and my dad would be in the next room.'

Like the women, partners could also have a rather rosy and unrealistic view of the situation and how things would turn out. In contrast, parents often feared the worst. They warned women to think about what they were doing before choosing a particular course of action. A woman who was living at home with her parents when she became pregnant recalled her boyfriend's suggestion that they should live together after hearing the news of the pregnancy: 'He said we should try to get a house together. He would get a mortgage.' Her mother was anxious that she should consider her options and avoid rushing into anything. She advised her: 'To sit down and think it through, talk to my boyfriend and put my name down at the Council.' She had not been convinced that her daughter's relationship would last: 'She told me to get my own place. She didn't want him to get a place (for both of them). She liked him but there were a lot of problems.' Having lived at home throughout most of her pregnancy, she moved into a flat with her boyfriend when she was 8 months pregnant, and after only 4 weeks together she moved back home again: 'I didn't get on with my boyfriend and he told me to leave.'

Although there was a strong desire amongst women for inde-pendence, and a place on their own or with their boyfriend, even the couples in stable relationships experienced problems and recognised the importance of having family support nearby. One woman moved away to live with her partner but later returned to live nearer her parents when she became ill during pregnancy: 'I was so ill, I lost 5 stone in 4 weeks and (partner) worked long hours. I couldn't be left at home alone so (partner) gave up his job and we moved back here to be near my mother.'

The issue of where and with whom women might live was not discussed by all the couples who spoke about the pregnancy and some avoided the issue. It was often taken for granted by women who were already living at home that they would or could continue to do so, like this woman who explained that she did not discuss it with her boyfriend: 'Because I knew I'd stay here, at home.' However, staying or living at home with parents was chosen by the women for very different reasons.

- First, staying at home was the most likely option for some young women, who were not in stable relationships and wanted to remain at home with their parents. Generally these women did not want to be independent yet, and indeed becoming pregnant had reinforced their desire to remain at home. Some did not feel ready to move away, or had never considered it as a realistic option. The pregnancy itself and their fears of being unable to cope with parenthood prompted these women to stay at home. This woman explained why: 'I knew I'd live with my mum because it was secure.'
- Other women weighed up their options and their situation and concluded that being pregnant was not a sufficient reason for moving in with the baby's father. Staying at home or living alone was a safer and a better option. These women might have been ready to leave home, but it simply did not make sense to them to do so. Sometimes the decision to live at home with parents was an expression of a lack of confidence in their relationship: 'I was only with (boyfriend) six months and then I fell pregnant. I didn't want to go living with him. I wanted to stay at home.' Other women knew that living with their boyfriend was not an option, such as one woman, who after assessing her situation, decided to stay at home: 'I knew that my mum would never throw me out. I knew that my boyfriend wasn't ready to live with me. I thought I'd be better off at home with my mum.'
- Staying at home was an option that women also chose for purely practical reasons. Some said that their parents had advised them to stay at home or agreed that they could do so until they found accommodation on their own or with their partner. This was a short term option and women usually stayed during pregnancy and moved away as soon as it was feasible. They were often committed to a relationship with the baby's father but felt that it was preferable to stay at home with their parents until after the baby was born or until they had an opportunity to move. One woman had planned to live with

her parents until she and her boyfriend could move into a house of their own: 'We'd live at home with my mum and dad until we could afford to buy our own house.' At the time of the interview, she and her boyfriend had bought a house together and were waiting to move into it. Another woman who was living with her boyfriend and his parents when she became pregnant said that they had decided to stay put and then move to a place of their own when they could: 'I was happy to stay where I was while I was pregnant... I told him we needed to get our own place (after the birth).'

Women in stable relationships and living with the baby's father said that they had not discussed where and with whom they might live because they assumed that things would continue as they were, like one woman who was 18 when she had her baby. She was living with the baby's father when she became pregnant and the pregnancy was planned: 'We were already living together – already here (in owner-occupied house).' Other women said that it was not a priority and that they just had not thought about it.

But a small group of women said that living arrangements were never discussed or had not arisen in the discussions with their boyfriend. For some of these women the news of the pregnancy was the beginning of the end of their relationship and some relationships ended shortly after their initial discussion. One woman recalled the unpleasant reaction of her boyfriend when she told him about the pregnancy: 'I spoke to my boyfriend too late and he shouted and bawled. That's how we split up really.' Another woman said that she did not talk to her boyfriend because he was not interested and she assumed that she could live at home with her parents: 'He just didn't want to know. It went without saying that I'd live with my mother.'

We have seen that nearly half the women who had discussed the pregnancy with their partner had also discussed where and with whom they might live during pregnancy (26 of the 53 women). We found that two-thirds (33 of the 53) discussed living arrangements after the birth with their partner. The most common option was living together. However, women were not always in agreement with their partner that this was the best option. Indeed, there was some evidence that couples wanted quite different living arrangements.

One woman described the divergent views of herself and her boyfriend: 'He wanted us to live together but I didn't want to.' Another woman did not have much faith in her relationship and felt that for the sake of her baby, she could not take any chances: 'He knew I wouldn't move in with him because I told him I wouldn't when I was pregnant. If you move in with someone with a baby and then split up, you've got nowhere.' But other women who thought things would work out were let down, as one woman who had hoped for a better outcome explained: 'I'd always known I'd be on my own. I had a sort of romantic notion about (baby's father) but he turned out not to be a very nice person.'

We asked the women who had helped them most in deciding where they might live after the baby was born. Less than a fifth of the women who had spoken to their boyfriend said that he had helped them most but many of these were cohabiting in any case when they became pregnant. One woman described what her boyfriend had done to help: 'He was always there. He said that he would definitely buy a house.'

It was clearly very important for some women to move into a place of their own. One woman was living with her boyfriend and his parents when she became pregnant and was anxious that he might not want to move: 'I don't think he really wanted to move away from his parents.' They moved into a housing association property when she was 34 weeks pregnant and she felt pleased that he had gone along with her wishes: 'He was very helpful about getting our own place. It was difficult for him to leave (his parents), but he supported me.'

Discussions with parents about where and with whom to live

Over half the women who had spoken to their mother and around a third who had spoken to their father discussed where and with whom they might live during pregnancy and after the birth. Not surprisingly, most of them were living at home and talked mainly about staying at home. Typically, mothers offered their daughter a place to stay or tried to persuade her to stay at home. However, women did not always agree with their parents. Some decided that they did not want to live at home, like this woman who explained why: 'I told my mum I'd think about whether I wanted to live with her. At the end of the day I wanted to live on my own.' Discussions at times seemed to involve the whole family while others were more one-sided, as this woman who spoke to her father noted: 'I just sat him down and told him what was going to happen and he was quite happy with that.'

Staying at home did not appeal to some women, and having to leave home was an unwelcome prospect facing others. It was clear from the women's accounts that their discussions became confrontational in a number of households, as anxious and angry parents reacted to the news of the pregnancy by insisting that their daughter stay with them. One father simply said when he was told of the pregnancy: 'Well you're stopping here while you're pregnant.' Another woman recalled what her father had to say on the matter: ' "If you choose to have the baby we'll kick you out." He didn't want a baby in the house.'

But not all women had the option of living at home. One woman who stopped working when she was pregnant described how she had to leave her rented accommodation because she could no longer afford the rent: 'I wanted to move back with my mum but she had no room... She said I should go into a hostel because she had no room at all.' Another woman had a similar experience and was also living away from home in privately rented accommodation when she became pregnant. She could not afford to pay her rent when she stopped working and said that her mother's advice was: 'Find myself a place... I didn't have anywhere to live and they all knew that.' She explained that her relationship with her mother had deteriorated when she told her that she was pregnant and that they had no further discussions: 'Because we had a big bust-up and I didn't talk to her nearly all the way through the pregnancy.'

Many of the women were already living with their parents but others who had left home decided to move back. One woman knew when she became pregnant that there would not be enough room in the flat she had shared with her boyfriend so she moved back home to her parents: 'I didn't really have any options. There wasn't enough room at the flat I was sharing with my boyfriend, so I had to move back to my mum's.'

It was clear that many of the cohabiting women would continue to live with the father of the baby. However, some parents were worried that their daughter was too young to cope with a baby. One woman said that although she and her partner were already living together her mother was not happy about the pregnancy: 'She wasn't very pleased. I think she more or less left it up to me. She didn't really advise me.'

Mothers often advised their daughter to think carefully about where and with whom they might live. One woman said that her mother was concerned that her relationship might not last: 'She said she wouldn't mind if I lived with him (boyfriend), but she'd rather I lived with her in case we split up.' Another woman who was living at home discussed the possibility of staying at home with her boyfriend and her parents until they could save enough money to buy a place of their own: 'We'd live with my mum and dad until we could afford to buy our own house.' Others talked about living with their partner's parents. Another arrangement which was discussed was the possibility of the couple staying with their respective parents: 'I would live with my family and he would live with his family until the baby was born. There was no reason to change anything.'

Again, the most common option discussed with parents about where women would live after the birth was staying or living at home. But it was clear that this would only be a temporary arrangement for some, and that sooner or later they would move away on their own or with their partner. Indeed, mothers themselves often knew that staying at home in the long term was not sustainable. One woman said that her mother agreed she could stay at home until she had a place of her own: 'She said,

"We'll stand by you." She was quite happy for me to stay till I got a council flat.'

Even women who had not discussed where they would live said that it was assumed that they would stay at home, like this woman who just took it for granted: 'I suppose I just thought I'd stay with my mum and dad.'

Mothers were mentioned more than any other source as being helpful to women in making a decision about where they might live after the baby was born. Nearly half the women who had spoken to their mother said that she had been the most helpful. This woman appreciated her mother's help in finding accommodation and the overall support she offered her: 'She came with me to look at houses and to buy furniture. My mum was always there. She's like my best friend really.' Another woman felt that having her mother with her made all the difference when she went to enquire about housing: 'She spoke up for me at the housing. When you're so young, they don't listen to you.'

Discussions with friends and other relatives

Less than half the women who had spoken to a key friend about the pregnancy discussed where and with whom they might live. One of the most common options discussed with friends was the possibility of staying or living at home with parents. Women also discussed applying for council accommodation and one woman described how her friend had advised her to go about getting accommodation quickly: 'She said, "Get a council flat." She told me exactly what to do in terms of getting mum to write a letter to the council to say she was kicking me out.' Women also talked to friends about the possibility of living with their boyfriend, like one woman who was living at home when she became pregnant. Her boyfriend had suggested living together but her mother had suggested that she stay at home: 'My friend said, "If you and (boyfriend) want to stay together, you stay together." '

Very few women who had spoken to their sister about the pregnancy discussed where they might live and only one woman who had spoken with her brother talked about it. During her discussion with her brother, this woman mentioned the possibility of staying at home but he made it quite clear to her that he did not want her and the baby there: 'He said, "Not here. You must leave here. I'm not staying here with you and a baby." '

A third of the 16 women who had spoken to other relatives said that they talked about where and with whom they might live. Some of the women appeared to have been rather isolated and to have had little contact or poor relationships with their parents. As a result, living with parents was rarely discussed and relatives often ended up offering women a place to stay while they were pregnant. Half the women who had spoken to other relatives talked about where they might live after the birth and usually discussed the possibility of staying with their relatives and applying for council accommodation.

Only 9 of the 27 women who spoke to their partner's relatives about the pregnancy also talked about their living arrangements. They were mainly advised to stay at home with their parents during the pregnancy but four were offered a place to stay.

A third of the women who had spoken to their GP talked about their living arrangements (7). They usually discussed the option of living at home or were asked where they planned to live. It was clear from the women's comments that some professionals wanted the women to understand the long-term commitment and responsibility they were taking on in deciding to keep their baby. One woman who was living with her parents when she became pregnant discussed the possibility of staying with them and recalled her GP's advice: 'He said, "Fair enough," if I wanted to live with my mum but I must remember at the end of the day, it's my baby, not my mum's. I mustn't lumber my mum with it. He also said I must remember that I've got the baby now for 18 years till he leaves home, not just for a few years.'

Most of the women who had spoken to a midwife about the pregnancy also discussed their living arrangements (7 of the 9). One woman said: 'I told her I was very worried about where I would live as I was registered homeless and just staying around. She said I should go and see the housing advice in town to see if I could get priority for a house or if I needed to move into a hostel.'

Women who spoke to housing officers (8) were primarily concerned about where to live. One woman who was living with her partner and had planned the pregnancy explained the housing problems they had encountered when she became ill during pregnancy. They had moved away to live in another part of the country because of her partner's job and returned to live nearer her parents when she became ill. They spoke to the local housing officer and explained that they had nowhere to live: 'He told us we had to wait two years even though we were homeless. I was ill and came back to Leeds but he said we'd made ourselves homeless and it was our fault. He said, "Stay with your parents." ' Another woman, who was asthmatic, was living with her partner when she became pregnant and renting an eighth floor flat from the local authority. She spoke to the housing officer about the possibility of getting a transfer to another property. She explained: 'I asked for certain areas. They said, "You just have to wait". I took my name off the transfer list.'

Overall, 3 of the 8 women who had spoken to a housing officer said that they had been particularly unhelpful and none of the women singled out a housing officer as being helpful in their advice in deciding where they might live.

Perceptions of support during the pregnancy and after the birth

We were interested in whom the women found to be most helpful overall in deciding what to do about their pregnancy. We also asked who had given them the most help in deciding where and with whom to live, the most financial support, the most practical help, and whether they had found anyone particularly unhelpful.

Mothers were generally rated more highly than anyone else for being helpful and supportive in their discussions about the pregnancy and what women should do about it. They were particularly singled out for the practical help they had provided during the pregnancy and after the birth. Women often depended on their mothers for advice on caring for their newborn baby and for their help with childcare and general household tasks in the early weeks and months after the birth. Women who were living at home spoke time and again of how they had appreciated the comforts and the security of home and how well they had been looked after by their mothers.

In contrast, partners were much less likely to be identified as helpful or sympathetic and emotionally supportive, and a substantial minority of women identified their boyfriend as being particularly unhelpful. However, women were rather more likely to say that their boyfriend had provided the most financial support.

It was clear that women differed in their assessment of who had been helpful and who had not. Indeed, women often reacted differently to the same kinds of advice. There also appeared to be a fine dividing line between advice and actions which were thought to be helpful and those which were less welcome or even unhelpful. Some women based their judgements on particular events, like this woman who said that her mother had been unhelpful because she had not accompanied her to a hospital appointment for her antenatal scan: 'I actually fell out with my mum for quite a while for being unhelpful. She doesn't like hospitals and she wouldn't come with me to have the scan.' Another woman said that although she had not found anyone particularly unhelpful, she added: 'Except then my parents took over a bit. They always wanted to hold him when I did, but in a way I enjoyed it as well, knowing they loved him.'

Support from mothers and fathers

Women consistently identified their mother as the most helpful person. Indeed, nearly two-thirds of the women who had spoken to their mother found her the most helpful, especially older teenagers, who also identified their mother as the most sympathetic. Overall, women appreciated many different forms of help and support, such as the emotional support of being comforted and listened to, or advice, or a different perspective, or encouragement to take action themselves. One woman recalled the extensive help and support her mother had given her throughout: 'She couldn't do enough for me. She offered me everything – converting the house, buying everything. She wanted to organise everything.' Another woman said how supportive her mother had been: 'She was completely supportive and she didn't try to force her opinions on me, and she helped me through them – whether she thought they were right or wrong.'

But not all women had the same experience and a few said that their mother had been particularly unhelpful. Some had had a poor relationship with their mother, father or both parents before the pregnancy in any case, and these relationships never really improved. In such circumstances, any parental advice was often unwelcome or unfavourably received. One woman whose own mother had been a teenage parent explained that she had left home when she was 15 and moved in with her aunt because she did not get on with her parents. She was single when she became pregnant unexpectedly and remarked that her aunt had been the most helpful person: 'She understands me and listens to me.' However, she felt let down by her mother whom she identified as particularly unhelpful and remarked: 'She just didn't want to help.' Another woman whose mother had also been a teenage parent said that she was particularly unhelpful because: 'She tried to force me into having an abortion.'

Although only 16 women had spoken to their father, 5 of them said that he had been the most helpful to them. It was clear that parents were a great source of help and support for many of the women who had been living with them when they became pregnant.

Parents also gave financial support. One third of the women who had spoken to their mother and as many as two-thirds who had spoken to their father said they had given the most financial support. One woman appreciated the financial support she had received from her parents throughout: 'I'd buy things and they'd buy two of what I'd bought. They were just there all the time.'

Over two-thirds of the women who had spoken to their mothers said that she had provided the most practical support. The comments made by some women indicated how dependent they had been on their mothers with little other practical help available. Some of them were not well enough to take care of themselves or the baby immediately after the birth. One woman had been unwell after the birth and relied almost completely on her mother's help and support: 'I got post-natal depression for 4 to 5 weeks. My mum was really good.' Another woman said that her mother took over her housework completely after the baby was born: 'She cleaned, washed and ironed, shopped and cooked.'

Support from partners

The picture was rather different with partners. 53 of the 75 women who had spoken to someone had spoken to a boyfriend and 6 of the 75 had spoken to their husband. Only 9 women had found their boyfriends the most helpful, and only 2 had found their husbands the most helpful. Very few of the women who were cohabiting when they became pregnant identified their boyfriend as the most helpful.

Partners were rarely singled out for the sympathy they had shown. Indeed, women were more likely to identify partners as being particularly unhelpful than helpful or sympathetic, and the lack of help and support from partners was a particular problem for some women. One woman who was single when she became pregnant and was living with a new partner at the time of the interview explained why she thought her boyfriend had been unhelpful: 'He never helped me through the pregnancy. He never came to the hospital or came with me to the midwife. He never bought me owt.'

Other women felt that they had been abandoned by their boyfriend once they announced their pregnancy, like one who explained that her boyfriend had been against her continuing with the pregnancy from the beginning and was adamant that he would not be there to support her or the baby: 'He wasn't interested in anything except getting rid of the baby. Although he's been to see (the baby), he's made it perfectly clear he's not helping in any way.'

On the more positive side, other women found that the small things their partners did were reassuring and supportive: 'If I was a bit down he'd make me a cup of tea. He was just great.' Women who were in less stable relationships when they became pregnant also valued the opportunity to discuss the future of their relationship, like this woman who was 17 when she became pregnant and had remained single throughout. Although she was living with her parents and had never moved, she had been waiting since she had become pregnant to be allocated a council property so that she and the baby could move in with her boyfriend: 'We just sat down and talked and talked about what we were going to do when (the baby) was born and if we were going to get married and get a house.'

A relatively small number of women said that their boyfriend had provided the most practical support: 'You name it – he did it! He's in a job where he had paternity leave so he was home.' Another woman who was single when she became pregnant but who started living with the baby's father after the birth recalled how involved her partner had been throughout her pregnancy: 'He went shopping with me. He read books with me. He went to all my classes. He was very supportive.' Only one of the married women said that her husband had provided the most practical help.

If partners were perceived to be helpful at all it was more often for their financial support. A quarter of the women who had spoken to a boyfriend and 4 of the 6 women who had spoken to their husband said they had provided the most financial support. A woman who was 18 when she had the baby said that the baby's father was a steady boyfriend when she became pregnant but the relationship had broken up after the birth after a short period of cohabitation. She said: 'He gave me half his wages when I was pregnant to buy things for (baby).' He had also given contributions to the baby's upkeep after the birth but could not afford to contribute when he was made redundant.

Support from relatives and friends

Some women identified a friend as the most helpful and the most sympathetic person they had spoken to. Friends were appreciated more for their emotional support, advice and sympathy than for their practical support or financial help, or for help and advice on where and with whom to live. Women asked their friends about the pregnancy rather than about what they should do afterwards. A woman whose relationship had ended after the birth had numerous conversations with people about the pregnancy, including parents, siblings and her boyfriend's parents, but had singled out a friend as the most helpful: 'She'd been through it all before and she told me what to do.'

But not all women appreciated their friends' candidness, particularly when they identified all the pitfalls that lay ahead, like this woman who thought a friend particularly unhelpful: 'She was really negative. She said I should live my life first and I wouldn't be able to go to college and I'd have no money.'

A few women identified their sister as the most helpful and sympathetic: 'She made me feel better about it all. I was confused in my head and she helped me sort it all out.' One woman whose sister had also recently become a teenage parent herself felt that their shared experience had been a great source of help and support, and that she had also given her the most practical support in caring for her baby: 'She'd just had a baby, so I bathed her baby and changed her, and I helped and learned.'

Three women had found a female relative the most helpful and sympathetic. One felt that everyone else had been unhelpful: 'Nobody

else wanted to help me. It was like me and my au
Women who had found female relatives helpful ger
or a poor relationship with their parents. One woma
relationship with her mother that had persisted thr
years. She had left home when she was 15 beca
divorced and she did not like her mother's new ʃ
single and living alone when she became pregnant anɑ saiɑ that she had
planned her pregnancy. She identified her aunt as the most helpful of all
the people she had spoken to while she was pregnant: 'She's closest to
me. I believe in her... She took me everywhere I needed to go. She took
me to the hospital and the doctor. She was there for me.'

Support from professionals

A few women felt that their discussions with their GP had been very
helpful. One woman who was 19 when she had her baby described the
negative reactions of both her mother and boyfriend to the news of the
pregnancy and recalled that they had both suggested that she have an
abortion. She appreciated her GP's assessment of the situation: 'He was
very helpful. He told me it wasn't the end of the world and that cheered
me up.' Another woman who was living with the baby's father when she
became pregnant and was 18 when she had had her baby had found her
GP particularly unhelpful: 'She didn't want to know. She never explained
anything.' Two women said that their GP had influenced their decision to
continue with the pregnancy.

One woman who was single and living at home with her parents when
she became pregnant thought her midwife had been the most helpful
overall and a few women appreciated the practical help they had received
from the midwife. Another woman said that her consultations with the
midwife made a difference to her decision to continue with the pregnancy.
Some women who had found their consultations with professionals
helpful often had little family support and were rather isolated. One
woman was 19 when she became pregnant and said that the baby's father
was a steady boyfriend but the relationship broke up after confirming the
pregnancy. She said that a friend who was also pregnant had been the
most helpful and that her mother had been particularly unhelpful. The
midwife had given her advice on where she might live and suggested that
she apply for hostel accommodation. She explained how the midwife's
advice made a difference to her decision to continue with the pregnancy:
'It made me feel a bit more secure in myself that I'd be able to manage
through the pregnancy.'

Three of the 6 women who had spoken to a social worker (all older
teenagers) said that they had been the most helpful and sympathetic, as

man explained: 'She was like a shoulder to lean on because I was right state.'

Only a few women had spoken to benefits or housing officers. Three women said that the benefits officer had provided the most financial support. A woman who was 17 when she had her baby and was living with her parents discussed the benefits she was eligible to claim and said that he had given her the most financial support: 'Because he advised me to apply for income support before the birth.' However, women were not as pleased with the advice and support that they had received from housing officers and most women said that they had been particularly unhelpful, as one woman in Leeds remarked: 'He wasn't helpful at all. It was like a ten minute chat and they wanted to get rid of me. I didn't want to go back.'

Conclusion

In this chapter we have seen how the wide variety of characteristics and relationships of the teenage mothers was reflected in the ways in which they made decisions about what to do about the pregnancy and their living arrangements during the pregnancy and after the birth. It was clear that few of them had actually made a decision to become pregnant, with only a quarter of the pregnancies having been planned. But only a quarter of the women had considered a termination of pregnancy, and few had sought any professional help. Continuing with the pregnancy was often not so much a decision as an acceptance of what had happened. There was evidence of considerable collusion, if not encouragement, in the continuation of the pregnancy, with partners often advising against termination of pregnancy and parents offering continuing support in whatever the women decided to do. It was perhaps not insignificant that relationships often broke down in spite of the advice of partners to continue with the pregnancy.

On the other hand, there were many indications of women continuing with the pregnancy when the relationship had already broken down or was in a very shaky state. There was clear evidence of unrealistic expectations about the future, in spite of the fact that some women realised that they would be on their own with the baby. Others understood that they could rely on their parents for support and shelter, and, as we will see in the next chapter, had never left home.

When women had discussed the pregnancy with their mothers they usually found them the most helpful and that they offered the most practical support. But again there was evidence of lack of contact or rapport with some mothers and some relationships had broken down completely.

It must be remembered that for a substantial proportion of women the pregnancy was welcome, even if unplanned, and they had neither found it necessary to discuss what to do about the pregnancy nor to discuss their living arrangements.

The complex pattern of discussions resulted in one decision which was common to all the women – to continue with the pregnancy – but the picture became much more complicated where living arrangements were concerned, as we demonstrate in the next chapter.

Chapter 4

Household Composition, Household Change and Housing

This chapter looks at the characteristics and composition of women's households when they became pregnant and at the time of the interview. We examine the changes which took place and explore the reasons and the factors affecting the moves made by women who moved. We have already seen in Chapter 3 the wide variety of advice and support received by women about where and with whom they might live during pregnancy and after the birth. The question of living arrangements was, not surprisingly, closely related to the development of the women's relationship with the father of the baby. As we have seen, only half the women were still in a relationship with the father of the baby at the time of the interview. This clearly had an impact not only on the extent to which women moved, for example, away from cohabiting relationships, but also on the extent to which they did not move, for example, when they remained at home with their parents. We identify a number of patterns of movement and staying put, but, again, the most striking finding is the extent to which patterns were difficult to establish.

The first part of the chapter looks at household composition, housing tenure and the type and size of accommodation women were living in when they became pregnant and at the time of the interview. We then examine the moves made by women before and after the birth of their babies and pay particular attention to the characteristics of the movers and the non-movers and their reasons for their actions. We look at the women's plans for future housing and the women on a waiting list for council housing. We then explore women's knowledge of housing before they became pregnant, and whether they thought that having a baby would give them housing priority.

Household composition

We asked women where and with whom they were living when they became pregnant and whether they were living in shared households (with their own family, their partner's family or with other relatives), or living independently (on their own with their partner or alone). Table 4.1 shows that the majority of women were living in shared households when they became pregnant. Just under half the women (39) were living with one or both parents (without a partner or husband). Just under a third (26) were living with their partner (5 of these were also living with their partner's parents and 1 was also living with her own parents). Nine women were living with their husbands, but 6 of these were also living with their husband's parents. Two women lived with other relatives, 2 were living with friends and only 6 were living alone when they became pregnant.

Table 4.1 shows a striking change in household composition between the time women became pregnant and the time of the interview. The proportion of women living alone had increased to more than a quarter (24). Eight of these had been cohabiting with their partner when they became pregnant. There was relatively little change in the actual number of women recorded as cohabiting with the father of the baby at the time they became pregnant (26) and at the time of the interview (23), mainly because, as we saw in Chapter 2, the number of women in cohabiting relationships at the time they became pregnant which subsequently broke up (11) was the same as the number of women in non-cohabiting relationships who were cohabiting by the time of the interview (11).

Of the 23 women cohabiting with the father of the baby at the time of the interview:

- 19 were living alone with him
- 3 were living with him and their own parents
- 1 was living with him and his parents.

There was a small increase in the number of women living with husbands (from 9 to 15). Of the 15 women living with their husbands at the time of the interview:

- 9 were living alone with him
- 4 were living with him and his parents
- 2 were living with him and their own parents.

Another notable change was a decrease in the number of women living with their parents (with or without a partner), from just under half at the time they became pregnant (40) to a quarter (22) at the time of the interview. We have seen above that 5 of the 22 were living with their partner or husband and their parents. Of the remaining 17, all but 1 (who was living with her parents and new partner) were single (16).

The fact that women chose to move away from their parents when they had a baby is not in itself surprising. However, the most important finding was the increased number of women living alone (24). At the time of the interview they were, of course, single parents.

Table 4.1 Household composition when women became pregnant and at the time of interview

numbers and column percentages

Women living with	At time of pregnancy					At time of interview				
	Total		H	S Nos	L	Total		H	S Nos	L
	Nos	%				Nos	%			
Husband alone	3	4	2	0	1	9	11	4	0	5
Husband and his parent(s)	6	7	2	4	0	4	5	2	2	0
Husband and own parent(s)	0	0	0	0	0	2	2	0	2	0
Partner alone	20	24	6	3	11	19	23	2	6	11
Partner and his parent(s)	5	6	1	0	4	1	1	0	0	1
Partner and own parent(s)	1	1	0	0	1	3	4	2	0	1
Living with new partner	0	0	0	0	0	3	4	2	0	1
Living with new partner and own parent(s)	0	0	0	0	0	1	1	0	0	1
Mother/father/parents	39	46	12	13	14	16	19	5	5	6
Other relatives	2	2	0	0	2	2	2	1	0	1
Friends	2	2	1	0	1	0	0	0	0	0
Living alone	6	7	3	3	0	24	29	9	8	7
Base: all women	(84)		(27)	(23)	(34)	(84)		(27)	(23)	(34)

In addition, 3 women were living with a new partner and 2 women were living with other relatives at the time of the interview.

Household size

Women were asked how many adults and children, including themselves, were living in the same household when they became pregnant. All but one woman, who was living in a hostel, were living in private households. There were no notable area differences in household size, but women were more likely to live in larger households (of 3 or more adults) than smaller households (of 1 or 2 adults) at the time that they became pregnant:

- Over a third (33) were in larger households with children
- Over a quarter (23) were in larger households without children
- Less than a third (25) were in smaller households without children
- Three were in smaller households with children.

When we examined changes in household size we found that women were more likely to be living in smaller households at the time of the interview than when they became pregnant. At the time of the interview over half the women (45) were living in households of one or two adults with children, although nearly half (39) were still in households of 3 or more adults with children.

Type of accommodation

Table 4.2 shows that two-thirds of the women were living in a house (57) and a quarter (22) in a flat or maisonette when they became pregnant. The picture was rather different across the areas, with women in Hackney more likely to live in a flat or maisonette, while in Solihull and Leeds the majority of women were living in a house. The rest were living in rooms (3 women), in a hostel (1) or had other living arrangements (1). Two women in Solihull were living outside the UK when they became pregnant.

Not surprisingly, there was a moderate increase in the proportion of the women who were living in flats and maisonettes at the time of the interview. Table 4.2 shows that the proportion of women in flats and maisonettes increased from a quarter at the time they became pregnant (22) to 40 per cent (34) at the time of the interview. The proportion of women living in a house decreased from two-thirds (57) to just over a half (47) and 3 women were living in a hostel or similar accommodation. Again, women in Hackney were more likely than women elsewhere to be living in a flat or maisonette.

Table 4.2 Type of accommodation women were living in when they became pregnant and at the time of interview

numbers and column percentages

| | At time of pregnancy | | | | | At time of interview | | | | |
| | Total | | H | S Nos | L | Total | | H | S Nos | L |
	Nos	%				Nos	%			
House	57	68	11	18	28	47	56	6	14	27
Flat/maisonette	22	26	14	3	5	34	40	18	9	7
Rooms	3	4	2	1	0	0	0	0	0	0
Hostel/similar accommodation	1	1	0	1	0	3	4	3	0	0
Other	1	1	0	0	1	0	0	0	0	0
Base: all women	(84)		(27)	(23)	(34)	(84)		(27)	(23)	(34)

Size of accommodation and number of rooms

Household size and number of rooms (excluding kitchen and bathroom) together give an index of overcrowding. This factor played an important part in the women's decision about whether to move or stay put, particularly after the birth when they wanted their own space and privacy. On average, women in Hackney were living in properties with fewer rooms when they became pregnant (4.0) than those in Solihull (5.1) and Leeds (4.3). Overall, around a sixth of the women (12) lived in small properties with 1 or 2 rooms but Table 4.3 shows that this was more common in Hackney where more women lived in flats and maisonettes. 40 per cent of the women (34) lived in properties with 3 or 4 rooms while 45 per cent (38) had 5 or more rooms.

Many women were already living in overcrowded conditions when they became pregnant, with a third living in households with more than one adult to a room. This was more common among women who were already living with their partner or partner's relatives than among women living with their parents. Half the women living with their partner, compared with just under a fifth living with their parents, were in overcrowded conditions when they became pregnant. All the women, except one in Leeds, had the use of a bath or shower when they became pregnant and all had the use of an inside toilet. Only a few women reported having to share these amenities with other households.

By the time of the interview, most women in all areas were living in smaller properties, not surprisingly because of the number who had moved away from parents to live with their partner or on their own with the baby. Table 4.3 shows an increase in the proportion of women living in properties with 3 or 4 rooms from 40 per cent (34 women) when they became pregnant to 61 per cent (51 women) at the time of the interview. There was a decrease in the number living in properties with 5 or more rooms from 38 to 24 women at the time of the interview.

Around a fifth of women (15) were living in overcrowded conditions at the time of the interview, which was a decrease on the proportion at the time they became pregnant.

Housing tenure

Previous research has shown that young mothers and their partners are heavily reliant on public sector housing (Simms and Smith, 1986). Wellings et al (1996) have noted that a birth at any age might result in women moving away from the family to set up a home of their own. In addition, poorer material circumstances which result in, or arise from, early parenthood are associated with a decreased likelihood of home ownership and an increased expectation of social or subsidised housing.

Table 4.3 Number of rooms in women's households when they became pregnant and at the time of interview

numbers and column percentages

	At time of pregnancy					At time of interview				
	Total		H	S	L	Total		H	S	L
	Nos	%	Nos	Nos		Nos	%	Nos	Nos	
One	4	5	2	1	1	0	0	0	0	0
Two	8	10	4	1	3	9	11	5	2	2
Three	10	12	4	2	4	31	37	8	9	14
Four	24	28	6	7	11	20	24	7	3	10
Five	22	26	7	5	10	16	19	5	5	6
Six	9	11	2	4	3	4	5	1	3	0
Seven or more	7	8	2	3	2	4	5	1	1	2
Mean number of rooms	4.4		4.0	5.1	4.3	3.9		3.7	4.2	3.8
Base: all women	(84)		(27)	(23)	(34)	(84)		(27)	(23)	(34)

However, there is little indication that the expectation of social housing is a driving force in the minds of teenagers who become pregnant.

We asked women about their housing tenure when they became pregnant and for each of their subsequent moves so that we could establish the prevalence of social and subsidised housing and home ownership and identify how housing tenure had changed over time.

Table 4.4 shows that at the time women became pregnant, most were living as lodgers or rent-free with their own family, their partner's family or with other relatives. Very few were owner-occupiers (3) and just under a sixth (12) were renting privately. Only 4 women were renting from a local authority and one was renting from a housing association.

Nearly half the women (40) were living alone with their parents (39) or with their partner and parents (1). Most were living rent-free (25) while the remainder were paying rent (15).

Just under a fifth (16) were living with non-relatives including their partner, partner's parents and friends. 8 women were living with other relatives including siblings, aunts and in-laws.

Table 4.4 shows that at the time of the interview the number of women living in local authority rented accommodation had increased from 4 to 28. Five women were renting housing association properties, just under a fifth (16) were renting privately and a quarter (22) were living with parents. There had been a small increase in the number of owner occupiers from 3 to 6 at the time of the interview. Five women were living rent-free with other relatives and 2 were living rent-free with non-relatives.

By the time we interviewed them, as many as two-thirds of the women (56) were living in local authority accommodation (28) or were on a waiting list for local authority accommodation (28).

There was a steady increase in the proportion of women claiming housing benefit: from 9 (11 per cent) when they became pregnant to 29 (35 per cent) during their pregnancy to 41 (49 per cent) at the time of the interview. This is important because it underlines how women who moved into their own accommodation were often reliant on social security benefits, as we shall see in Chapter 5.

Movers and non-movers

Although we have seen that many women move during their pregnancy or in the first year after the birth of their babies (Hopkinson, 1976; Clark, 1989), there is a lack of information on women who do not move. We asked women who had not moved about their living arrangements and plans. We also asked those who had moved about each of their moves, including when they moved, their reasons for moving, where they moved, whom they lived with, their household composition and housing

Table 4.4   Housing tenure when women became pregnant and at the time of interview

numbers and column percentages

	At time of pregnancy					At time of interview				
	Total		H	S	L	Total		H	S	L
	Nos	%		Nos		Nos	%		Nos	
Owner-occupier	3	4	1	0	2	6	7	0	1	5
Renting from local authority	4	5	1	0	3	28	33	8	9	11
Renting from housing association	1	1	1	0	0	5	6	2	0	3
Renting privately	12	14	5	5	2	16	19	9	4	3
Living with parents (paying rent)	15	18	3	5	7	10	12	3	2	5
Living with parents (rent-free)	25	30	9	8	8	12	14	4	5	3
Living with other relatives (paying rent)	1	1	0	0	1	0	0	0	0	0
Living with other relatives (rent-free)	7	8	2	4	1	5	6	1	2	2
Living with non-relative (paying rent)	5	6	3	1	1	0	0	0	0	0
Living with non-relative (rent-free)	11	13	2	0	9	2	2	0	0	2
Base: all women	(84)		(27)	(23)	(34)	(84)		(27)	(23)	(34)

tenure, how long they stayed or planned to stay in that accommodation and their satisfaction with the accommodation.

The extent to which women moved was closely related to their living arrangements when they became pregnant. Only one in six of the women who were living with their parents when they became pregnant moved during pregnancy, compared with nearly one in two of the women who were cohabiting. However, this picture changed after the birth. Around two-thirds of the women living with their parents when they became pregnant and two-thirds of the cohabiting women moved at least once after the birth. The age of the women was not an important factor in the frequency or timing of moves.

Number of moves during pregnancy and after the birth

Table 4.5 shows the proportion of women who had moved before the birth or after the birth only and those who had moved both before and after the birth. The table shows that moving was more common after the birth than during pregnancy. Three-quarters of the women (61) moved at least once between the time they became pregnant and the time of the interview. Just under a third of all the women (25) moved at some stage during their pregnancy, mostly only once. Nearly two-thirds of the women (51) moved after the birth, again mostly only once.

Table 4.5   Whether women moved during pregnancy and/or after the birth or not at all

numbers and column percentages

	Total Nos	%	Hackney Nos	Solihull Nos	Leeds Nos
Moved					
During pregnancy only	10	12	2	4	4
After the birth only	36	43	12	12	12
During pregnancy *and* after the birth	15	18	7	2	6
Did not move	23	27	6	5	12
Base: all women	*(84)*		*(27)*	*(23)*	*(34)*

Of the 61 women who moved, 10 moved during pregnancy only, 36 moved after the birth only and 15 moved both during pregnancy and after the birth.

Table 4.6   Number of moves by women between the time they
            became pregnant and the time of the interview

numbers and column percentages

	Nos	%
None	23	27
One	29	35
Two	18	21
Three	10	12
Four	2	2
Five	0	0
Six	0	0
Seven	0	0
Eight	0	0
Nine	1	1
Ten	0	0
Eleven	1	1
Base: all women	*(84)*	

Non-movers

A quarter of the women (23) had not moved between the time they became pregnant and the time of the interview, with the Leeds women more likely to stay put than those in the other areas (6 in Hackney, 5 in Solihull and 12 in Leeds). At the time they became pregnant, the women who did not move were either living at home with their parents (13) or with their husband (5) or their boyfriend (4) or an aunt (1). Although there was no age difference among non-movers overall, not surprisingly, the younger teenagers who had not moved were more likely than the older teenagers to be living with their parents.

It was clear that some of the women who had stayed put had not done so by choice, but simply had nowhere else to go. Others had had no reason to move and had taken a decision to stay where they were, at least in the short term. We asked women about their accommodation and whether they had ever thought of moving, and if so, what had stopped them. Of the 23 women who had never moved, the majority were very satisfied or satisfied with their accommodation (16), 3 were fairly satisfied, and 4 expressed dissatisfaction.

Many of the women who were satisfied were living at home with their parents in pleasant accommodation with all the comforts of home. One woman (who was 16 when she became pregnant and whose boyfriend was a casual partner) was still living with her parents and was very satisfied because: 'It's secure. It's mum and dad's house and the rent is paid. There are no worries about being kicked out and there is always company in the evenings.' Another woman who was 18 when she had had her baby and was living with her parents when she became pregnant also reflected this view. The baby's father had been a steady boyfriend but their relationship had broken up shortly after she announced that she was pregnant. She explained: 'I love living with my mum. I have all I need. I'm very comfortable here... She (mother) helps me endlessly. She babysits a couple of nights a week so I can go out. She helps me when I'm tired. She's just brilliant.'

It was clear that living with parents had some practical benefits, particularly for women who were living rent-free. Women also valued the help with childcare from family members and a few women spoke of their 'built-in baby sitting service'. But these benefits were often short-lived: women appreciated the company at home but still wanted their own space and independence, and a chance to set up a home of their own for their new family. Our interviews with the grandparents suggested that they too had some reservations about whether staying at home was sustainable in the long term. The burden of living with a young baby or a noisy toddler and the associated problem of overcrowding inevitably created tensions within households. Indeed, some grandparents appeared to have taken on parental responsibilities.

Not surprisingly, women who were living at home but having to share the accommodation with parents and other siblings, described overcrowded conditions. A woman who was 17 when she had had her baby and was living at home with her parents when she became pregnant felt that living at home was unsatisfactory, but the disruption had been particularly marked since the birth: 'I'm in the same room with (baby). I had to swop bedrooms with my sister and now when her boyfriend comes to stay at weekends, they have to sleep in a single bed in her bedroom.'

Some of the women who were living with their partner and his relatives also described similar problems of overcrowding, a lack of space and a lack of privacy. One woman who was married to the baby's father when she became pregnant and who had planned her pregnancy, had lived with her husband's relatives since they were married. She was pregnant with her second baby at the time of the interview and explained that they had not moved because they were waiting to be housed by the council. However, she felt that her husband was not as eager to move as she was: 'He has been supportive but he doesn't realise how desperate I am.'

Some women who had expressed a lack of satisfaction with their accommodation spoke of financial problems. A woman who was living with the baby's father when she became pregnant and had planned the pregnancy, felt that their owner-occupied house was fairly satisfactory but added: 'There's so much I want to do with it but we can't afford it.'

Plans to move away

Despite the fact that the majority of women who had not moved were satisfied with where they lived, almost all of them (20 of the 23) said that they had thought of moving, mainly because they wanted their own place alone with their baby or together with their partner. A woman who was living with her parents explained why she wanted to move: 'I want me and (partner) and (baby) to be like a family, because we're not at present. And to have our own little house.' Women also said that they wanted more space and to live in a better area.

Some women had not moved mainly because they could not afford to or because they were waiting to be allocated a council property (12). Some, like this woman who had been on the council's waiting list for only two months, were hopeful of being housed quickly. She was 19 when she had her baby and said that she knew her partner had not wanted a baby when she planned to become pregnant. She had been living with her aunt since she was 15, and although she had never moved, she thought that the accommodation and the area were unsatisfactory: 'There's no garden and (baby) can't play outside. I don't like this house anyway. It's not a very safe area.' At the time of the interview she was hoping to be reassessed by the council and remarked: 'I'd move tomorrow if I got another house.'

Others had also taken steps to find new accommodation, and buying or renting privately were the preferred options for some like this woman who had recently bought a house and was waiting to move in with her partner and baby. She lived in her parents' home with her partner and baby until they had saved enough money for a deposit on a house. She said that the accommodation was very satisfactory, but that they wanted to move because: '(Baby) is too big now to stay here with mum and dad and we want our own house.' A few women had looked for other accommodation but had not found anywhere affordable and suitable, and one woman summarised why she had not moved: 'It's house prices really.'

One woman whose baby was 11 months old at the time of the interview was not in any hurry to leave home and remarked that her mother was pleased to have her stay indefinitely: 'She told me I could stay here as long as I like, till I'm 50 if I want!' Although she had no immediate plans to move, she had thought about what she might do in the future and added that she might stay at home: 'Until (baby) is old enough to go to school and I can get a proper full-time job and get a house.'

The movers

We have seen that 61 women had moved between the time they became pregnant and the time of the interview. Most of them were not frequent movers, but there was a small group of women (14 women) who moved three times or more. We will discuss them in more detail later in the chapter.

Why women moved when they did

We asked women the single most important reason for each move and we were able to identify a number of themes. The main reason for moving was that women wanted to be independent. This woman, who was living with her parents when she became pregnant but was cohabiting at the time of the interview, explained that her main reason for moving was: 'Independence. I needed to stand on my own two feet.' Another woman who had moved once and had lived with her partner and parents before they moved into a place of their own with their baby remarked: 'We wanted to be a family of our own. I was happy where I was, but I think he (partner) wanted to support us himself.'

The first move was clearly a big step for many women. Some women whose main reason for moving was to gain independence were also influenced by other factors like relationship problems with their partner or family, overcrowded conditions at home, the poor state of repair of their accommodation or the undesirable area they were living in. One woman who had moved only once was living with her parents when she became pregnant and said that the father of the baby was a steady boyfriend. They had discussed living with their respective parents during the pregnancy and had planned to buy a house and move in together with the baby after the birth. They lived temporarily with her parents until the baby was three months old. She explained why she wanted to move: 'Privacy. You need to establish your own family unit really,' but added: 'We were very cramped at my parents, all in one bedroom. And we had our own house (owner-occupied) just being finished.'

We have already seen in Chapter 2 that relationship breakdown was common and that as many as half the women were single lone parents at the time of the interview. It is not surprising, therefore, that relationship problems were cited by some women as the most important reason for moving and for their dissatisfaction with accommodation. However, some experienced more serious problems than others and described frequent, acrimonious and sometimes violent encounters with the father of the baby, like a woman who was 17 when she had her baby and was living with the baby's father when she became pregnant. She moved into a mother and baby hostel when her son was five months old and explained why: 'To get away from my baby's dad. He started taking drugs and stealing money from me. He was aggressive and always shouting.' But despite the physical attacks and their partner's abusive behaviour, some women did not leave immediately. Another woman was living with a violent partner but stayed, against her mother's advice, before leaving him to live with her mother: 'Mum kept telling me to come back (home) because he started hitting me.'

Relationship problems were the main reason for moving for a substantial minority of women who were already living with their partner when they became pregnant (7 of the 23 women living with their partner). One woman was 17 when she had her baby and was living with her partner when she became pregnant. Although she assumed that they would always stay together, their relationship ran into problems when she decided to continue with the pregnancy against her partner's wishes: 'He never wanted kids. He said if I had an abortion I could stay but I never wanted that.' The relationship broke up when she was 20 weeks pregnant and she went to live with her parents.

In contrast, another woman knew almost immediately that the relationship was heading for trouble when her partner heard she was pregnant. She was also 17 when she had her baby and moved four times: from living with her partner to living with a friend; from there to living with an aunt; from there to living alone in local authority accommodation; and again to living alone in other local authority accommodation. She said that she had thought the pregnancy would lead to a break-up of their relationship: 'I didn't know what the next day would bring. I'd nowhere to live really. I knew I'd be living on my own.' Two weeks after confirming the pregnancy, their relationship ended and she moved away from her partner into rent-free accommodation with a friend when she was 8 weeks pregnant.

Not all the difficult relationships were with the baby's father. Tense and strained relationships with parents and siblings characterised some households, particularly among women living at home after the birth. One woman described the arguments which resulted at night when her sister was disturbed by the baby: 'My sister and dad were arguing about the baby all night because my sister and I shared a room. He said, "That's how babies are." '

The poor state of repair and the perceived unsuitability of accommodation for young children were other reasons for moving. This problem was found both in council accommodation and privately rented properties. One woman who was privately renting an unfurnished property identified a number of problems which she felt were unacceptable: 'It's damp and freezing cold in the winter. There are gaps around the windows, even though there is double-glazing. There's no hot running water in the kitchen. The stairs leading upstairs to my flat are disgusting – they're filthy.'

But another reason for moving was a change in women's personal circumstances. For example, those who had been working when they became pregnant but had not returned to paid employment after the birth could not afford to pay high rents. This was particularly difficult for women who had lived in privately rented accommodation. We will see in Chapter 5 that the majority of respondents were reliant on social security benefits as their sole source of income at the time of the interview and, not surprisingly, the necessity to live within their means limited their choice of housing.

Sometimes a number of factors operated simultaneously and affected the timing of women's moves and with whom they lived. One woman who left home when she was 18 to live with her boyfriend became pregnant shortly afterwards. Although he advised her to keep the baby initially, she did not believe that the relationship would last because he was involved in drug dealing. She considered returning home to live with her parents but they had left the area. She was 24 weeks pregnant when she first moved and said that the condition of their privately rented unfurnished flat was her main reason for doing so: 'The state of the flat. It was damp, cold, wet and horrible.' However, following the break-up of their relationship she moved into privately rented accommodation on her own.

Changing patterns of household composition

Women were asked how long they had planned to stay in each place. It was clear from their comments that they had often expected to stay longer than they did, but that circumstances had forced them to move earlier. Some appeared to have had little control over the type and condition of the accommodation to which they moved, where they lived and with whom.

We summarised the household composition for the movers and non-movers at the time the women became pregnant and at the time of the interview by the number of times they moved. This material is presented in tabular form in Table 4.7. It is important also to refer to Table 4.8, which documents the household composition of the women at the time of the interview by the number of moves they made and whether they were still in a relationship with the father of the baby. We thought it useful to document the changes in the summary below which follows the women through the process.

Non-movers

When they became pregnant 5 of the 23 non-movers were married, 4 were cohabiting, 13 were living alone with their parents and 1 with an aunt.

Table 4.7 Household composition when women became pregnant and at the time of the interview, for movers and non-movers

numbers and column percentages

| | At time of pregnancy | | | | | | At time of interview | | | | | |
| | Total | | Not moved | Moved once | Moved twice | Moved 3+ times | Total | | Not moved | Moved once | Moved twice | Moved 3+ times |
	Nos	%					Nos	%				
Husband alone	3	4	2	0	0	1	9	11	3	4	0	2
Husband and his parent(s)	6	7	3	3	0	0	4	5	3	1	0	0
Husband and own parent(s)	0	0	0	0	0	0	2	2	0	2	0	0
Partner alone	20	24	3	9	3	5	19	23	2	12	5	0
Partner and his parent(s)	5	6	1	1	2	1	1	1	1	0	0	0
Partner and own parent(s)	1	1	0	0	1	0	3	4	1	1	1	0
Living with new partner	0	0	0	0	0	0	3	4	0	0	1	2
Living with new partner and own parent(s)	0	0	0	0	0	0	1	1	1	0	0	0
Mother/father/parents	39	46	13	15	8	3	16	19	11	1	2	2
Other relatives	2	2	1	0	0	1	2	2	1	0	1	0
Friends	2	2	0	0	1	1	0	0	0	0	0	0
Living alone	6	7	0	1	3	2	24	29	0	8	8	8
Base: all women	*(84)*		*(23)*	*(29)*	*(18)*	*(14)*	*(84)*		*(23)*	*(29)*	*(18)*	*(14)*

Table 4.8 Household composition at the time of the interview by whether women still with father of the baby

numbers and column percentages

	Still with father of the baby					Not with father of the baby				
	Total	Not moved	Moved once	Moved twice	Moved 3+ times	Total	Not moved	Moved once	Moved twice	Moved 3+ times
Husband alone	9	3	4	0	2	0	0	0	0	0
Husband and his parent(s)	4	3	1	0	0	0	0	0	0	0
Husband and own parent(s)	2	0	2	0	0	0	0	0	0	0
Partner alone	19	2	12	5	0	0	0	0	0	0
Partner and his parent(s)	1	1	0	0	0	0	0	0	0	0
Partner and own parent(s)	3	1	1	1	0	0	0	0	0	0
Living with new partner	0	0	0	0	0	3	0	0	1	2
Living with new partner and own parent(s)	0	0	0	0	0	1	1	0	0	0
Mother/father/parents	3	2	0	1	0	13	9	1	1	2
Other relatives	0	0	0	0	0	2	1	0	1	0
Living alone	2	0	0	1	1	22	0	8	7	7
Base: all women	*(43)*	*(12)*	*(20)*	*(8)*	*(3)*	*(41)*	*(11)*	*(9)*	*(10)*	*(11)*

At the time of the interview there was little change. Two of the women who had been living alone with their parents continued to live there with their partner or new partner. One woman who had been cohabiting subsequently married the baby's father. At the time of the interview:

- 6 were married – 3 living alone with their husband and 3 with their husband and his parents
- 4 were cohabiting – 2 living alone with their partner, 1 with her partner and her parents and another with her partner and his parents
- 1 was living with a new partner and her parents
- 11 were living with their parents
- 1 was living with an aunt.

Few of the non-movers were living independently at the time of the interview. For instance, only 5 of the 10 married or cohabiting women were living independently with their husband or partner. The rest were living with their own relatives or their husband's or partner's relatives. One woman who was living with a new partner was also living with her parents. All the other women (12) were living in shared households with their parents (11) or an aunt (1).

However, most of the women who had not moved had thought about moving (20). Over half (12) were waiting to be allocated council housing. 7 of these were living with their parents, 1 with an aunt, 1 with her husband, and 3 with their husband and his relatives.

As Table 4.8 shows, 12 of the 23 non-movers were still in a relationship with the baby's father and 11 were not, with most of the latter group living at home with their parents.

Women who had moved once

When they became pregnant, 3 of the 29 women who moved only once were married, 10 were cohabiting, 15 were living with their parents and 1 was living alone.

At the time of the interview, 7 women were living with their husbands, 13 with their partner, 8 were living alone and only 1 woman was living with her parents.

In contrast to the women who had not moved, most of the married and cohabiting women (16 of the 20) were living independently at the time of the interview. Only 4 women were living with their husband or partner and their own parents (3) or with his parents (1). The 9 women who were not married or cohabiting were almost all living independently, with only 1 woman living with her parents.

As Table 4.8 shows, relationship breakdown was relatively uncommon among women who had moved only once, in that 20 of the 29 were still in a relationship with the baby's father and most of their moves had been from living with parents to cohabiting. Of the 9 women who were not still in a relationship with the baby's father, 8 had moved to live alone and one had moved back to her parents.

Women who had moved twice

When they became pregnant, 6 of the 18 women who had moved twice were cohabiting, none were married, 8 were living with their parents, 1 with friends and 3 were living alone.

At the time of the interview, 5 were living with their partner, 1 with her partner and her own parents, 1 with a new partner, 1 with other relatives, 2 with their parents and 8 were living alone.

These women were less likely than those who had moved only once or those who had not moved still to be in a relationship with the baby's father. As Table 4.8 shows, only 8 of the 18 were still in relationship with him. Of the 10 who were not, 7 were living alone.

Women who had moved three or more times

When they became pregnant, 6 of the 14 women who had moved three or more times were cohabiting (5 alone with their partner and 1 with her partner and his parents), 1 was living with her husband, 3 with their parents, 2 with other relatives or friends and 2 were living alone.

At the time of the interview, 2 were living with their husband, 2 with a new partner, 2 with their parents and 8 were living alone.

Relationship breakdown had been common in this group, with only 3 of the 14 still in a relationship with the baby's father, as Table 4.8 shows. Of the 11 who were not, 7 were living alone, 2 were with their parents and 2 were living with a new partner. 6 of the 14 had lived with the baby's father at some stage since becoming pregnant but their relationship had broken down by the time of the interview.

We looked in some detail at the moves made by women according to the number of moves they had made.

Women who had moved once only

Table 4.5 shows that three-quarters of the women (61) moved between the time they became pregnant and the time of the interview. Table 4.6 shows that just under half of the movers (29) moved only once.

We asked them with whom they went to live when they moved and with whom they had been living before. We also noted with whom they were living at the time of the interview, bearing in mind that they themselves might not have moved but that their household composition might have changed by someone moving in or out. We found that when they moved:

- 18 women went to live with their partner (17) or with their partner and her parents (1). At the time they became pregnant:
  - 9 were already cohabiting (and moved with their partner to different accommodation)
  - 8 were in a steady relationship with the father of the baby and living with their parents
  - 1 woman was in a steady relationship with the father of the baby and living alone.

Most of the 18 women (15) were still cohabiting (12) or married (3) at the time of the interview but 3 said that their relationship had broken up although they had not moved again.

- 2 women moved to live with their husbands: one was already married when she became pregnant; the other was in a steady relationship and living with her parents before she married the father of the baby. Both were still married at the time of the interview.
- 7 women went to live alone, 6 of whom had been in steady relationships with the father of the baby and had been living with their parents when they became pregnant. One woman had been cohabiting when she became pregnant but the relationship had broken up. At the time of the interview, 6 of the women were single and living alone and 1 was cohabiting with the father of the baby who had moved in with her.
- 2 women went to live with their parents. Both were married and living with their husbands outside the UK when they became pregnant. They returned home alone to live with their parents during the pregnancy and were joined later by their husbands.

Women who moved twice

Just under a third of all movers (18) moved twice between the time they became pregnant and the time of the interview. We asked the women with whom they went to live at each of their moves.

- Half the women (9) went to live with their partner at the first move, of whom 6 were single and living with their parents and the rest (3) were already cohabiting when they became pregnant.
  - On their second move, 5 of the 9 women moved again with their partner. 2 women moved back to live with their parents, one of whom still had a steady relationship with the father of the baby at the time of the interview. 2 women moved to live alone, but one retained a steady relationship with the father of the baby at the time of the interview.

- 4 women moved to live alone at their first move: 2 had already been living alone when they became pregnant, 1 had been cohabiting and 1 had been living with her parents.
  - On their second move, all 4 women moved to live alone. At the time of the interview, one was cohabiting with a new partner and the other 3 were still single and living alone.
- 3 women went to live with their parents at their first move:
  - the first had been cohabiting when she became pregnant, moved to live with her parents and then moved back to live with her partner after the birth, where she was still living at the time of the interview.
  - the second, who had also been cohabiting when she became pregnant, went to live alone on her second move and was still alone at the time of the interview.
  - the third had been single and living alone when she became pregnant and subsequently moved away from her parents to live alone again and was still alone at the time of the interview.
- 1 woman who was in a steady relationship with the father of the baby had been living with a friend when she became pregnant and went to live with another friend before moving again to live on her own.
- 1 woman who was living with her parents when she became pregnant moved to live with her sister at her first move and moved again with her.

Half of the women who had moved twice (9) went to live alone on their second move. Seven of them were single and living alone at the time of the interview, 1 had a steady non-cohabiting relationship with the father of the baby and was also living alone, while the other woman was cohabiting with a new partner who had moved in with her.

Women who had moved three times or more

Table 4.6 shows that just under a quarter of all movers (14) had moved three or more times between the time they became pregnant and the time of the interview. These women were a rather diverse group, mostly older teenagers (10).

We asked the women with whom they went to live at each of their moves:

- 3 women went to live with their partner at their first move. 2 of these were living with their parents (1 in a steady relationship and 1 in a casual relationship with the father of the baby) when they became pregnant. One of these women moved again 7 times with the father of the baby and then, following the break-up of their relationship, she moved again to live with a new partner. The other woman returned to live with her parents following the breakdown of her relationship before moving a third time to live alone. The third woman was already cohabiting when she became pregnant and moved with her partner to live with her parents. She moved twice more with her partner, to whom she was married at the time of the interview.

- One woman who was already married and living outside the UK when she became pregnant returned to live with her husband and parents before moving twice more with her husband alone.
- 3 women went to live with their parents at their first move. 2 of them had been cohabiting when they became pregnant: one moved twice again to live alone, while the other, who had also made two more moves, went to live alone before returning to live with her parents. The third woman had had a casual relationship with the father of the baby and was living outside the UK with her parents when she became pregnant. She also moved twice again, moving house with her parents before moving to live alone. All 3 women were single at the time of the interview.
- 2 women went to live with a friend at their first move: one had been cohabiting with the father of the baby when she became pregnant. She moved another three times, living with her aunt, moving alone before moving into other accommodation alone. The other woman was living alone when she became pregnant. She moved to live with a friend and then moved again to live with her aunt before moving another nine times – on each move to live alone.
- 5 women went to live alone at their first move: 2 had been cohabiting when they became pregnant. One of these women moved twice again, on both occasions alone. The other woman went to live with her parents on her second move before moving again to live alone. The third woman had been living with a friend when she became pregnant and on each of her moves she went to live alone. The fourth woman was living with her sister when she became pregnant and after living alone she returned to live with her sister before moving again to live with a new partner.

There was no particular pattern in the moves of this small group of women. Almost all of them (11) had returned to live with their parents (8) or another relative (3) on at least one of their moves – particularly after the breakdown of cohabiting relationships. Most had lived alone at some stage since becoming pregnant or were living alone at the time of the interview.

Patterns of moving

We can see from this analysis how difficult it was to establish a clear pattern of moves and relationship breakdown during pregnancy and after the birth among these teenage mothers.

We have seen that 11 of the 16 living alone with their parents at the time of the interview had never moved, and that only 2 of these were still in a relationship with the baby's father. We can see that 8 of the 24 women who were living alone at the time of the interview had been in a cohabiting relationship when they became pregnant. We can also see that all the 24 women living alone at the time of the interview had moved at least once and 8 of them had moved three or more times. We can see that 12 of the 19 women cohabiting with the baby's father at the time of the interview had moved only once, and a further 5 had moved twice.

We have also seen that few of the women who had moved were still living with their parents at the time of the interview, but 5 of the 18 women who had moved twice and 7 of the 14 women who moved 3 or more times had moved to live with their parents (alone or with their husband or partner) before moving again. This illustrates how much many women depended on their parents for practical assistance and support, particularly at a time of relationship breakdown.

We can see that the women who moved only once were more likely than the others still to be in a relationship with the baby's father and that relationship breakdown was generally related to more frequent moves, although, on the other hand, only around half of those who had never moved were still in a relationship with the baby's father.

There are clearly a number of factors which have to be taken into consideration when assessing the complex pattern of moving, household composition and relationship breakdown.

Changing patterns of housing tenure

We also looked at the women's housing tenure for the first three moves:

- On their *first move* over a third of the women (22 of the 61) moved into local authority housing. Just under a fifth (12) moved to their parents, a sixth (8) moved to privately rented accommodation and 5 women moved to housing association properties. Two women moved to live with other relatives and 7 with non-relatives. As expected, relatively few women became owner occupiers (5).

We found that most women who moved into local authority accommodation on their first move had not moved again (16). The rest either moved on to another local authority property, moved to other relatives or back to their parents. Most women moving into local authority accommodation on their first move were living with their parents when they became pregnant while a few had lived with relatives or friends.

In contrast, women who were already living in private rented accommodation rarely moved directly into local authority accommodation on their first move, but generally moved to other privately rented properties on subsequent moves.

- On their *second move* over a third (11) of the women moved to local authority accommodation. There was an increase in the proportion of women renting privately and a slight increase in the proportion living with parents, which generally coincided with the break-up of relationships. Women moving to local authority accommodation had usually moved from their parents or from one local authority property to another.
- 8 of the 14 women making a *third move* went to local authority accommodation while 3 moved to privately rented accommodation, 2 moved to their parents and 1 to a housing association property.

Satisfaction with accommodation

Not surprisingly, there was a relationship between the reasons for moving and women's satisfaction with the accommodation.

Less than half the women had been satisfied with their accommodation on their first move (27 of the 61 women). Another third were fairly satisfied (18 women) but a quarter were dissatisfied.

Around half the women were satisfied with their accommodation on their second move but satisfaction levels were higher on the third move. 9 of the 14 women who moved had been satisfied with their accommodation, 2 were fairly satisfied and 3 were dissatisfied.

Reasons for satisfaction or dissatisfaction

There were no notable differences in satisfaction levels between women living in local authority and privately rented accommodation. Not surprisingly, women were more critical of rented accommodation than other forms of housing, particularly with parents and relatives. Even women who had been fairly satisfied with local authority and privately rented accommodation repeatedly spoke of the problems and delays they had encountered in getting basic repairs carried out.

We have seen that women moved or were dissatisfied with accommodation for a variety of reasons. One woman was living with her parents when she became pregnant and moved into local authority rented accommodation with her boyfriend when her baby was 9 months old. She thought they would stay there 'forever' but she moved home after three months when their relationship broke up: 'I didn't get on with him any more.' She said that the accommodation had been fairly satisfactory but commented: 'It was in bad repair. The sockets were off the walls and the electricity was very bad. I would get electric shocks, but it was never sorted out.' She thought that the accommodation at her parents' house where she returned to live as a lodger was fairly satisfactory also and added: 'It's not as good as having your own place, is it?'

Another woman who had lived in a hostel during her pregnancy moved into local authority rented accommodation with her baby when he was one month old. She had been living there for just over a year and said that the accommodation was unsatisfactory because: 'I live on the eighth floor and the windows aren't fixed, and I told them (the council) over a year ago. The lift's not working and the neighbours aren't nice.' Other women reflected the same concerns about the safety aspect of high-rise flats: 'It's horrible. I refused it three times. It's really dangerous. If a child climbed up on the windows, it could swing out. And it's on the fourth floor.'

Women also spoke of practical problems such as keeping their accommodation warm and comfortable. One woman described the problems she had experienced living in her local authority rented flat: 'I don't like it at all. The flats need to be done up. They were going to knock them down. They're too old. The heating's broken down three times and it's still not working.' Another woman living in privately rented accommodation was fairly satisfied but remarked: 'The landlord doesn't do anything here. It's very cold. The fire is electric, so it's expensive. There's not many facilities. There's no washing machine or anything like that.'

Dissatisfaction with accommodation often resulted in women moving elsewhere. Some stayed for very short periods before moving again, while others who were equally dissatisfied had fewer options and had to stay put, like a woman who was living with her parents when she became pregnant and was 17 when she had her baby. She left home to live with her boyfriend when her baby was eight months old: 'I wanted to live with (partner). I just wanted space of my own.' She moved into a three bedroomed flat and had been living there for 8 months at the time of the interview but felt that it was not satisfactory: 'It's a terrible area. The flats are falling apart. I'm on the seventh floor. I just don't want to live in a flat.' Although she had already lived at home, returning there was not a realistic option: 'It was just hard at my mum's with the two kids as well (her brother and sister who were still living at home were both young). It was causing stress.' She could not say how long she would stay in the flat but added: 'It's a dump... We just want to get out as soon as possible.'

Another woman who had lived alone throughout was dissatisfied with her accommodation and had moved three times from one privately rented property to another. She was living in a privately rented flat when she became pregnant and moved shortly after the birth because she had been sharing a bathroom and wanted one of her own. She moved to another privately rented property but stayed for only three months because she found living on the third floor without a lift impractical: 'I was scared the baby would fall out (of the window) and it was very difficult with all the stairs.' She had been living in another privately rented flat for one month at the time of the interview and said that the accommodation was satisfactory because: 'It's on the ground floor.'

Other women were more concerned about the area they lived in than the accommodation itself, particularly those living alone with their baby. One woman explained that she had found her council house unsatisfactory because it was damp: 'There were leaks in the bathroom and all the windows leaked.' However, the condition of the house was not her main reason for moving when she left to live as a lodger with relatives: 'I moved because I got burgled three times in one week.' Another woman who was an owner occupier did not like the area she lived in either: 'The area is a bit rough, it's a bit scruffy and there's lots of derelict housing around. We want him (baby) to grow up speaking nicely, which he won't learn around here.'

Choice and satisfaction

It was clear that women who were intending to stay put for the foreseeable future were not necessarily satisfied with their accommodation, while others who had moved were not always dissatisfied with theirs. Some of the women who were living in temporary accommodation would have stayed there had they been given the option to do so, and other women who were living in comfortable accommodation with relatives and friends had often been offered a place to stay on the condition that it would be a short-term arrangement only.

One woman who had moved three times had been living with her partner when she became pregnant before moving to a mother and baby hostel when their relationship broke up. She found the accommodation satisfactory but stayed for only five months because she did not like the other women living there: 'It was clean but the people there were horrible. It was just the atmosphere. It made you feel uncomfortable. Everyone was bitching all the time and the staff never did anything about it. I really had no-one to talk to and I was getting bored and depressed. The actual accommodation was all right. You had everything you needed.' She moved temporarily to live with her friend's parents and said that the accommodation was very satisfactory: 'It was always nice and tidy and they were always friendly to me. I couldn't have asked for a better place to live.' However, she could only stay there for four months and moved home with her 12 month old baby to live temporarily with her mother until she could find a place of her own. She had been living there for two months at the time of the interview and said that the accommodation was very satisfactory: 'I get well looked after. It's brilliant here. It's all clean and lovely. She (mother) never stops cleaning.'

We have seen how important it was for women to be independent and how much they valued having their own privacy. This woman made the decision to leave her parents where she and her partner had lived until the baby was 11 months old. She wanted to live with her partner alone and have 'my own space'. She was very satisfied with her owner occupied house and liked: 'Having my house, being able to do my own thing, not having to rely on my mum the whole time. I could never go back home.'

Indeed, it was not uncommon for women to leave accommodation they felt was satisfactory in order to live independently. Unfortunately, things did not always turn out as they had hoped and independence was often accompanied by isolation, particularly for women living alone. This woman had lived with her boyfriend when she was pregnant and went to live with her friend when their relationship broke up. She stayed with her friend for two months and went to live as a lodger with her aunt. She described the accommodation as very satisfactory but left after five months when her baby was only one week old to live in a council house on her own with her baby. In the event, she stayed there for only four months and had applied for a transfer as soon as she moved in because she felt isolated: 'I didn't want to live down there. I didn't know nobody.'

Although many of the women wanted to be independent, there was no doubt that very few had enough resources to bring this about in reality. We have seen time and time again that the romantic picture of independence that some women had had of living with their partner never materialised. For other women, the difficulties they had experienced in settling down on their own with their baby were often related to the lack of suitable and affordable housing. One of the concerns expressed by women living in local authority accommodation was that it was often located in poor and isolated areas without basic amenities and a long distance from their parents. Some areas were said to be notorious for housing a high number of single mothers and women felt ghettoised as a result.

It was clear that some women had had reservations about their accommodation from the beginning but said that they felt they had no choice. This was particularly the case with local authority accommodation. One woman who had already moved twice lived in a hostel for 11 weeks as a statutory homeless person and had to move when she was 26 weeks pregnant because the council had located a property for her. She had not wanted to move and recalled: 'I was told in my letter from the council that if I didn't take it I'd lose priority... I didn't want to get out of the hostel and I didn't want to move into the house they'd given me, but I had to or I'd lose priority and go to the bottom of the list.' She spent nine months in the accommodation and moved again when her baby was six months old. She said that her accommodation had been unsatisfactory and explained why: 'It had damp streaming down the walls. There was a hole in the roof that the council didn't fix for six months. The kitchen was so small, you couldn't turn around in it. The walls were crumbling and the floor had wood rot. It really stank in autumn and winter and the windows rattled. There was no garden and it went straight onto the road. And just after I left, the ceiling fell in.'

From some women's accounts of their discussions with their relatives and friends about where and with whom they might live during their pregnancy and after the birth, it was clear that they had thought of all possible routes into local authority housing. One was the non-statutory homeless route, discussed particularly by women living at home with their parents, like this woman who wanted to move out: 'I thought I would go to the council. My mum said she would kick me out, or tell them she had because we were overcrowded.'

One woman had moved seven times since she became pregnant and typified the older teenager who had moved frequently, who was isolated and had had little family support. Indeed, it seemed that the problems she had encountered in her efforts to become independent were enduring. She had not planned to become pregnant and her relationship with her boyfriend ended after the birth. She had been in paid employment when she became pregnant but when she left her job at the end of her pregnancy, she could not afford to pay the rent in her privately rented flat. She lived with a friend's family for eight weeks during her pregnancy and said that the accommodation was very satisfactory: 'Nobody else would have me move in. I was on my own and I was scared.' She stayed with her aunt for a few weeks before taking temporary accommodation while she was waiting to be housed by the local authority. Her account of how housing allocation had worked for her was nothing more than Hobson's choice: 'You get one choice when you're in a hostel. If you don't take it, you're out on your ear.' She left the local authority flat where she had lived alone with her baby because her ex-boyfriend (the baby's father) had: 'Wrecked my home. I had to have the police in.' She was housed temporarily in another hostel before being allocated another council flat but left there after three months: 'It was three floors up so I couldn't go up and down the stairs.' At the time of the interview she was living in another privately rented flat but did not know how long she would be able to afford to stay.

Women's knowledge of housing before they became pregnant

We asked women if they had known before becoming pregnant whether or not having a baby would give them housing priority. Three-quarters of the women (61) said that they had not known whether it would, but 23 said that they had known. Nearly all of the women who said they knew went on to say that they thought that having a baby would give them priority, but two women said that they knew before they became pregnant that having a baby would not give them housing priority. This is an important finding and suggests that a significant minority of these women were mistakenly under the impression, before they became pregnant, that having a baby would give them housing priority. This does not suggest that women became pregnant to obtain housing but it does highlight the misconceptions that women had about the way the system actually works.

One of the women in Leeds explained why she had not known anything about housing priorities: 'I didn't know nothing about having kids. I was more interested in school.' Most of the women who said they did know said that they had heard that they would get priority from a number of different sources, including friends and relatives (some of whom had been housed themselves), the media and from school. One woman in Hackney explained that although she knew that her friend had been housed it was not something she thought of when she realised she was pregnant: 'My friend had got somewhere to live. But I didn't think when I got pregnant, "Yippee! I can get a council flat!".'

Other women said that they had heard it reported in the media generally, as this woman's comment illustrates: 'Actually I'd heard it on the news as well, that they were coming down on single mothers that were having babies just to get a flat.' Seven of the women said that they heard that it was easier to be housed if they had a baby and another five thought that they would get priority over others. A few women said that they knew that the housing department would give them extra points if they had a child.

Local authority housing

At the time of the interview, two-thirds of the women (56) were living in local authority accommodation (28) or were on a waiting list (28) for local authority housing.

Only 4 women had been living in local authority accommodation when they became pregnant, three with partners and one with her husband. Three of the four were still in local authority accommodation at the time of the interview, while the fourth had moved to a housing association property with her partner.

Of the 28 women in local authority accommodation at the time of the interview:

- 13 were living alone
- 7 were cohabiting with the baby's father
- 4 were living with their husbands alone
- 1 was living with her husband and his relatives
- 1 was living with her sister
- 2 were living with new partners.

Five of the 28 women had lived in another local authority property on a previous move since they had become pregnant.

Overall 35 of the 84 women interviewed had lived in local authority accommodation since they had become pregnant. Of the 7 who were living in other forms of accommodation at the time of the interview, two had moved more than 9 times since they had become pregnant.

A higher proportion of women in Hackney were on a waiting list than elsewhere and younger teenagers (11 of the 27) were more likely to be on a waiting list than older teenagers. Of the 28 women on waiting lists:

- 6 women were living alone (1 was in a steady non-cohabiting relationship with the father of the baby and 5 were single)
- 1 was living with her aunt
- 7 were living with their husbands (2 alone with him, 2 with him and her own parents and 3 with him and his relatives)
- 4 were cohabiting with the father of the baby (3 alone with him and 1 with him and her own parents)
- 1 was living with a new partner
- 9 women were living with their parents (2 were in a non-cohabiting relationship with the father of the baby; 1 was in a non-cohabiting relationship with a new partner; 6 were single).

Most of the women had never moved (12) or had only moved once (7). Four women had moved twice and another four had moved 3 times. One woman had moved as many as nine times.

Although only a third of the women on waiting lists were expecting to be housed in the next six months, two-thirds had had their names down for over a year, while 2 women had already been waiting for more than two years. A further third had been waiting for less than a year.

One woman had applied for council housing when she was pregnant. She was 19 when she had her baby and said that the baby's father was a steady boyfriend when she became pregnant. However, their relationship broke up when she decided to keep the baby: 'I wanted to keep it and he decided to finish with me.' She was living alone in privately rented accommodation when she became pregnant and had moved to three privately rented properties before she could get suitable accommodation on the ground floor. Although she expected to be housed by the council within the next six months, she said that she had been told this when she applied for housing almost two years earlier: 'They tell me I will, but I'm not hopeful. They've always said that I will get somewhere in the next six months.'

Conclusion

We have already noted the lack of a clear pattern in the living arrangements, the extent to which women moved during pregnancy and after the birth, and the extent to which their relationships with the father of the baby had broken down. It is perhaps not surprising that so much depended on the nature of the relationship with the baby's father, rather than on the actual living arrangements of the young women. Although there can be little doubt that unsatisfactory accommodation could exacerbate relationship problems, it was apparent that many of the relationships which collapsed were based on shaky foundations in any case.

The young women who lived in their parents' home at the time of the interview, including those who had never left it, were often in the most comfortable surroundings with considerable support. Those who were living alone were not always in satisfactory accommodation, even if they valued their independence, and indeed, many of them felt isolated and lonely. On the other hand, the living accommodation shared with partners or husbands was not always satisfactory either, especially when it was also shared with other family members.

It was quite clear that many of these young women had embarked on pregnancy with little idea of what was awaiting them in terms of where and with whom they might end up living a year after the birth of their babies. There was certainly little evidence that they had become pregnant in order to get council housing, although a third of them were in local authority accommodation by the time of the interview and a further third were on a council housing list. A lack of planning and foresight was a characteristic of most of these young women and was also found in relation to their financial arrangements, as we will see in the next chapter.

Chapter 5

Social Security Benefits

One of the many concerns surrounding teenage pregnancy is the possibility of long-term negative outcomes for both the mother and baby. Previous studies have found that teenage mothers are more likely to suffer adverse health, educational, social and economic outcomes (Wellings et al, 1996). The financial implications and the long-term costs of supporting teenage mothers and their families have also been highlighted (Burt, 1986; McGuire and Hughes, 1995). It is against this background that we examined social security benefits in the interviews with the women and the fathers and grandparents of the babies.

In this chapter we look in detail at the extent to which women claimed benefits and how much they knew about benefits before they became pregnant, during their pregnancy and after the birth of the baby. We were particularly interested in the changes over time. Perhaps not surprisingly, we found that a much higher proportion of women were claiming benefits at the time of the interview than at the time they became pregnant. Benefits were by then the sole or primary source of income for many of them, reflecting the findings of other studies.

The first part of the chapter looks at how much women knew about benefits before they became pregnant and how they had first heard about them. The second part of the chapter looks more closely at the numbers of women claiming benefits at different times: before they became pregnant, during pregnancy and after the birth. We asked them at what stage in pregnancy and after the birth they had received or tried to claim benefits and how they had learnt about the benefits they had claimed. Most women gave details of their total weekly income from benefits and any deductions such as those made as part of a repayment of a social fund loan. We also asked them about other regular or irregular sources of income. Almost all the women reported the exact amount of their weekly income.

The context

In Chapter 2 we looked at the employment status and occupational history of the women and the fathers of the babies. We found that over half the women in this study had become single lone parents by the time of the interview.

This added to the probability that increasing numbers of the women interviewed would become dependent on benefits. Previous research has shown that paid employment is likely to account for only a small proportion of the net weekly income of lone parents (Burghes and Brown, 1995). We were also interested in the level of income of the women, particularly since so many of them had become dependent on benefits. In their study of lone parents, work and benefits, Marsh, Ford and Finlayson (1997) reported that the incomes of lone parents were only half those of other families with children, and that even lone parents in full-time employment had incomes lower than those typical of two-parent families. The research also showed that, disregarding housing benefit and those receiving disability benefits, the great majority of lone parents who were out of work and reliant on income support generally had to manage on less than £100 a week. In addition, the bulk of lone parents' net income came from social security benefits, with only a fifth of their net income coming from their own earnings.

The situation was even more pronounced for single, never-married lone mothers. Income from their own earnings amounted to only 13 per cent of their overall net income, a very small proportion came from maintenance payments, while the rest was made up of social security benefits.

Pre-pregnancy knowledge of benefits

We asked women what they had known about benefits before they became pregnant and found ample evidence that they were poorly informed. Indeed, it was not until after many of them had become pregnant or had had their babies that they sought advice about benefits, in particular those they might be eligible to claim.

We saw in Chapter 3 that the majority of women (61) said that they had not planned to become pregnant. With this widespread lack of planning it seems unlikely that these young women had become pregnant in order to claim social security benefits, but in this respect they were not unique. Ford et al (1995) examined the circumstances surrounding the entry into single lone parenthood, and noted a 'striking absence of purpose' amongst younger single lone parents.

We asked women if they had known before they became pregnant whether having a baby would enable them to claim social security benefits. Over half the women (47) said that they had not known whether it would or not, including most of those who were married before they became pregnant (8), around half of the single (24) and cohabiting women (13) and one third (2) of those in casual relationships. But even women who said they knew something had no detailed knowledge of the benefits they might be able to claim or how much they might be entitled to.

Sources of information on social security benefits

Most women who knew something about benefits before they became pregnant had heard by word of mouth, mainly from relatives and friends. More than half of them said that they had first heard that they could claim benefits from family and friends who were also claiming them. It is not surprising that many women said that they had heard it mentioned on television or in the media, while others had been told by friends and relatives who were not claiming benefits themselves or by various professionals.

It is important to reiterate that these women came from a wide variety of backgrounds with differences not only in their age, family composition, ethnic group, educational achievements and employment status but also in their expectations for their future. The majority had not planned to become pregnant and often had detailed plans for paid employment or further studies. Many of those who had planned their pregnancies were in stable relationships and were working or studying when they became pregnant. It was clear that few women had become pregnant with the idea of becoming dependent on social security benefits.

We saw in Chapter 2 that around two-thirds of the women (54) felt that their work, study or training plans had changed as a result of their pregnancy. Of these 54 women, half said that they had not known whether or not having a baby would enable them to claim social security benefits. In addition, only a third of them (17) had been in receipt of social security benefits before they became pregnant.

Of the 30 women whose work, study or training plans had not changed as a result of their pregnancy, around half had *not* known whether having a baby would enable them to claim benefits, but 13 of them were already receiving benefits.

Women in receipt of benefits before they became pregnant

Table 5.1 shows that over a third of the women (30) were receiving benefits before they became pregnant and Table 5.4 shows that married women were less likely than others to fall into this category.

Table 5.2 shows that most of the women (21) claiming benefits when they became pregnant were receiving income support. The rest (9) were receiving benefits such as the jobseeker's allowance (3), housing benefit (4), council tax benefit (1) and sickness/ disability benefit (1). Clearly, as the table shows, some of the women receiving income support were also receiving some of these benefits. We looked at these women receiving income support in more detail, and examined factors such as their school-leaving age, their educational qualifications and their employment status at the time of the interview.

Table 5.1 Women receiving benefits (excluding child benefit) before and during pregnancy and after the birth

numbers and column percentages

	When became pregnant		During pregnancy		After birth	
	Nos	%	Nos	%	Nos	%
Benefits	30	36	61	73	78	93
Statutory maternity pay only	0	0	9	11	3	4
Maternity allowance only	0	0	4	5	0	0
Not receiving benefits	54	64	10	12	3	4
Base: all women	*(84)*		*(84)*		*(84)*	

Table 5.2 Benefits received before and during pregnancy and after the birth

numbers and column percentages

	When became pregnant		During pregnancy		After birth	
	Nos	%	Nos	%	Nos	%
Income support	21	25	51	61	68	81
Housing benefit	9	11	24	29	41	49
Council tax benefit	5	6	18	21	41	49
One parent benefit	0	0	0	0	27	32
Lone parent premium	0	0	0	0	18	21
Social fund loans/grants	0	0	12	14	24	29
Family credit	0	0	0	0	14	17
Maternity grant	0	0	47	56	5	6
Statutory maternity pay	0	0	11	13	11	13
Maternity allowance	0	0	11	13	11	13
Jobseeker's allowance	3	4	9	11	2	2
Community care grant	0	0	0	0	2	2
Sickness/disability benefit	2	2	4	5	3	4
Child benefit	0	0	0	0	84	100
Base: all women	*(84)*		*(84)*		*(84)*	

Women receiving income support at the time they became pregnant were more likely than others to have left school before the statutory school-leaving age, but were as likely as others to have educational qualifications. However, they were less likely than others still to be in full-time or part-time education at the time of the interview.

19 of the 21 women were still receiving income support at the time of the interview, illustrating the extent to which these women had become dependent on social security benefits. Of the 19, 17 were not in paid work/unemployed, 1 was on a Government Training Scheme and 1 was a student at the time of the interview. In contrast, just under a fifth of the women who were not receiving income support when they became pregnant were in full-time or part-time paid employment at the time of the interview.

We asked the women whether there were any benefits they had tried unsuccessfully to claim before they became pregnant. Five women said that they had tried to claim benefits, one of whom was already receiving housing benefit. Four women tried to claim income support and one tried to claim a social fund payment.

Benefits received when pregnant

Table 5.1 shows that the proportion of women claiming benefits increased from just over a third (30) before they became pregnant to just under three-quarters (61) during their pregnancy, excluding the women who were receiving statutory maternity pay or maternity allowance only (13). Only 10 women did not receive any benefits during their pregnancy, of whom 5 were married, 2 were cohabiting, 2 were in steady relationships and 1 was in a casual relationship with the father of the baby when they became pregnant. Looking in more detail at the women who received benefits during pregnancy by their relationship with the father at the time they became pregnant, they accounted for:

- 3 of the 9 married women; of the others, 1 received statutory maternity or maternity allowance only and 5 received no benefits;
- 21 of the 26 cohabiting women; of the others, 3 received statutory maternity pay or maternity allowance only and 2 did not receive any benefits;
- 32 of the 43 in steady non-cohabiting relationships; of the others, 9 received statutory maternity pay or maternity allowance only and 2 received no benefits;
- 5 of the 6 women who were in casual relationships with the father of the baby; the other 1 received no benefits.

Some women who were already claiming benefits sought advice on how pregnancy and parenthood would change their entitlements, while others who had never claimed benefits looked at what was available to them. The interaction between social security benefits, social accommodation and employment was heavily influenced by a number of factors, such as women's personal circumstances, the availability of family support and particularly by the status and the stability of their relationships with the father of the baby and subsequent changes in their relationships over time.

Table 5.3   **Receipt of benefits before women became pregnant, by relationship with the baby's father at the time**

numbers and column percentages

	Total Nos	%	Married Nos	Cohabiting with baby's father Nos	Steady non-cohabiting relationship Nos	Casual relationship Nos
In receipt of benefits	30	36	1	15	12	2
Not in receipt of benefits	54	64	8	11	31	4
Base: all women	*(84)*		*(9)*	*(26)*	*(43)*	*(6)*

Table 5.2 shows that the number of women claiming income support increased from 21 before becoming pregnant to 51 women during their pregnancy. Table 5.5 shows the marital status of the women receiving benefits during pregnancy. Comparing these data with those in Table 5.4 we can see that the increase was particularly marked for women in steady non-cohabiting relationships with the father of the baby, where four times as many were claiming income support as before their pregnancy.

Table 5.2 shows an increase in the number of women claiming housing benefit from 9 women before they became pregnant to 24 during their pregnancy. Not surprisingly, women cohabiting when they became pregnant were more likely than women in steady or casual relationships to claim housing benefit. None of the married women claimed housing benefit, mainly because they were often living as lodgers with his parents (5) or her parents (1) or because they were owner occupiers (2). A fifth of the women (18) claimed council tax benefit during pregnancy, again mainly cohabiting women.

Recipients of income support, income-based jobseeker's allowance and family credit may be eligible to a maternity grant or maternity expenses payment from the social fund to cover the costs associated with a new baby. We found that just under two-thirds of all the women (52) had received this benefit (47 during pregnancy and 5 after the birth). A sixth of the women (12), all but one of whom were single, had received loans or grants from the social fund.

A quarter of the women (22) received statutory maternity pay (11) or the maternity allowance (11).

Table 5.4   **Benefits received before women became pregnant,
by relationship with the baby's father at the time**

numbers and column percentages

	Total Nos	%	Married Nos	Cohabiting with baby's father Nos	Steady non-cohabiting relationship Nos	Casual relationship Nos
Income support	21	25	1	12	6	2
Housing benefit	9	11	0	5	3	1
Council tax benefit	5	6	0	3	1	1
Jobseeker's allowance	3	4	0	2	1	0
Sickness/disability benefit	2	2	0	1	1	0
Not receiving benefits	54	64	8	11	31	4
Base: all women	*(84)*		*(9)*	*(26)*	*(43)*	*(6)*

Table 5.5   **Benefits received during pregnancy, by relationship with
the baby's father when women became pregnant**

numbers and column percentages

	Total Nos	%	Married Nos	Cohabiting with baby's father Nos	Steady non-cohabiting relationship Nos	Casual relationship Nos
Income support	51	61	2	19	26	4
Housing benefit	24	29	0	13	9	2
Council tax benefit	18	21	0	10	6	2
Social fund loans/ grants	12	14	0	1	8	3
Maternity grant	47	56	2	17	23	5
Statutory maternity pay	11	13	1	5	5	0
Maternity allowance	11	13	0	3	8	0
Jobseeker's allowance	9	11	0	3	4	2
Sickness/disability benefit	4	5	0	1	3	0
Base: all women	*(84)*		*(9)*	*(26)*	*(43)*	*(6)*

We asked the women if they had tried unsuccessfully to claim any benefits during their pregnancy. 14 women said that they had, three of whom were not claiming any other benefits. Of the 14 women, 7 had tried to claim maternity grant, 3 income support, 2 jobseeker's allowance and 2 a loan or grant from the social fund. Two of the three who were not claiming other benefits had tried to claim a maternity grant and one had tried to claim income support.

Benefits received after the birth

We were interested in how the picture had changed after the baby was born and asked women what benefits they had received as parents. As Table 5.1 shows, excluding child benefit, statutory maternity pay and maternity allowance, almost all of the women (78) had received at least one other benefit. Of the remaining 6 women, 3 had received child benefit only and 3 had received statutory maternity pay.

By the time of the interview the number of women receiving child benefit only had increased to 6, of whom 1 was married, 4 cohabiting and 1 was single. All the women were in paid employment. The other 78 women were receiving at least one other benefit, apart from child benefit, and just under two-thirds of these (47) said that benefits were their sole source of income. Their net weekly income from benefits and their overall net weekly income from all sources will be discussed later.

We looked at the number of benefits (excluding child benefit, statutory maternity pay and maternity allowance) that women had received after the birth, not necessarily concurrently. Overall, a third of the women (26) had received 1 or 2 benefits, over a third (32) had received 3 or 4 and over a quarter (23) had received 5 or 6 benefits.

Disregarding child benefit which all the women received after the birth, Table 5.2 shows that there had been a marked increase in benefit claimants, particularly those claiming income support, housing benefit and council tax benefit. There was also a twofold increase in the number of women who had received loans or grants from the social fund, giving some indication of the limited resources of some women. Other benefits such as family credit, one parent benefit and lone parent premium, and of course, child benefit were claimed by women for the first time after the birth of the baby.

68 of the 78 women receiving benefits after the birth received income support. Of the 10 women who did not receive income support but received other benefits, 7 received family credit (4 family credit only and 3 family credit and another benefit), 2 received the jobseeker's allowance and 1 received a maternity grant which had been claimed during pregnancy and had been paid late.

Table 5.6 shows that the overwhelming majority of single and cohabiting women were claiming income support after the birth but married women were less likely to do so.

We looked at the 68 women receiving income support at the time of the interview in more detail: their school-leaving age, educational qualifications and their employment status at the time of the interview. We found that all of those (16) who had left school before the statutory school-leaving age were receiving income support. Just under two-thirds had educational qualifications compared with almost all the women (94 per cent) who were not receiving income support. Of the 13 women who were employed at the time of the interview, 5 (all in part-time employment) were receiving income support and 8 were not.

The move towards single parent status was especially marked by the fact that a third of women (27) said that they were receiving the one parent benefit. They represented:

- 7 of the 23 women cohabiting with the father of the baby;
- 1 of the 5 women in a steady non-cohabiting relationship with the father of the baby;
- 15 of the 35 single women;
- 3 of the 4 women cohabiting with a new partner;
- 1 of the 2 women in a steady non-cohabiting relationship with a new partner.

Of the 27 women claiming one parent benefit after the birth, 10 were cohabiting with the father of the baby (7) or with a new partner (3). Only one of the women reported that the benefit had subsequently been withdrawn. One woman explained why she had not reported that she was living with the father of the baby: 'You have to say you're on your own or there's no chance of benefits.' Another woman remarked: 'He (father of the baby) doesn't really live here. It's been through the CSA and they don't really know what's happening.'

18 women were receiving the lone parent premium on top of their income support payments, of whom 5 were cohabiting.

14 women said that they were receiving family credit – available to low paid wage earners with children – but this was claimed by a higher proportion of married than cohabiting or single women. It is possible that some of the women might not have intended working while their baby was young, but with the 1992 ruling which reduced the hourly qualification threshold from 24 to 16 hours employment a week, they might have been encouraged to work (see Ford et al, 1995 for a discussion).

Table 5.6 Benefits received after the birth, by relationship with the baby's father at the time of the interview

numbers and column percentages

	Total		Married	Cohabiting with baby's father	Steady non-cohabiting relationship	Single and alone	Cohabiting with new partner	Steady relationship with new partner
	Nos	%	Nos	Nos	Nos	Nos	Nos	Nos
Income support	68	81	6	18	5	33	4	2
Housing benefit	41	49	3	12	2	21	2	1
Council tax benefit	41	49	6	10	0	22	2	1
One parent benefit	27	32	0	7	1	15	3	1
Lone parent premium	18	21	0	4	0	13	0	1
Social fund loans/grants	24	29	1	5	1	15	2	0
Family credit	14	17	6	2	0	6	0	0
Maternity grant	5	6	1	1	0	3	0	0
Statutory maternity pay	11	13	2	4	1	3	1	0
Maternity allowance	11	13	0	4	1	5	0	1
Jobseeker's allowance	2	2	1	1	0	0	0	0
Community care grant	2	2	0	1	0	1	0	0
Child benefit	84	100	15	23	5	35	4	2
Base: all women	(84)		(15)	(23)	(5)	(35)	(4)	(2)

The number of women claiming housing benefit had risen sub-stantially from 9 before pregnancy to nearly half of all the women (41) at the time of the interview.

The rise in the number of women receiving grants or loans from the social fund also indicates how poorly equipped many of them were to meet the expenses of setting up their own home and the basic costs of family living, particularly given their almost complete reliance on social security benefits. Over a quarter of the women (24) had received loans or grants from the social fund, two-thirds of whom were single (15). None of them mentioned having received more than one loan or grant. The data did not differentiate between those receiving grants which did not have to be repaid and those receiving loans which did. Although the amount awarded may be between £30 and £1,000, the women did not state the actual amount received. The most common method of repayment mentioned for loans was through deductions from their income support payments of up to 22 per cent of the overall weekly payment.

We asked women if they had tried unsuccessfully to claim benefits after the birth. 14 women said that they had, 6 of whom had tried to claim two benefits. 12 of the women were already receiving other benefits, but one who had tried unsuccessfully to claim income support and family credit was receiving no benefits and another, who tried to claim family credit, was only receiving statutory maternity pay.

Sources of information about benefits

The most common source of information for women about social security benefits was either face-to-face advice or from leaflets picked up at a local DSS office or the local post office. A small number of women contacted the benefits enquiry line (BEL) or Citizens Advice Bureaux or job centres. Women often got advice from relatives and friends who either told them about the benefits they were claiming themselves or advised them to get information through the sources above. We saw that in some cases, parents found out about benefits on behalf of their daughter and then advised them on the benefits they could apply for, how to apply for them and when to do so.

Net weekly income from benefits and other sources of income

We were interested in determining whether women were reliant on social security benefits as their primary or sole source of income, or whether they had any additional regular or irregular sources of income. We have already seen that just under two-thirds (47) of the women who were receiving one or more benefits apart from child benefit said that social security benefits were their only source of income. They were more likely to be single than married or cohabiting women.

The remaining 37 women had other income sources including:

• their own income from paid employment
• their partner's income from paid employment
• regular or infrequent contributions from the baby's father
• regular or infrequent contributions from their parents.

We also asked the women about their current net weekly income from benefits and whether the income was only for themselves and their baby or whether it was shared with someone else, such as their partner. The responses varied according to the financial arrangements operating within their households.

Overall, the average net weekly income from benefits (including child benefit) was just under £70. Over three-quarters of the women (65) were receiving £60 or more in benefits per week. Eight of these women, three of whom were receiving disability benefits, received over £100.

The majority of women (69) said that their income from benefits (including child benefit) was just for themselves and their baby, while the remainder (15) said that their income from benefits was shared with their partner.

Other sources of income

Table 5.7 shows the women's sources of income by their marital status at the time of the interview. The table shows that single women were more likely than married or cohabiting women to cite social security benefits as their sole source of income. They also often had less reliable sources of additional income, such as contributions from the father of the baby or from relatives.

Of the 37 women who had another income source apart from benefits:

• 18 had income from their own (4) or their partner's earnings only (8), or from their joint earnings (6). These were usually married (8) or cohabiting women (8) while 2 were single.
• Another 3 single women had earnings from their own paid employment plus a contribution from the baby's father (regular or infrequent).
• 9 of the women received a contribution from the baby's father but had no other income source apart from benefits.
• 7 women received contributions from their parents, their partner's parents or other relatives, but had no other income source apart from benefits.

We also looked at the total weekly earnings from all sources including benefits, paid employment, and contributions from the father of the baby or other relatives. The average net weekly income was just over £100

Table 5.7 All sources of income, by relationship with the baby's father at the time of the interview

numbers and column percentages

	Total Nos	Total %	Married Nos	Cohabiting with baby's father Nos	Steady non-cohabiting relationship Nos	Single and alone Nos	Cohabiting with new partner Nos	Steady relationship with new partner Nos
Benefits only	47	56	5	12	2	23	3	2
Benefits plus support from baby's father only	9	11	0	2	3	4	0	0
Benefits plus support from baby's father plus woman's wage	3	4	0	0	0	3	0	0
Benefits plus woman's wage only	4	5	0	2	0	2	0	0
Benefits plus partner's wage only	8	10	6	2	0	0	0	0
Benefits plus both partners' wages	6	7	2	4	0	0	0	0
Benefits plus parental or relatives' contribution	7	8	2	1	0	3	1	0
Base: all women	(84)		(15)	(23)	(5)	(35)	(4)	(2)

but there was a striking difference between the women according to marital status. Married women had almost twice as much income per week (£148.30) as single women (£76.80). Just under a quarter of all the women (20) had a net weekly income in excess of £100, but only two of them were single.

The number of women who referred to infrequent contributions from parents does not adequately reflect the support and assistance that some received. Some parents provided continuous material and moral support, often at great financial and personal expense to themselves, as will be discussed more fully in the chapter covering the interviews with the grandparents themselves. Many of the women, and sometimes their partners, had lived rent-free with parents at some stage since becoming pregnant and, as we have seen, some women were still living with parents when we interviewed them.

Maintenance payments

A recent study of lone parents by Marsh, Ford and Finlayson (1997) which looked at maintenance payments and the effects of the Child Support Agency (CSA) noted that less than half of parents had an agreement of some kind in place for payments which included court orders, voluntary agreements and assessments made by the CSA itself. They found that agreements to pay maintenance were less common among single never-married lone parents of whom over three-quarters had no agreement at all. We found that maintenance payments were not often mentioned by the women as a source of income, although some had mentioned that assessments had been carried out by the CSA. Only two women mentioned court orders. Given that applications for income support and family credit from lone parents trigger procedures to recover maintenance payments by the CSA, it is surprising that so few women spoke of maintenance assessments and payments. Even where agreements are in place, not all women receive regular payments and some payments are handled by the DSS through deductions, which was the experience of one of the women in our study.

Chapter 6

Interviews with the Fathers

Our interviews with the fathers and mothers covered the same topics so that we could look at their different perspectives on a number of important issues, for example, whether the pregnancy had been planned and their reactions to the pregnancy. We were also interested in the extent to which the fathers were involved in deciding what to do about the pregnancy and where and with whom the women would live during pregnancy and after the birth. We asked them about their involvement in looking after the baby and their contribution to the baby's upkeep. We looked at how much they knew about social security benefits and housing before their partner became pregnant, and we explored their views and perceptions of teenage mothers which we report on in Chapter 8.

We were able to achieve interviews with markedly different numbers of fathers in the three areas. The overwhelming majority of fathers interviewed were from Leeds (20 of the 24) and only four fathers were interviewed in Hackney and Solihull (two in each area). We therefore treat the fathers interviewed as one group, acknowledging that they are mainly from Leeds, and we note that there were important characteristics in this sub-sample which distinguished them from the fathers in the sample as a whole, as described by the teenage mothers in their interviews.

Our achievement of more interviews with fathers in Leeds was undoubtedly related to the fact that nearly two-thirds of the women in Leeds were still in a relationship with the baby's father, compared with less than half of the women in Hackney and Solihull. The fathers interviewed were mostly in steady relationships, living with or married to the baby's mother, and only a few relationships had broken up since the pregnancy occurred, in marked contrast to the sample as a whole where half of the relationships had broken up. There was ample evidence to suggest that many of the couples where the father was interviewed had planned the pregnancy, while others who had not planned in the same way had wanted a family at some stage. There was usually a high degree of consensus between couples about having a baby, so that even if the pregnancy was not planned it was almost always wanted.

These important differences from the rest of the main sample of fathers must be borne in mind in reading this chapter. The fathers interviewed undoubtedly expressed views typical of a much more committed and stable group than those which might have been found taking the sample as a whole.

Age of the fathers when the baby was born and whether they had had other children

Two-thirds of the fathers were under 25 and five (2 in Solihull and 3 in Leeds) were teenagers themselves at the time of the birth. The rest were under 30 apart from one who was 43.

Only one father had had children before the present baby.

Marital status at the time of the interview

20 of the 24 fathers interviewed were living with (13) or married to (7) the baby's mother at the time of the interview. The remaining 4 fathers were single, but two of them had lived with the baby's mother and had subsequently split up.

Ethnic group, country of birth and religion

The majority of fathers, like those in the main sample, were of white ethnic origin. 20 were white, two were Indian, one was Pakistani and one Middle Eastern. 20 were born in the United Kingdom, two in Africa, one in Europe and one in Australia. All but four said that English was their first language.

14 of the fathers had no religion, 5 were Church of England, 4 were Muslim and 1 was a Roman Catholic.

Age of father's mother when she had her first baby

We asked the fathers for the age of their own mother when she had her first baby. The average age was 21.8 years and a quarter said that their mother was a teenager when she had her first baby, a lower proportion than we found among the mothers of the women interviewed. Nearly half of their mothers were aged between 20 and 24, two between 25 and 29, and one was over 30. Five respondents said that they did not know how old their mother was when she had her first baby.

Marital status of father's parents

We asked the fathers about the present marital status of their parents and whether any had entered new relationships. We found a similar picture among both the fathers and the women interviewed: relationship break-up among their parents was very common and only just over a third of the fathers interviewed (9) said that their parents were still married. Nearly half of them (11) said that their parents were divorced or separated, and another four said that a parent had died.

Of the 11 respondents whose parents were separated:

- 3 said their mother had a different husband/partner
- 4 said their father had a different wife/partner
- 1 said that both parents had different spouses/partners
- 1 said that his parents were separated and alone
- 2 said their parents were separated but did not know whether either or both had new partners.

One man in Leeds who did not know whether his parents had new partners commented: 'I don't know. I keep out of it.' A married man said that his parents had separated when he was 9 years old and both were with different partners at the time of the interview. He felt that the break-up of his parents' relationship had influenced his own outlook and commented: 'Don't you find that people who come from a broken home are the ones who really want their relationship to work?'

Of the 11 respondents whose parents were no longer together, 2 were aged 5 or under when their parents separated, 8 were between 6 and 10 and 1 was between 16 and 20.

There appeared to be close links between many of the fathers and their own parents. Half of them said that they had regular contact with both their parents and a third had contact with one parent. Two did not have regular contact with either parent and one said that both parents were dead.

Number of siblings

Family size among both the teenage mothers and the fathers interviewed was well above the national average. The average number of siblings reported by the fathers was 3.8.

Age on completion of full-time education, educational and vocational qualifications

We found a similar picture among the main sample of fathers and those interviewed. A quarter of those interviewed had left school before the age of 16. Over half had left school at 16 while 3 had left school at 17 or 18. Two were still in full-time education.

One third of the fathers interviewed (9) had no educational qualifications – a similar proportion to that found in the main sample of fathers. 12 of the 15 with qualifications had GCSE or an equivalent qualification. Of the remaining three, one had A-levels and was studying for a degree, and two had obtained first degrees, with one studying for another degree.

10 of the 24 fathers had vocational qualifications – a slightly higher proportion than that found in the main sample. The qualifications included City and Guilds, NVQ Levels 1 and 2, BTEC (OND), London Chamber of Commerce certificates and an Assistant Accounting Technician certificate.

Current employment status, social class and occupational history

Over a quarter of fathers were unemployed (7) which was slightly lower than in the main sample. Over half (13) were in full-time employment and 2 were in part-time employment, which was slightly higher than in the main sample. Only 3 of the 7 unemployed men had educational or vocational qualifications.

The majority of fathers in paid employment were in manual occupations: 10 in skilled and 3 in semi-skilled occupations. Two were in managerial occupations, two were students and the rest (7) were unemployed.

We were interested in the fathers' employment history and asked those who were working how long they had been in their current job. Half of them had been in their current job for 12 months or less, a quarter for between one and two years and the rest for more than three years.

All but one of the unemployed men had been in paid employment at some time, all in manual occupations. Three had left their jobs for health reasons, two had moved area, one had gone to college and one was laid off.

Effects of baby on father's work, study or training plans

Only one third of the fathers interviewed felt that having a baby had changed their work, study or training plans, which was the reverse of what we found among the mothers, two-thirds of whom had changed their plans as a result of the pregnancy. The main reason for this difference was the fact that the mothers usually had to look after the baby, but it was also important that relatively few of the fathers were teenagers themselves when they became parents, so that they were more likely than the mothers to have established themselves in employment and to have finished their studies.

How had plans changed? Some of the fathers' comments echoed those of the mothers, but fathers were more likely to mention the added financial pressures of having a baby, particularly if both partners had been earning before the pregnancy. The loss of earnings coupled with the additional expense of a family prompted some fathers to work longer hours or extra days or overtime.

A Leeds father who was married to the baby's mother when she became pregnant felt that his work plans had changed. He said that although the pregnancy had not been planned it had not been avoided either: 'I felt I had to work more and bring in a lot of money doing overtime.' But he added that having to work so much might have created more problems than it had solved: 'I ended up working seven days a week and it put a terrible strain on our marriage.'

Another Leeds man who was 19 and living with the baby's mother when she became pregnant said that he was forced to take the first job he was offered because he needed one quickly. For him, an unplanned pregnancy meant '...going into a job that I didn't really like just for the money,' and added, 'I'm still looking for another job. I'm not really happy in this job, but because of the baby, I can't afford to give it up.'

An unplanned pregnancy also had an impact on further study and training so that plans to start further studies did not materialise or courses were abandoned or put on hold before their completion. A man in Solihull who was 18 and living with the baby's mother when she became pregnant described how the unplanned pregnancy had changed his study plans: 'I was going to do a course in mechanics, but I couldn't afford to.' Another man in Leeds, who also said that the pregnancy was unplanned, explained how things had changed for him: 'I was studying two nights a week on a five-year BTEC course. I've put that on hold because of time. It's too difficult to do right now.'

Planned and unplanned pregnancies

One third of the fathers interviewed said that the pregnancy was planned (8), which is rather higher than the proportion found in the main sample, and two said that although it was not planned it was not avoided either. The remainder described the pregnancy as unplanned (14), ranging from men who had discussed having a baby with their partner and agreed they would like one at some stage, to others who had never thought of having a baby or discussed it with their girlfriend or partner.

As a result, an unplanned pregnancy for some fathers was something they had never contemplated and did not want. For others, however, unplanned simply meant unexpected. Indeed, one of the fathers in Leeds who said that the pregnancy was not planned explained that he and his partner had already tried unsuccessfully to have a baby.

Not surprisingly, none of the eight men who had planned the pregnancy felt that their study, work and training plans had changed as a result. As we have seen, couples who had planned the pregnancy were usually married or cohabiting and the pregnancy appeared to have been a joint decision by both partners.

Of the eight men who had planned the pregnancy, none were teenagers, 5 were in paid employment, 2 were unemployed and 1 was a student, 5 were cohabiting, 2 were married and 1 was single but subsequently married the baby's mother.

Another two men said that the pregnancy was semi-planned. Both were cohabiting with the baby's mother when the pregnancy occurred and were married at the time of the interview. One said that when his girlfriend became pregnant: 'Our main concern was getting married and then she was pregnant so we brought the wedding forward.' The other said: 'We didn't mind if he (baby) came along.'

We asked the babies' fathers why they decided to have a baby at this time. A few fathers appeared to have accepted that they were running the risk of their partner becoming pregnant rather than actively setting out for her to conceive. One said: 'We weren't using any contraception so I suppose we must have done (planned the pregnancy). She (mother of the baby) says we didn't plan, but if we didn't plan we'd have used contraception. We went into it with open eyes.' Another man who was living with his mother when his partner became pregnant said: 'She was out of work and she'd finished college so I suppose we thought we'd try.'

Other men were clear both about the planning and the timing of the pregnancy, like one who was living with his partner when she became pregnant: 'I felt it was the right thing to do. I wanted us to be a family.' A married man said: 'My parents wanted a grandchild and I was wanting to have a child. It strengthens the family bond.'

Eight fathers said that the pregnancy had been planned and two said that it had been semi-planned. We compared this with what the women had said and found a high degree of consistency between the accounts of the fathers and mothers but some inconsistencies. The two women whose partners had said that the pregnancy had been semi-planned both said that it had been planned. In addition, one father said that it had not been planned but his wife said it had. However, both said they were overjoyed about it.

Another father, who was living with the mother of the baby when she became pregnant but whose relationship had split up after the birth, said that the pregnancy had been planned but the mother said that it had not. She explained: 'We were planning to marry and we were going to move to another flat.' Her first reaction when she suspected the pregnancy was: ' "I'm not." I didn't know whether to laugh or cry, it was sort of mixed.' Although he was pleased about the pregnancy he said that he had considered a termination of pregnancy but she had not. Their relationship had broken up after the birth.

Reactions of fathers to news of the pregnancy

Three-quarters of the fathers interviewed said that they were delighted, overjoyed or pleased when they had heard the news and their partners usually expressed similar reactions. One man who said that the pregnancy had neither been planned nor avoided described his reaction: 'I jumped for joy. I went to the shop and bought a load of brandy and got extremely drunk. I've wanted to be a father from the age of 18 (was 26 when baby was born). I was over the moon.'

Another man said that the pregnancy was not planned although he and his partner knew they wanted children. He explained how he felt: 'Surprised, and a little bit scared. I was pleased – we did want kids, but it was a bit earlier than we had planned.' Another man who said that they had planned the pregnancy described what had happened: 'Both of us laughed and then we cried. I was definitely feeling happy about it.'

With so few planned pregnancies, it was not surprising that some fathers were shocked and surprised. One man explained how surprised he was because he and his partner had tried and failed to have a baby before, and were using contraception when the pregnancy occurred: 'I actually said to her, "Whose is it?" because we had actually stopped trying and we were taking precautions, so it was a shock!' Another man was pleased about the pregnancy but was annoyed that everyone else knew before he did: 'I was, like, second from last to know.'

Only two men had felt anxious and confused about the pregnancy initially. One father, who was only 18 when the baby was born, explained that the pregnancy was not planned. He was living with his parents when his girlfriend became pregnant and said: 'I was shocked and frightened.' His partner was also anxious: 'I was scared. I daren't tell my mum. Although she knew before I did.'

Another man, who was 20 when the baby was born, explained that the pregnancy had not been planned. He too was living with his parents when his girlfriend became pregnant and was married at the time of the interview: 'I was in two minds. I didn't know what to do. I told her to have an abortion. I was really against it (the pregnancy) but when I got home and talked to my mum, I changed my mind.' His partner was equally distraught: 'I couldn't believe it. I was shocked. I thought my life was going to end.'

Although couples usually reacted similarly to the news of the pregnancy, some did not. Women often reacted less favourably to the news of the pregnancy than the father of the baby. One couple who were in a casual relationship at the time of the pregnancy were cohabiting at the time of the interview. The father, who was just 18 when the baby was born, reacted positively to the news of the pregnancy, but his partner, who was 17 when the baby was born, was less positive: 'I was really shocked. I couldn't believe it. I didn't think it could happen. I took the morning-after pill and it didn't work.'

Another teenage couple also reacted differently to the news of the pregnancy. They were cohabiting at the time of the pregnancy and had split up after the birth. The father of the baby was 18 when the baby was born and described his reaction as: 'Shock. I was pleased but shocked.' His partner, who was 17 when the baby was born, recalled her reaction: 'I was gutted. I didn't really want to be pregnant.'

What fathers wanted the baby's mother to do about the pregnancy

We asked fathers what they wanted their partner to do about the pregnancy and whether they had discussed options other than keeping the baby. All the men said they had wanted the women to have the baby, apart from the two fathers who wanted their girlfriend to have a termination of pregnancy.

However, a further two men said that they had considered the possibility of a termination of pregnancy, in spite of the fact that they were pleased about the pregnancy, because they felt that all options needed to be discussed. One (who was 21 when the baby was born) said: 'That or adoption were the only other alternatives and we had to discuss it. I didn't tell her to do it (have a termination) but it had to be discussed.' The other man (who was 27 when the baby was born) echoed this view: 'Not for my own reasons. More for hers. I think she was stuck in the middle. I was delighted, but her parents weren't keen. It was hard for her, especially being so young.' In both cases the women said that they had not considered having a termination and although they discussed the possibility of having one they did not want to go ahead with it.

One of the men (who was 18 when the baby was born) who had wanted his girlfriend to have a termination of pregnancy explained why it was never discussed: 'I just didn't want to bring it up.' She had not considered having a termination herself and said: 'I couldn't have got rid of it. Even if (partner) had stayed around, I'd still have kept it.'

The other man (who was 20 when the baby was born) discussed the possibility of having a termination and described his girlfriend's confusion: 'She didn't really know herself. She didn't really want to keep it but she couldn't see herself having an abortion.' Although she had considered the possibility, she explained that after discussing it with her partner and mother: 'I just didn't think I could go through with it. I love children and my mother said, "Whatever decision you make, it will be with you for the rest of your life", and (partner) didn't want me to have an abortion.' She said that her mother and partner had influenced her to continue with the pregnancy: 'Because I knew he would support me, it made it easy to continue with having the baby.'

We compared the views of both fathers and mothers on the possibility of a termination of pregnancy. Only two women had considered it. One of these women's partner had also considered it, but the other partner had not. The couple were in a casual relationship at the time of the pregnancy and were cohabiting at the time of the interview. She was shocked when she suspected she was pregnant and made an appointment with a counsellor which she did not keep. She recalled her conversation about having a TOP with her partner who said: 'No. It's murder.' He was 16 when the baby was born and explained: 'I don't agree with abortions.' She said that her discussion with him had influenced her decision to continue with the pregnancy because she felt that he would support her.

Nearly half the fathers said that they had not considered a termination because they wanted the baby. One man who was married when his wife became pregnant explained that a termination had '...never been a question for us'. Another man who was living with his girlfriend when she became pregnant said: 'We wanted a baby. I would never consider it my place to suggest to a mother-to-be to have a termination.'

In some cases termination was not considered for religious reasons. A few fathers said that they did not agree with abortions, reflected in the comments from this man: 'I don't agree with things like that unless there's something wrong.' A few fathers were completely against abortion, like this man: 'There was no question of an abortion. There was nothing to discuss.'

Adoption was not even considered by the overwhelming majority of fathers. Only one man in Leeds, who had considered a termination of pregnancy, said that he had also considered adoption. Again, he felt that all options needed be discussed but his partner had said that adoption was out of the question. Most of the fathers said that they wanted the baby or could not have given it up. A man explained: 'I couldn't do it really because I'd be thinking about him too much. I love him too much anyway to give him away.' Another father said: 'It didn't even enter our minds. There was no way we could have it and then give it away.'

Decision-making

We have seen how important sources of support were to women in the early days and weeks after first suspecting and confirming their pregnancy. The majority of women talked to at least one person about their pregnancy, but we saw that women in more stable relationships were less likely to mention discussions with their partners about the pregnancy than those in less stable relationships.

We asked the fathers how closely they had been involved in the decision about what to do about the pregnancy, and if they had discussed where and with whom their partner might live during pregnancy and after the birth of the baby.

Two-thirds of the fathers (16 fathers) said that they were closely involved in the decision about what to do about the pregnancy. Two said that they had some involvement and two had no involvement. One said that he was involved in the discussions but the decision was not for him to make, and three said that there was no decision, mainly because they wanted the baby.

- The three men who said that there was no decision were happy with the pregnancy. Two were living with their partner and one was married when she became pregnant. Two had planned the pregnancy and the other couple had already tried unsuccessfully for some time to have a child.
- The two men who said they were not involved in the decision said that, although the pregnancy had not been planned, they were happy to have the baby, and that no decision was necessary.
- The man who felt the decision was not his to take had planned the pregnancy and was living with his partner when she became pregnant. He felt that they should discuss all the options, including a termination and adoption, but that his partner should take the final decision.

One man described his involvement in the discussion but not the final decision: 'I was involved but if she hadn't wanted the baby there would have been nothing I could have done – but she did want it.' He was living with his partner and his parents when she became pregnant. Another man who had only had some involvement said that he had planned the pregnancy, but that when it came to making decisions: 'I've had no say – she's organised it all.'

Although the responses of the fathers give a mixed impression, it is clear that many of the fathers were closely involved in discussions and decisions about the pregnancy. There appeared to have been a good understanding between some of these couples before the pregnancy about whether they wanted children at all and when they should have them, even if the baby came a little earlier than expected.

However, the views expressed in the interviews with the fathers were by no means typical of the sample as a whole, as we have seen in the interviews with women, where it was quite clear that some women had made a decision to become pregnant or have the baby against the wishes of their partners. Not surprisingly, there was no indication of this in the interviews with the fathers, who frequently talked about joint decision-making, reflected in one man's comments: 'It was a mutual decision. We agreed on everything.'

Discussions about where and with whom the baby's mother would live during pregnancy

Half the fathers (12) said that they had discussed where and with whom the baby's mother was going to live during pregnancy. Those who were already married or cohabiting usually discussed where they would live together. One father in Leeds said: 'We'd already bought a house and were living together.'

A father who was living with his partner and her parents when she became pregnant said: 'We knew we could stay here with her mum but we thought we should try the council as well.' Another man who was living with his partner and his own parents said they had discussed getting a place of their own: 'We planned to get our own place together. We were together then, but not on our own.'

Some agreed that they would continue to live together but also live with their parents until they could get a place of their own. A Leeds man who was living with his girlfriend's parents when she became pregnant explained why he decided that they should continue to live with them: 'We agreed that we needed some finance behind us. I didn't want to be put in a council house in the middle of an estate and get trapped. Her parents said we could stay with them till we got some money together.'

What did couples decide?

- Three couples decided to remain apart and live with their respective parents during the pregnancy and then look for a place together. A man in Leeds explained what he and his girlfriend had decided: 'We would continue to live as we were (living with respective parents). I didn't want to get into debt so we went along with it as long as we got somewhere eventually.'
- Another four couples decided to live together, but to move in with his or her parents during the pregnancy and then look for their own place after the baby was born.
- One was living with his wife and his parents and they decided to continue with this arrangement.
- Two were already living together and decided to continue to do so.
- One couple were living together with the father's parents and decided to remain together but to look for a place of their own.
- One couple who were living with their respective parents decided to look for a place to live together.

Of the 12 fathers who had had no discussion about living arrangements, 8 said that there was no need because they were already living together. One man who was living with his partner said: 'We knew we would just stay here as we were before. Eventually this house will be mine anyway.' A married man explained why there had been no discussion: 'We were married and had our own house, so there was nothing to discuss.' Two said that there was no discussion because it was assumed that their girlfriends would live at home with their parents and one said that he and his partner had already made plans to be together and had applied for council accommodation.

The majority of fathers said that they had not spoken to anyone else about where and with whom the baby's mother would live. Some said that they had spoken to their own parents or their partner's parents. Many of these people offered advice about getting a place of their own. Some suggested applying for council accommodation while others said that they should buy their own place. One man in Leeds said that his father advised him to: 'Put my name down for council accommodation because it will help (girlfriend) being pregnant. He thought a mortgage would be a good idea too.' Another Leeds man said that all his friends and family gave similar advice: 'They all said the same – "Go get a mortgage." I was hoping for work accommodation but it didn't work out and then we pushed the council as hard as we could. A mortgage was too scary at the time.'

Decisions about where to live were not always simple and clearcut. Many of the fathers were still living with their parents (some with their partner as well) when the pregnancy occurred and had not expected to be faced for some time with the prospect of parenthood, not to mention their own mortgage or their own home. It was clear that discussions and decisions about the relative merits of buying a property, renting privately, seeking council accommodation or remaining at home with parents caused considerable stress among some of the fathers, not least because they were still coming to terms with the pregnancy and impending parenthood. It was not surprising that some fathers found the idea of taking out a mortgage an unwelcome responsibility.

Discussions about where and with whom the women would live after the baby was born

We have seen that half the fathers discussed where and with whom their partners would live during the pregnancy and we found that half also discussed her living arrangements after the birth. It was clear from the father's accounts that there was a definite shift away from the option of living with parents to living together. Those who were already living together were concerned that they would need more space once the baby was born. A man in Leeds was already living in council accommodation when his partner became pregnant and explained why he wanted to move: 'The flat had only one bedroom and it was damp. We'd complained. I was pushing the council to get us somewhere else. I assumed we would continue to live together.'

Another man in Leeds who was living with his partner and his parents when she became pregnant explained that although they had talked about staying together, their relationship came under a great strain when they encountered problems in finding accommodation of their own, and they had subsequently split up: 'We went to find a house, but it was no good because there was damp everywhere. So we had to leave and we went to my mum's and then we went to her dad's, but we had to leave there because there wasn't enough room. We found a house, but we split up. She went to a friend and I went to my friend, then I went back to my mum and she went back to her mum's. We're together again now, not living together, but we see each other a few times a week.'

Where fathers were living when the woman became pregnant

Of the 24 fathers:

- 13 were cohabiting with the baby's mother when she became pregnant:
  - 3 with their partner and his parent(s)
  - 2 with his girlfriend's parent(s)
  - 7 alone with the baby's mother
  - 1 was sharing accommodation with another couple
- 3 fathers were living with their wives (1 with his wife and his parents)
- 5 were living with their parents
- 3 were living with friends.

Type of accommodation fathers were living in before the pregnancy

- 17 of the fathers were living in a house when their partner became pregnant:
  - 6 with their partner and parents
  - 5 with their parents only
  - 3 with their girlfriend only
  - 1 with his wife
  - 2 with friends
- 5 were living in a flat or maisonette (4 with their partner and 1 with friends)
- 1 was living in accommodation abroad with his wife
- 1 was living in a mobile home with his partner.

Relationship changes since the pregnancy

It must be constantly borne in mind that the fathers interviewed were not typical of the fathers as a whole. Among the fathers interviewed, very few relationships had broken down by the time of the interview and many had become more stable. This is, of course, a different picture from that found in the interviews with women, which showed that almost half of them were single and alone at the time of the interview. We looked at changes in the relationships of this sub-sample.

Married relationships
3 couples were married at the time the pregnancy occurred and were still married at the time of the interview.

Cohabiting relationships
13 were cohabiting at the time the pregnancy occurred. At the time of the interview, 3 were married, 8 were still cohabiting and 2 were single.

Other relationships
7 couples were in steady relationships and 1 in a casual relationship at the time the pregnancy occurred. At the time of the interview, 1 was married, 5 were cohabiting, and 2 were single (although one was still in a steady relationship with the baby's mother).

How often did the fathers see their baby?

The fathers interviewed were much more likely to see their babies than those in the main sample, mainly because a high proportion of them were living with the baby and the baby's mother. 20 of the 24 fathers interviewed were cohabiting with (13) or married to the baby's mother (7) at the time of the interview. One father saw the baby once a week and two saw the baby twice a week. Another father who had lived with his parents throughout explained that he saw his daughter: 'As much as possible. I used to work away all week, but now I'm back I see her every Sunday, and if I can I see her during the week. I do try to see her.'

Contribution to the upkeep of the baby

22 of the 24 fathers made a contribution to the baby's upkeep. One father who had lived with his parents throughout explained that he had contributed to the baby's upkeep until the baby's mother stopped seeing him: 'There is a court action about contributions at present. It was £25 a week before. It'll be the same again I suppose.' Another father who was living with the baby's mother said that he had made contributions when he was in full-time employment: 'I paid when I was working full-time but

I'm not paying now. If I was in full-time employment I'd be quite willing to pay and I do, but unfortunately I can't at the moment.'

Most of the fathers living with or married to the baby's mother said that they supported both mother and baby. Many said that their contributions varied and few were able to put an exact figure on them. A handful of fathers said that they gave all their earnings to the baby's mother, like a Leeds man who was unemployed and living with the baby's mother: 'Every fortnight. She gets everything. £92 a fortnight.'

Another man who was also receiving social security benefits said: 'When I get money, she gets half of it.' Another man who was living with the baby's mother said that they were both working: 'All our money is pooled. Everything is shared.' One man who was living with his parents explained that in addition to paying maintenance payments he gave the baby's mother more money when he could afford to: 'I give through the CSA – £20 a week and if there's anything else she asks me. If I can give, I do.'

Involvement in looking after the baby

We asked fathers if they had any involvement in looking after the baby. Many of the fathers who were living with or married to the baby's mother spoke of caring for their baby or doing as much as they could. Many described how they shared household duties and childcare, and often referred to involvement after work and at weekends, reflected in one man's comments in Hackney: 'In the evenings, yes, and at weekends. I take him out and do his shopping and I look after him while (wife) does the housework. I take on the responsibility of doing the shopping myself.'

One man explained that he did whatever he could and added: 'It's a give and take relationship.' Another father who was living with the baby's mother explained: 'I bath him, feed him, change his nappy and look after him when (baby's mother) goes to college.' Where both parents were working there were also systems of shared tasks: 'I do everything necessary. She works two nights a week and I have him all the time while she's sleeping.' Another said: 'I change him and feed him, and at the weekends we take it in turns to get up if he wakes up.'

One man who had lived with the baby's mother and the baby until it was 9 months old said that he took the baby: 'Overnight sometimes.' Another man who had lived with the baby's mother and the baby until it was two months old was no longer involved in looking after the baby. Two of the fathers had never lived with the baby's mother. One of them who saw his baby once a week said that he was not involved in looking after the baby. The other saw his daughter at least once a week and said: 'I play with her. I've bathed her once. I'll mind her if her mother has to go out.

On Sundays I change her nappy, I feed her and do everything for her, when I have her to myself, but when her mother is there, she does it all.'

Pre-pregnancy knowledge of benefits and housing

We asked fathers if they knew before the baby's mother became pregnant whether having a baby would allow her or both of them to claim social security benefits. We found that the fathers knew as little as the mothers about social security benefits. For instance, only five fathers said that they knew whether having a baby would allow the baby's mother or both of them to claim social security benefits. One man who was a welfare rights officer married to the baby's mother said: 'I knew what she could claim. It's my job!' Another man said he did not know because he had only moved to England when his wife was pregnant: 'Coming here was something unknown. I never knew how the system worked here.' But many of the fathers who had been born in England were equally unclear about the benefits system.

Nine of the 24 fathers said that they knew before the baby's mother became pregnant whether having a baby would give her or both of them housing priority. However, as we had found with the mothers, some fathers were mistakenly under the impression that being a single parent would give the baby's mother housing priority. One man's comments showed a wrong assumption that housing applicants were assessed on the basis of marital status rather than housing need: 'If she'd been a lone mother I think she'd have been able to get housing priority, but as we were living together, it wouldn't apply.' Another man in Leeds said that his sister was a single parent and that this automatically gave her housing priority: 'My sister's got two kids and she got a house when she had her first. She more or less went to the top of the list.'

The Institute of Housing (1993) has pointed out that local authorities have a statutory duty towards women with dependent children and those fleeing from violence but that it is the presence of dependent children which entitles households to housing and not simply the presence of only one parent. Some fathers knew that having a child was a key criterion: 'If you've got a baby you're entitled to housing. I heard it through my mum.' Another said: 'We had a rough idea. We knew that if you had a kid you could get a house.' Another also believed that they would be entitled to housing if they had a child but added: 'I never considered it because the housing they give you is pretty awful. This house we're in isn't in a wonderful area, but at least it's ours.'

Chapter 7

Interviews with Grandparents

In this chapter we examine the views of the grandparents of the baby. We achieved interviews with 41 grandparents (8 in Hackney, 13 in Solihull and 20 in Leeds), most of whom were maternal grandmothers (35), but we also interviewed two paternal grandmothers in Solihull and four maternal grandfathers (one in Hackney, one in Leeds and two in Solihull). In two cases both the baby's maternal grandparents were interviewed, so that the 41 interviews with grandparents related to 39 of the 84 women in the sample.

We explored many of the same issues raised in interviews with the baby's mother and father. We looked at the reactions of grandparents when they first became aware of the pregnancy and asked them what they wanted the baby's mother to do at the time, both in terms of continuing with the pregnancy and where and with whom she might live during the pregnancy and after the birth. We also asked them about their own knowledge of social security benefits and housing before the teenage mother had become pregnant. We were particularly interested in their assessment of how things had worked out in the end.

We were more successful in recruiting both fathers and grandparents to the study in Leeds than in Solihull or Hackney. It is difficult to say exactly why this was so, but it almost certainly reflected the closer family ties we found in Leeds. In addition, the data suggest that Leeds women were in more settled relationships and fewer were single, both at the time of the pregnancy and at the time of the interview. This could have contributed to the higher number of both fathers and grandparents whom we could interview, although we cannot account fully for the differences between the three areas.

The grandparents, like the fathers interviewed, undoubtedly represented a different group from the grandparents as a whole, although, unlike the fathers, we have little information from the women on the characteristics of the whole sample of grandparents, other than their present marital status, whether the women were living with them and whether the maternal grandmothers had been teenage mothers themselves.

We interviewed one or both parents of 17 women currently living with their parents. In 5 of these cases the woman's husband or partner was also living in the household. (This accounted for 18 of the interviews with grandparents since both maternal grandparents were interviewed in one case.) We interviewed one or both parents of 22 women who were not living with their parents. Of these, 4 were living with their husbands, 2 with their husband and his relatives, 11 were cohabiting, 1 was living with her partner and his relatives, 1 with another relative, and 3 were living alone with their baby. (This accounted for 23 of the interviews with grandparents, since, again both maternal grandparents were interviewed in one case.)

Just over half of the grandmothers interviewed (19) had been teenage parents themselves, which was a similar proportion to that reported by women about their mothers in the main sample. In one third of the cases where the grandparents were interviewed (13) the women had planned their pregnancies, which was a higher proportion than we found in the main sample.

Characteristics of grandparents

Ethnic group, country of birth, religion and first language

There was little ethnic diversity among the grandparents, with the overwhelming majority of white ethnic origin: 35 of the 41 interviewed. 4 grandparents in Solihull were Pakistani, 1 grandparent in Hackney was Indian, and another grandparent in Leeds described herself as Anglo-Indian.

Most of the grandparents (32 of the 41) were born in the UK: 2 Leeds grandparents were born in Ireland and 1 in India; 4 grandparents in Solihull were born in Pakistan and 1 in China, and 1 grandparent in Hackney was born in India.

Very few grandparents (4) said that they had no religion, in complete contrast with the baby's mother and father, around half of whom had no religion. 20 of the 41 grandparents were Church of England, 11 were Roman Catholic, 5 were Muslim and 1 was a Quaker.

English was the first language of all but five of the grandparents (1 in Hackney and 4 in Solihull).

Housing tenure at the time of the pregnancy

Of the 41 grandparents, 24 were owner occupiers, 14 were in local authority properties and 3 in housing association properties at the time that the baby's mother became pregnant.

Frequency of contact between grandparents and the baby and the baby's mother

We have seen that 17 of the 39 women were still living with their parents at the time of the interview. (Indeed 11 of them had never moved since becoming pregnant.) In all these cases the grandparents saw the baby and its mother every day. In 2 cases the baby and its mother were living with the paternal grandparents interviewed who also saw them every day. The women who were not living with the baby's grandparents all had regular contact with them. In 9 of the 20 cases the grandparents saw the baby and its mother every day and the rest saw them once or twice a week.

The interviews with the baby's grandparents and the women showed that some families had been shaken by the pregnancy but many more had rallied around to help and support the baby's mother and her partner. The fact that so many of the grandparents reported frequent contact with mother and baby suggests strong family ties. However, the comments made by some grandparents indicated that relationships had deteriorated since the pregnancy.

Current employment, social class and occupational history

Just under half the grandparents (19 grandmothers and 1 grandfather) were in full-time or part-time employment, 1 was a full-time student, and another 2 (both grandfathers) were on job training or placement schemes. The rest (17 grandmothers and 1 grandfather) were unemployed.

The majority of working grandparents (12 of the 20) were in manual occupations, mostly semi-skilled, one was in a skilled non-manual occupation, 7 were in managerial level occupations and none were in professional occupations.

14 of the 18 who were unemployed at the time of the interview had worked before, mostly in semi-skilled or unskilled manual occupations. Some had left their last job for health reasons, while some grandmothers had not worked since they had become pregnant themselves. Other grandmothers who had returned to work after they had had their children had subsequently left because of unsuitable or expensive childcare arrangements or because they had decided to look

after their children themselves. A handful had left because they did not like their job. The unemployed grandfather had lost his job following restructuring of his firm.

We have already seen from the interviews with the baby's father and mother that both pregnancy and parenthood had changed their work, study and training plans. We were interested in what impact the baby had had on the grandparents. It was clear that the birth of the baby could have brought about major changes in their lives, and indeed, in the interviews, grandparents referred time and again to the effects it had had on their own lives, and on the whole household, particularly if the mother and baby had lived at home after the birth. 21 of the women where the grandparents were interviewed were living with their parents when they became pregnant and 17 were living with them at the time of the interview (11 of these had never moved out). Two-thirds of them had not planned their pregnancies.

Eight of the 41 grandparents (7 grandmothers and 1 grandfather) felt that their own work plans had changed as a result of the baby. They had often abandoned their own plans for re-entry into employment or had remained in part-time rather than full-time employment in order to give the baby's mother the opportunity to work or study. Of these 8 grandparents, 2 were in full-time employment, 2 were in part-time employment and 4 were unemployed. The three unemployed grandmothers said that they had planned to return to work but decided instead to look after the baby so that their daughters could work or study. One explained how her own plans had changed: 'I would have gone back to work. Our youngest is 12 now and I thought I'd get a full-time job, but (baby's mother) is working full-time now so I said I'd have the baby to help them out.'

One grandfather had previously been in full-time employment and felt that the pressures of unemployment and having to find other work were exacerbated by the added demands of family life: 'It's made (work plans) harder to cope with. It's hard enough anyway but now I can't get out. I have spent all my time sorting my daughter out. It reduces the mental time and energy left and I have no space for myself. I can't cope with starting something myself, what with my daughter and the baby.'

The two women in full-time employment said that they were working more flexible hours and were also helping with childcare, while the two in part-time employment said that they had decided not to work full-time so that they could help look after the baby. One woman said: 'I just work during the evenings now rather than during the day. I look after (baby) four days a week. It's altered my social life more than anything!'

It was clear from the interviews that a number of grandparents were faced with a second round of parental responsibilities at a time when they had only just finished bringing up their own children.

When and how grandparents first heard about the pregnancy

Most of the grandparents (31) knew about the pregnancy by the time the mother was 10 weeks pregnant, with an average of 7.3 weeks. It appeared from the interviews that many were told as soon as the young women first suspected it themselves. However, five of the grandparents did not know until their daughter was more than 11 weeks pregnant, with three of these not knowing until she was 16 weeks pregnant.

Most grandparents (26) first learned about the pregnancy from the baby's mother. Another 7 suspected before they were told, or even before the baby's mother had suspected it herself. One grandmother in Hackney 'just guessed' when her daughter was 16 weeks pregnant. Another had suspected the pregnancy before her daughter did when she started to be sick at six weeks: 'I had to encourage her to go to the doctor's at eight weeks.' The rest of the grandparents were told by the baby's father, the paternal grandmother or other relatives.

Reaction of grandparents to news of the pregnancy

Many of the grandparents had not suspected the pregnancy and over a third said that they were shocked and surprised when they first heard about it. Some grandparents had not expected that this would ever happen to their daughter and others had hoped that history would not repeat itself. A grandmother in Leeds said that another daughter had also become pregnant, and thought: 'Oh Lord! Not again! Because my other daughter was a single parent and it was a bit of a shock when it happened again.'

For other grandmothers who had been teenage parents themselves, the news of their daughter's pregnancy brought back some unwelcome memories. A Leeds grandmother reacted with: 'Shock! The wedding was supposed to go ahead, then it was cancelled, then she was pregnant. Everything had gone flat. She'd done the same as me all those years ago and I didn't want her to go through what I'd been through.'

One third of the grandparents said that they were disappointed or upset when they had heard of the pregnancy and some said that they were annoyed or angry. Some grandparents felt a sense of frustration and disappointment that their daughter had become pregnant, or a concern that the pregnancy would limit her opportunities for a career or further studies. One grandmother said that her daughter had become pregnant despite being advised of the risks and said she felt: 'Annoyed that she should get herself into that situation when she'd been advised all about it and all her friends had got pregnant.' Another grandmother explained: 'It was a shock because she'd planned to go to university, so I thought about that and what her dad would say.'

Some grandparents were acutely aware that becoming a parent at this young age signalled a loss of youth and freedom. Many of them were worried that their daughter was not ready for the commitment and the responsibilities of parenthood, such as one who described her reaction to the news of the pregnancy: 'I can't deny I was a bit disappointed. She's extremely bright, extremely beautiful and beautiful on the inside too, so I'm lucky with her. I wanted more for her out of life. I didn't think she was ready. She's very young.'

But it was not just the parents of single women who voiced their concerns about the pregnancy. Some parents were also concerned about married or cohabiting women who had planned the pregnancy. A Pakistani grandmother explained that she and her daughter had travelled to Pakistan for an arranged marriage. Her daughter had became pregnant within two months of getting married and when she was told about the pregnancy she felt her daughter was: 'Too young really. I would have liked her to be older (was 17 when the baby was born). I had an awful time. I have looked after babies for years now. I looked after my brothers and sisters, my own, and now my grandchildren.'

A grandmother who had been a teenage mother herself was also concerned. Her daughter had also planned her pregnancy and was married when she became pregnant: 'I was horrified. She was so young and we wanted her to have a bit of a career before she settled down.' Another grandparent reflected this view: 'She was a bit young,' but added: 'I was only seventeen when I had her. But she wanted it.'

Most of the grandparents interviewed expressed less positive and optimistic reactions to the pregnancy than the baby's mothers or the fathers we interviewed. Some grandparents clearly had different plans and hopes for the baby's mother than she had for herself. However, negative reactions were not only about the pregnancy but also related to concerns about unsuitable relationships with partners of whom parents disapproved. Some grandparents were concerned that the baby's mother would get caught up in a cycle of bad decisions.

Only a quarter of grandparents said that they were happy, pleased or delighted when they heard of the pregnancy, in contrast to many of the fathers interviewed. But even the grandparents who were pleased often had mixed feelings about the pregnancy, such as a Leeds grandfather who described how he felt when he was told about the pregnancy: 'A typical parent's reaction – "Oh dear!" I was pleased in many ways and apprehensive in others.'

What grandparents wanted the baby's mother to do about the pregnancy

We asked grandparents what they wanted the baby's mother to do about the pregnancy and whether they had discussed options apart from keeping the baby. Although relatively few had been pleased when they had heard about the pregnancy, over half said that they wanted the baby's mother to have the baby (24 of the 41). A quarter (10) said that it was not their decision or it was not for them to say. Very few (5) said that they wanted the baby's mother to have a termination of pregnancy, and 2 said that she should have the baby and then have it adopted.

Half of the grandparents said that they had discussed other options with the baby's mother but many felt that only she could decide whether to continue with the pregnancy or not. Some grandparents who were not in favour of a termination of pregnancy felt that it should still be discussed as an option. One grandmother whose daughter's pregnancy was unplanned thought that only she could decide what to do, but accompanied her to see her GP: 'I went with her for her first doctor's appointment. He faced her with the issues but he found it very difficult to discuss them. She certainly did not want to have an abortion and was angry at his attempt to discuss it. I'm very against abortion myself anyway so it's not something I would suggest.'

A grandmother whose daughter had planned her pregnancy wanted her to have the baby but had discussed other options with her: 'I asked her how she felt about it. We discussed if there were any other options and we agreed that we didn't believe in abortion. I would have backed her if she wanted one but I would have been disgusted. She was chuffed to buttons. She wanted to have the baby.'

Five of the grandparents had wanted the baby's mother to have a termination of pregnancy, but one explained: 'Because of her age, I'd rather she'd have an abortion, but it wasn't up to me. It was her choice.' A grandfather described his conversation with the baby's mother and about the decision she subsequently made: 'I said we'd support her financially if she decided to go ahead (with the TOP). She said, "I'll have to think about it." She came back a few days later and said, "I'm keeping it." I said, "OK, that's it then. You've made your mind up. That's it." '

Some of the grandparents who had discussed other options felt the baby's mother had already decided what she wanted to do. One grandfather wanted the baby's mother to have the baby and then have it adopted and said: 'We wanted her to do what she wanted to do. She wouldn't have contemplated an abortion. She never mentioned adoption. As far as she was concerned she was going to have the baby and that was that. We wanted what was best for her and it wouldn't have been best to insist on anything.'

Others emphasised that they would support their daughter, whatever she decided: 'I asked her if she'd thought about adoption and she said, "fleetingly". I wanted her to keep it. She knew I'd stand by her no matter what. It was just an unfortunate mistake.' But grandparents were also often more concerned that the baby's mother could live with her decision, whatever it might be, like this grandmother: 'I said she could have a termination but it was entirely up to her. I wouldn't want her to regret it later. She was the one who must face it.' Another said: 'We never discussed adoption but abortion was mentioned. It wasn't what she wanted. I thought if she had an abortion, she might hate us for the rest of her life. She had to decide.'

Time and again the grandparents commented that they would support the baby's mother in whatever decision she made. Having discussed the options with her, they were often resigned to the fact that she would continue with the pregnancy and accepted that this was her decision. One grandmother said that once her daughter had indicated that she wanted to continue with the pregnancy her own response was: 'Well, that was her decision. I said we'd back her up and support her as much as possible.' Another grandparent commented: 'I didn't want her to come back and say, "You pushed me into having a termination." She was only 18. She had her whole life ahead of her. It had to be her decision, to be her choice. But I said, whatever happened, we'd support her.'

In many instances no-one else was involved in the discussion about the pregnancy, but in other cases (13) some or all of the family members were involved. The grandmothers often referred to the grandfather's involvement. A grandmother who had been a teenage mother herself described her husband's reaction to the news of the pregnancy: 'He was shocked. He was frightened for her and didn't want her to make a mistake like I had done.'

It was clear that grandparents did not always give the same advice, as this comment from a grandmother illustrates. She wanted the baby's mother to continue with the pregnancy but her husband: 'Wanted her to have an abortion. He said it would ruin her life. A lot of dads seem to react that way from what I hear. They think of them as a little girl and not a woman.' Another grandmother recalled what her husband said: 'Initially he put the pros and cons to her and also discussed abortion. He said that it's not all rosy and you don't get money thrown at you. We both said we'd support her whatever her decision.'

We have seen from the interviews with the women that conflicting advice from different family members was not uncommon, creating tension and arguments within some households. One grandmother described the different reactions and advice about the pregnancy within her household: 'Her brothers said, "You're mad (to have a termination)" and the girls said, "We'll babysit." Her father was thoroughly disgusted – I don't know why. He was never there for her (baby's mother) anyway.'

Other grandparents adopted a more united and directive stance as one grandmother's comments indicate: 'We sat down for a family discussion (including the baby's father). I said, "You've got to think about it. This is where growing up begins. It's not playing with dolls, this is a lifetime's responsibility." I didn't advise her to make the decision quickly, but that if she was going to have an abortion it needed to be fairly soon. I did tell her I was against abortion. We dismissed adoption as almost distasteful. My husband and I agreed that if she couldn't cope we would bring up the baby as our own.'

Half of the grandparents did not discuss other options, some because the baby's mother had already decided she wanted to continue with the pregnancy and there seemed to be no point in having any discussion. Moreover, far from having the opportunity to discuss the pregnancy and consider other options, some felt that the pregnancy had been presented to them by the baby's mother as a *fait accompli*, giving little opportunity to open up the discussion. One grandmother whose daughter had planned to become pregnant explained why she had not discussed any other options with her: 'There was no talk about it at all. Even if I had wanted to talk about it she wouldn't have taken any notice.' Another said that her daughter had decided she wanted to have the baby and described her resigned reaction: 'OK. There was not a lot we could do. Just stand by them and help them.'

For others (12) there was nothing to discuss: they wanted the baby's mother to continue with the pregnancy and they did not believe in or agree with a termination of pregnancy. A woman whose daughter had not planned her pregnancy explained: 'I knew she would keep it. I don't believe in abortions just for the sake of them. It's very different if there's something radically wrong, but I don't believe in aborting a baby just for convenience. I knew she would have the baby, so I just had to be there to support her.' A few grandparents were quite clear about keeping the baby, as one explained: 'I don't believe in it (termination of pregnancy). Definitely not adoption either. If she hadn't wanted to keep it, we would have adopted it.'

Where the pregnancy had been planned, other options were rarely discussed. One grandparent explained how her daughter simply altered her wedding plans after becoming pregnant unexpectedly: 'She was glad, she wanted to go ahead (with the pregnancy). She just brought her wedding forward.'

Involvement of grandparents in the decision about the pregnancy

Many grandparents said that the baby's mother must make the final decision herself. Although nearly half of the grandparents said that they had no involvement in the decision about what to do about the pregnancy, it was clear that they were involved to some extent in discussions about it. One grandmother discussed what her daughter might do, including having a termination if the baby was deformed, but said that she had no involvement in the final decision: 'Basically it was just her decision and whatever she'd decided, I'd go along with her and support her. I'll back her one hundred per cent – that's what I'm here for.'

Another grandmother said that she had no involvement but was equally supportive: 'I left the decision totally up to her. I wouldn't sway her anyway. I mean I didn't want her to have the abortion but I told her I'd stick by her whatever she decided.'

Other grandparents felt they were closely involved. One grandmother described what had happened: 'I was involved, but not that I made the decision for her. In fact, I'm almost sure one of the first things she said to me was that she was going to keep it.' Another grandmother who said that she had wanted her daughter to decide for herself said she was closely involved in the decision, adding: 'But I had little influence. I didn't have much alternative but to cope with it.' And yet another described how she had resisted telling her daughter what to do because she felt that she had to decide for herself: 'She used to say, "What do you think?" and I gave my opinion, but I said that it was her choice and whatever she decided we'd support her. She knew we were there for her.'

One grandmother who said that she had some involvement noted: 'I just pointed the options out to her and let her make her own mind up.'

Another who wanted her daughter to have a termination of pregnancy said: 'I knew really from day one she wouldn't have an abortion because she's always been against abortion, but we tried to put the other side to her.'

Discussions about where and with whom the baby's mother might live during pregnancy

We have seen that 21 women were living at home when they became pregnant and 17 were living with their parents (alone or with their husband or partner) at the time of the interview. 28 of the grandparents had not discussed where and with whom the baby's mother would live during pregnancy, in many cases because it was assumed that she would continue to live at home. One grandmother simply said: 'We just took it for granted she'd live here.' Another grandmother reflected this view: 'I knew she'd stay with me. There was nothing to talk about.'

Some grandparents saw no reason to discuss living arrangements because their daughters were already married (4) or cohabiting with the father of the baby (6). Although this grandmother was shocked to hear her daughter was pregnant she did not discuss her living arrangements because she was already living with the baby's father: 'She was happy where she was and who she was with.'

Another grandmother said that she was '...fuming – I was livid...' when she heard her daughter was pregnant but had not discussed her future living arrangements: 'She (daughter) seemed to have it all worked out herself – where she was living. So I didn't interfere.'

The grandparents (13) who had discussed where and with whom the baby's mother would live during pregnancy mostly talked about her staying at home or returning home to live. A grandmother commented: 'I asked her if she'd discussed it with the father. I made it clear she could stay with me. She was quite pleased.' One grandfather accepted that his daughter had already decided where she wanted to live and felt that there was no reason for the pregnancy to change this: 'She stayed where she was. There was no point in upsetting the applecart. She was living with her boyfriend and quite happy there.'

But a few grandparents spoke of already strained relations with their daughter, like one grandmother who made it clear that the baby's mother could continue to live at home during pregnancy but would have to move out after the birth: 'She could stay till after the baby was born. I couldn't put up with all the arguments.'

Others were concerned that their daughter would feel supported, like a grandmother who said: 'She discussed it with me and said she would stay here while she was pregnant and then live with (baby's father) after the baby was born. But it was her decision. She would not be easily led and you cannot pass on wisdom – just pick up the pieces if there are problems.'

It appeared that some of the young women who wanted to live with the father of the baby had overestimated the stability of their relationships and their parents were not always convinced that the relationships would last. One grandfather described what happened and the concern he had felt: 'I asked her what she was going to do. She wanted to live with the father but it dawned on her that the relationship was not that good... She realised that they did not get on that well... We tried to support her. We thought she would stay with the baby's father but later she broke it off and stayed at home.' He added: 'Her mother and I discussed it endlessly. (Baby's mother) didn't realise what it meant for her life. She still doesn't really.' Another grandparent also felt that her daughter did not appreciate that responsibility she had taken on: 'It's hard work (being a parent). You forget what it's like after all those years. They don't realise what hard work it is do they? They think it's all a game."

Another grandmother whose daughter stayed at home with the father of the baby became concerned about their relationship and was pleased when it broke up: 'She said she'd stay with me and I let him stay here. She was delighted. He didn't have anywhere to go... It was really up to us. I was able to keep an eye on her and I knew she was safe. She was already pregnant so he could stay. She couldn't get pregnant again.'

Another recalled how her daughter's intention to leave home and live alone with the baby's father never materialised: 'She said she would get a house with him (baby's father) but I don't think they tried very hard. I just took it for granted she'd be here with us anyway.'

Other grandparents described how their daughter was pleased to stay at home either because they did not want to leave home or because they had nowhere else to live. Some parents agreed that the father of the baby could also live with them: 'We (parents) both decided she'd live here. Her boyfriend could stay here a couple of nights. She was happy about that. I think she was frightened to be on her own with the baby.'

Involvement of the grandparents in the decision about where and with whom the woman should live during the pregnancy

Over half the grandparents had no involvement in the decision about where the woman should live during the pregnancy, while over a quarter said they were closely involved and just under a quarter had a limited amount of involvement.

Some grandparents described living at home as taken for granted. One grandmother who had been closely involved in the decision said that her daughter would live at home with them and said: 'There was never any question. There was nowhere else to go.'

On the other hand a grandmother who said that she had no involvement in the decision also described living at home as a decision that arose by default rather than by design and explained: 'There was no discussion. There were no other options.'

Discussions about where and with whom the baby's mother would live after the baby was born

Many of the grandparents had not discussed where and with whom the baby's mother might live after the baby was born, mainly because they had assumed that she would stay at home or where she was. Some were concerned about how the baby's mother would cope: 'I didn't think she was old enough to live on her own with a baby.' Another grandmother said that she discussed the possibility of finding a place for her daughter to live alone: 'I think she was a bit nervous about being on her own, but that's what she wants now. Privacy and her own breathing space.'

Others said they had looked at all possibilities with the baby's mother: 'I just offered her all the options really. She could stop here, or I'd help her buy a house, or I'd alter the house so she could stop here.' Another grandmother described how they had helped: 'She and (baby's father) were trying to get a mortgage but they couldn't so we said he could move in with us. She said they'd have to get a place of their own. They would try for a mortgage and put their names down (for a council property) and I said we'd help them as much as we could... We'd said we'd act as guarantors. In the end, we gave them the deposit on the house.'

But not all the young women had the same options, as this grandmother illustrated: 'I said perhaps the council might give her a flat. She wanted to live with her boyfriend. Her dad wouldn't let her live here.' Other grandparents agreed to have the mother and baby to stay until they could get somewhere else. One grandmother said that her daughter wanted her own place: 'She thought about renting but it's too expensive. She's got her name on the council list and applied to the housing associations.'

Pre-pregnancy knowledge of social security benefits and housing

We were interested in how much grandparents knew before the baby's mother became pregnant about the eligibility of teenage mothers for housing or social security benefits.

Over half the grandparents said that they had not known whether having a baby would give teenage mothers housing priority. Some felt that their daughter would receive priority if she was a lone mother. One grandmother said that it was not relevant in her daughter's case but thought that she would have been given priority if she had been a single mother on her own: 'If she'd been on her own, probably. We've a three-bedroom house here, so in my daughter's case, she would have lived with us.'

It appeared from the interviews that many respondents had the impression that lone parents received preferential treatment, as this grandmother's comments indicate: 'I know that there have been changes in government policy to produce housing for lone mothers. It's well publicised.'

Another grandmother who had been a teenage mother herself reflected the common belief that housing was allocated on the basis of marital status rather than housing need: 'I was in the same situation myself before I got married to my first husband. I knew that single mums got a lot of help and they got priority with housing if they had a young baby.'

We also asked grandparents if they had known before the baby's mother became pregnant whether having a baby would allow her to claim social security benefits. Around half of grandparents said that they had known, but even these were only generally aware that benefits could be claimed but had no firm details about types of benefits or levels of income. Even grandparents who were claiming social security benefits themselves said that they did not know exactly which benefits which could be claimed: 'We are on income support ourselves but it wasn't an issue. I didn't know the ins and outs.' Another grandmother had more detailed knowledge about some of the benefits which might be claimed: 'I knew she was entitled to income support and if she worked she could claim family credit.'

How had things worked out?

Over half the grandparents felt that things had worked out well, but others had reservations. Although some had expressed disappointment, anger or worry about the pregnancy initially, they felt pleased with the overall outcome, feeling that their daughter had coped well with parenthood and that her relationship with the baby's father had survived and become more stable.

One Leeds grandmother was delighted with the outcome and explained: 'I'm over the moon. She's done absolutely marvellously. She's got her own place and she's not going to be conned again.' Another said: 'It's worked out well. She's a good mum – it's like watching myself all over again. They're coping really well and (baby's father) has kept his job down. It was sad she had to leave home but they wanted to be together.'

But one grandmother spoke of her disappointment that her daughter was single, alone and had become dependent on social security benefits: 'She's a single mother. I'd have preferred her to be settled down and married before she had a baby. It's no picnic. You're living on a tight budget all the time, and she's dependent on benefit now. The £240 didn't pay for the furniture. I had to pay out quite a lot myself.' Another said: 'I'm a bit disappointed about where she lives. It's not what I'd hoped for her.'

Others were even less pleased with the way things had turned out for the baby's mother and for themselves. Indeed, some parents had developed greater concern after the baby was born because, in their view, things had gone from bad to worse. While some grandparents expressed their satisfaction that relationships had lasted, others had hoped for the opposite and were deeply worried about relationships which they felt were unsuitable, unstable and sometimes violent.

We have already seen that half the relationships had broken down by the time of the interview. One grandmother explained why she was pleased when the relationship with the baby's father ended: 'She seems to be managing fine. I'm less worried now that he's gone. I thought she was in danger.' (She thought that the baby's father had been violent.) Another grandmother remarked: 'It has worked out for the best, genuinely. She's (baby's mother) very strong minded. She'd have suffered if she'd have attempted to move out with him (baby's father).' And another felt that the break-up of her daughter's relationship was for the best: 'It couldn't have worked out better. She's away from him and she's got her own little house now.'

Some grandparents (14) spoke of the pressures they had experienced or were still experiencing, particularly if both the mother and baby had lived at home. A few felt that the pressure of having them both at home was becoming too much for them: 'It's been very tense. We get very tired and we look after him a lot because (baby's mother) is not around. She's at college or out. We are the ones who get up in the night.'

A grandmother in Hackney explained that her daughter had never moved away from home. She had decided not to work full-time herself so that she could look after the baby for her daughter, but had a number of concerns about how things had worked out: 'It's getting a bit much now. He's a toddler, into everything. And I seem to be in the mother role. As much as I love him, he's her baby. I think I get taken for granted. I'll be sad when he goes – I love him to bits. And the thing is, he seems to want me all the time – hanging on my legs. But she's ready to go now and have her own home.'

Another grandmother who was looking after her grandchild and was not working so that the baby's mother could work also spoke of the dependent relationship that her grandchild had developed: 'I want them to stay here but now I understand they want to find somewhere of their own. But who is going to look after (baby), and he looks to me before he will settle to sleep.'

Other grandparents were clear that their support had been very important and felt sure that the baby's mother would have coped less well without it: 'I wouldn't say it's been a bed of roses but I think it's worked out fairly well. She's got a lot of support here. The baby's got his grandfather as a father figure. He's got his uncle as a plaything and he's got two mums! What more could you want?' Another grandmother remarked: 'Over the last 19 months it has occurred to me that it has been hard work for the whole family. Without that family I don't know how they survive, if they don't have care and support – financial or otherwise. If the mothers are blamed or victimised then the children suffer and become our damaged adults of the future.'

Chapter 8

Perceptions about Teenage Mothers, Housing and Benefits

We asked the women, the fathers and the baby's grandparents to comment on a number of statements which have been made in recent years about single teenage or young mothers. We were interested first in their views on the statement that teenage or young mothers become pregnant in order to get housing or their own home; secondly, on the statement that single teenage or young mothers who become pregnant find it easier than married couples to get housing or their own home; and thirdly on the statement that teenage or young mothers have a baby because they know they will get extra social security benefits. We wanted to assess the views of each group of respondents about these statements and to see whether they thought that they were true.

We have seen in this report that the *women interviewed* came from a wide variety of backgrounds with a considerable diversity in educational achievement and employment. We also saw great changes in their circumstances between the time that they became pregnant and the time of the interview when their babies were mainly around a year old. Only a quarter of the women (23) had planned their pregnancies. Their relationships with the fathers of their babies when they became pregnant ranged from married to casual relationships, with most women either cohabiting or in a steady relationship. However, by the time of the interview nearly half of the women had split up with the father of the baby and were single and mostly living alone. We found a big increase in the proportion living in local authority accommodation from 5 per cent when they became pregnant to one third (28) at the time of the interview, with a further third (28) on a local authority waiting list. The proportion of women receiving benefits had increased from one third (30) when they became pregnant to over 90 per cent (78) at the time of the interview, excluding those receiving statutory maternity pay, maternity allowance or child benefit only.

The majority of *fathers interviewed* were from one area (Leeds) and were different from those described by the women in the main sample in that they were usually married or cohabiting with the baby's mother. Pregnancies had seldom been planned but were often wanted. Around half of the fathers interviewed were living in owner-occupied houses (6) or in local authority accommodation (7). In many respects, their views reflected the views of the married or cohabiting women in the main sample. We compared the views of the fathers interviewed with those of their partners in this analysis.

The overwhelming majority of *grandparents interviewed* were maternal grandmothers. One factor which undoubtedly influenced their views of single teenage or young mothers was that just over half of the grandmothers (19) had been teenage mothers themselves: a similar proportion to that found among the mothers of the women interviewed in the main sample. However, the parents of married or cohabiting women were rather over-represented in the sample of grandparents interviewed. The parents of over half of the married women (8) or those cohabiting with the father of the baby (14) or a new partner (1) were interviewed compared with the parents of around one third of the single women (16). The parents of women still living at home were also rather over-represented, as we saw in Chapter 7. The grandparents' views were also compared with those of their daughters in this analysis.

Whether teenage or young mothers become pregnant in order to get housing

Views of the women

We asked the women what they thought of the statement that teenage or young mothers became pregnant in order to get housing. As Table 8.1 shows, over half of them (46) thought that it was true, with single and cohabiting women rather more likely than married women to think so.

Table 8.1   **Respondents' views on whether teenage women get pregnant in order to get housing**

					numbers and column percentages	
	Women		Fathers interviewed		Grandparents interviewed	
	Nos	%	Nos	%	Nos	%
Yes	7	8	7	29	6	15
Yes some but not all	39	46	9	38	14	34
No	35	42	6	25	18	44
Don't know	3	4	2	8	3	7
Base: women, fathers and grandparents interviewed	*(84)*		*(24)*		*(41)*	

However, most of those who thought it was true (39) added that it applied to some but not all teenage women who become pregnant. A woman who was 19 when her baby was born and living with a new partner at the time of the interview said: 'Some do. Some that aren't working or haven't got an education. They think it's an easy way out.' Another woman who was 19 when she had her baby and was married at the time of the interview remarked: 'I think you shouldn't have children unless you want them. As I say, ours was planned. We were just waiting till I got my hairdressing qualifications. Some of them do use a baby to get a house or a flat. They use a baby as an excuse.'

Single women often said that it was true of other women but not themselves, like an 18 year old: 'Yes, I think some of them do, but I know I didn't. My friend didn't get on with her step-dad but the council said that you had to be pregnant to get housing.' Another single woman who had left her parents' home and was living alone at the time of the interview agreed: 'Well some do, but I definitely didn't because I didn't want to leave home. Some think it's great fun to have a home, but the reality is, all your friends give up on you.'

A sixth of the women (13) said that they knew others who had become pregnant in order to get housed. One woman who was 18 when she had her baby was single at the time of the interview: 'It's a difficult question. In my case, it's not true, but I do know people who've done it. I suppose if you're having problems with your parents it's an easy option, but I don't think it's fair to say it about everybody in the category I'm in, because everybody's different.' Another woman who was 17 when the baby was born and cohabiting at the time of the interview said: 'I wouldn't say that of all, but I would say it of some. I know girls at school, I don't know if they did it to get a house but I do know they got pregnant deliberately. And they're younger than me. They're 15 and 16.'

Even if women thought that teenagers became pregnant in order to get housing, they did not always agree that this was an 'easy option'. Some believed that these women had not always taken into account the difficulties that lay ahead, like a woman who was living at home with her parents and had split up with the father of the baby with whom she had lived after becoming pregnant. She was living alone in local authority accommodation at the time of the interview and said: 'I think there's probably quite a few teenagers who do that (become pregnant) to get out (from their parents). I had no reason to do that. I think some probably do but it wasn't the case for me. To be honest, I think they're a bit crazy – all that aggravation, just for a flat.'

Another single woman who had lived with a relative throughout said: 'Teenage girls want to get away from home and think that a baby will get them their own house. It doesn't work like that though.' A woman who had planned to become pregnant and was cohabiting throughout described how some women had no other options: 'I do know people who have done that. I think it's to get security. A lot of them don't have much to live for. If they get a place, it's a home. It's some security isn't it?' Her comments crystallised the perverse incentive to become pregnant which Phoenix (1991) has described as the perceived absence of positive alternatives to motherhood.

Just under half the women (35) disagreed with the statement that teenagers became pregnant to get housing. Some said that it was not true because they had not done so, like a single 16 year old who had lived with her parents throughout: 'No. It weren't true for me because it was an accident. I didn't think about housing or nothing and I haven't tried to get my own house.'

Others did not think that housing was the primary reason for becoming pregnant. One woman was living with her parents when she became pregnant and was living with a relative in local authority accommodation at the time of the interview: 'You wouldn't get pregnant to get a council place. They make it sound like the council put you in palaces but they don't. I haven't done so bad, but who'd want to get pregnant for the sake of being put in a council flat?'

Many of the women who disagreed with the statement did so with the benefit of hindsight. They could readily identify the difficulties and hardships associated with young parenthood which they said they had not been fully aware of when they became pregnant themselves. One woman who was cohabiting at the time of the interview thought that teenagers did not become pregnant to get housed and remarked: 'Why would anyone want to do that? You have all the bills and expenses when you live in your own house.' A married woman said: 'No. It'd be too expensive and they'd have loads of responsibilities – rent, bills, the baby. A headache!'

Views of the fathers interviewed

The fathers interviewed were rather less sympathetic towards teenage mothers. As Table 8.1 shows, two-thirds of them (16 of the 24) agreed with the statement that teenage women got pregnant in order to get housing, with little difference according to their marital status.

However, over one third of them said that it was true of some rather than all teenagers who became pregnant. One man remarked: 'I'm sure some of them do, but you can't generalise and say everyone does. I think it depends on their social background. Certainly some of the people round here are an example of it.' Another cohabiting father agreed: 'I think some teenagers do, yes, because I know some. But it's wrong to generalise.'

Others felt the tendency was more widespread like this man who was 43 when the baby was born and was living with the baby's mother throughout: 'I think possibly most of them, yes. Not necessarily all of them. It depends on the circumstances. A lot of young people do it without thinking of the consequences.' Another cohabiting father commented: 'I think a lot probably do. It seems an easy way to get a place. Otherwise you're just waiting forever.'

Like the women, the fathers differed in their views about whether becoming pregnant in order to get housing was an easy option. Some felt that women carefully weighed up their options, while others felt that it was a lack of thought and planning which resulted in women becoming pregnant.

However, a single father who was 20 when the baby was born felt that becoming pregnant was the result of a calculated decision by some women: 'Some do (become pregnant in order to get housing), some don't. Some have no option. If they want out, they look at what they can do to get away from their parents, and having a baby is the easy option.' Another cohabiting father remarked: 'I do think it's true. I think some of them are a bit foolish and they think it's an easy way to live on their own.'

Getting away from their family to become independent was also mentioned by fathers as one of the reasons why teenage women became pregnant. A married man said: 'People who are unhappy at home go out and get pregnant and they get a house.' Another man who was cohabiting explained that although his sister who was also a teenage parent had not become pregnant to get housed, other women might do so: 'My sister had a baby when she was 17 and she went on living with my mum and dad. Maybe some might do it if they're with a family they don't want. A baby is a lot of commitment though.'

Like the mothers, the fathers who disagreed with the view that teenagers became pregnant in order to get housing felt that if women had planned to become pregnant, housing was unlikely to be a primary motivation. One man who was 19 when the baby was born and living with the baby's mother throughout noted: 'If you plan to have a baby you wouldn't do it on purpose to get a house.' Another man commented: 'I think that is a bit harsh, isn't it. Reproducing is a natural thing.'

One man who had lived with the baby's mother before the relationship broke up remarked: 'That's stupid, we couldn't get a house, and we tried.'

We compared the views of the fathers with those of their partners and found that two-thirds (16) of the women whose partners were interviewed thought that teenage women became pregnant to get housing compared with around half of the main sample, even if they thought it was true of only some. However, around half the women expressed different views from their partners. One father thought that teenage mothers became pregnant in order to get housing: 'Some do, I know some women who have done that.' But his partner said that she did not know whether it was true or not. Another woman commented: 'Some of them do, they use a baby as an excuse.' But her partner was not sure: 'I don't know what they think. A lot of the time it just happens.'

Views of the grandparents interviewed

As Table 8.1 shows, just under half (20) of the grandparents interviewed thought that teenage or young mothers became pregnant in order to get housing, although most thought it was true of some rather than all. Nearly half of them (9) had been teenage mothers themselves. But over half the grandparents disagreed with the statement or felt unable to comment.

Grandparents felt that there were many different reasons why women became pregnant and spoke of some women's lack of judgement, their lack of planning and their unrealistic expectations and poor understanding of the additional responsibilities of parenthood. Unlike the fathers, grandparents rarely referred to becoming pregnant in order to get housing as an easy option.

One woman who had been a teenage mother herself commented: 'I suppose in some cases. I don't think they realise how serious it is to have a baby. It might be a way of getting away from home.' Another woman with a cohabiting daughter reflected this view: 'There might be some if they're not happy at home. I think a lot of them are silly – they don't take precautions. They don't think of the consequences.'

Another woman who had been a teenage mother herself and whose daughter was single and living with her at the time of the interview remarked: 'Well it may be true in some cases but generally, girls get pregnant for wrong reasons. I don't think any girl would get pregnant to get a house – that's nonsense. It's bitter talk.'

Others said that, while some women did this, their own daughters had not. A woman who had also been a teenage mother had two teenage daughters with babies. The one we interviewed was living with her parents and the father of the baby. The grandmother commented: 'In a lot of circumstances yes, it is true. But I can't say that about my two daughters. But yes – in a lot of cases it is true.'

A woman whose daughter had become pregnant in a casual relationship and was living at home at the time of the interview explained that housing had not been an issue for her daughter: 'Maybe in some cases (it is true) but not always. It depends on the person. It depends on their home life. (Daughter) never did that, otherwise she wouldn't be here now.'

However, around half the grandparents thought that teenagers did not become pregnant to get housing. Many of them felt that there were more plausible explanations for teenagers becoming pregnant. One woman spoke of her daughter who was in a steady relationship with the father of the baby when she became pregnant, then lived with him until their relationship broke up and was living at home with her parents at the time of the interview: 'I don't think anyone becomes pregnant to get housing or their own home. Ignorance and carelessness possibly but not housing – No!'

Another woman whose daughter was living with her at the time of the interview referred to her daughter's lack of planning: 'No, from my experience (daughter) didn't do it for that reason. It was a complete mistake. They need to use reliable contraception and know where to get it.' This woman also felt that teenagers did not become pregnant deliberately: 'I think it's a load of rubbish. There's a lot of teenage mothers that get pregnant but they don't do it deliberately.'

Other grandparents were quite clear that housing was not the primary motivation, like this woman who had been a teenage mother herself. Her daughter was married at the time of the interview: 'I don't think so. I think that's extreme – just to get somewhere to live.' Another woman whose daughter was also married noted: 'If they do (become pregnant in order to get housing) they must be mad. It's no fun having a child on your own.'

Some grandparents who felt the statement was untrue spoke about their daughters. One woman who had been a teenage parent herself said: 'I wouldn't have thought so. I didn't and (daughter) didn't. It might seem like that sometimes.' Another woman commented: 'It's a load of rubbish. My daughter certainly didn't do it deliberately.'

We compared the views of the grandparents with those of their daughters, and found that, like their parents, around half of their daughters (22) thought that teenage mothers became pregnant in order to get housing while half did not. Most individual women agreed with the views of their parents on this issue.

Whether single teenage mothers find it easier than married couples to get housing or their own home

Views of the women

Women's views were more divided on the issue of whether single teenage mothers found it easier than married couples to get housing or their own home. As Table 8.2 shows, 44 per cent of women (37) thought that they did, with single and married women more likely to think so than the others. On the other hand just over a third of the women (33) thought that single teenage mothers did not find it easier than married couples to be housed and a sixth (14) did not know whether they did or not.

One woman had been living with her parents when she became pregnant and was living alone in local authority accommodation at the time of the interview. She felt that single mothers found it easier to be housed, not because they were given priority over married couples, but because they were more likely than married couples actually to apply for council housing: 'It might be easier (to be housed) because married couples tend to go for mortgages.'

Table 8.2   **Respondents' views on whether teenage women who become pregnant find it easier than married couples to get housing**

numbers and column percentages

	Women		Fathers interviewed		Grandparents interviewed	
	Nos	%	Nos	%	Nos	%
Yes	21	25	13	54	12	29
Yes some but not all	16	19	4	17	3	7
No	33	39	3	13	17	41
Don't know	14	17	4	17	9	22
Base: women, fathers and grandparents interviewed	*(84)*		*(24)*		*(41)*	

There were some differences among women's views according to their current housing tenure. For instance, 5 of the 6 women living in owner-occupied houses thought that single teenage mothers found it easier than married couples to be housed. One said: 'I think personally, with us being married, we get penalised because we are married. We can't claim anything because we are married. The girl who used to live next door used to be able to claim everything because she was single.'

In contrast, less than half of the women living in privately rented or local authority accommodation at the time of the interview thought that single teenage mothers found it easier to be housed than married women. Nevertheless a married woman living in privately rented accommodation at the time of the interview thought that single teenage mothers were given priority for council housing: 'They probably are. We were told that there weren't any houses because single mothers get their pick. I think that's disgusting really.'

A few women said they had personal knowledge to back up their views. One married woman said she knew of single mothers who had been housed by the local authority before her and remarked: 'Before, they used to give them (single teenage mothers) flats but now they're giving them houses. I know all my friends got pregnant at 16 and put their names down after me and got places straight away, even if there was room at their parents' house. There's no doubt that the fact that I got pregnant probably helped.'

We often found that the perceptions of some married or cohabiting women that single women had housing priority or the 'pick' of accommodation were not borne out by the experience of the single mothers interviewed. A sixth of the women (12), most of whom were single at the time of the interview, said that they themselves had not found it easier to be housed.

One woman who had planned her pregnancy was living with the father of the baby when she became pregnant but was single, alone and living in local authority accommodation at the time of the interview. She had not expected her relationship to break up and had not found it easy to be housed: 'I had to fight for what I have now. I wrote to MPs and everything. I'd never have got pregnant with (baby) if I'd known I wasn't going to stay with (the father of the baby).'

Another woman whose steady relationship with the father of the baby had broken up had a new partner at the time of the interview. She was living in privately rented accommodation and was not on a council housing waiting list. She did not think that single teenage mothers found it easier to get housing: 'No. Where's my house then? I'm single. I'm a mother. There's married couples out there with houses. Where's my house then?'

A single woman who had lived with her aunt throughout was on a waiting list for council housing and thought that single and married couples were treated the same: 'I don't think it makes any difference. There's no priority for single mothers any more.'

We have already seen that being housed in poor and run-down areas was a cause of concern for some women who had been housed in local authority accommodation but felt that they had little or no choice about where they would live. One cohabiting woman had refused to take a local authority property three times before eventually accepting it. She felt that she had had no choice in the matter and did not think that single teenage mothers found it easier than marrier couples to be housed: 'No. I think they're given rubbish areas. This is a terrible area. I was offered a flat in an area I didn't even put down on the form to the council.'

Another woman was single, alone and living in local authority accommodation at the time of the interview. She did not know if single teenage mothers found it easier to be housed, but had also had little housing choice: 'I think there's just different situations, isn't there? They give priority, don't they, to people having babies. If you're not, then you're last on the list. The only problem is, you get put somewhere like this (an area with a high proportion of single mothers). If you're a single mum, this is where you get put.'

Views of the fathers interviewed

The fathers were more likely than either their own partners or the women in the main sample to think that single teenage mothers found it easier than married couples to get housing. As Table 8.2 shows, nearly three-quarters thought they did, with the single men as likely as the others to think so. Some could not comment on the statement while only three thought that single teenage mothers did not find it easier than married couples.

Just over a third of the fathers interviewed were living in local authority accommodation or were on a waiting list: a smaller proportion than the two-thirds of the main sample of women interviewed. In fact, nearly as many of the fathers interviewed were living in owner-occupied houses as in local authority accommodation.

Some fathers had formed the view that single teenagers received preferential treatment as a result of their own experiences or those of relatives and friends. Not surprisingly, the more negative the experience the more likely they were to conclude that single women had fared better than they had. Three of the fathers described how married relatives had waited longer than single parents to be housed. One married man described his married sister's experience: 'My sister and her husband and two kids were having a hard time getting a council house and they were seeing others (single women) getting houses all the time.'

Another married man who was living in privately rented accommodation said that he was sure that single women were given priority over married couples and knew of single women who had been housed: 'They definitely find it easier to be housed. My wife has got friends who have got houses. They were given them when they left school.'

Rather surprisingly, two fathers said that housing officers had suggested to them that housing was allocated on the basis of marital status and that single mothers found it easier to be housed. One man who was cohabiting with the baby's mother when she became pregnant but had split up with her after the birth said: 'I think it would be easier (for single women). We were told that by the housing officer.'

Other fathers thought that single teenage women found it easier to be housed because of their vulnerability which gave them higher priority than two-parent families. A cohabiting man said: 'I suppose it is easier in a way because I suppose they'll need a house more than other people if they're on their own with a baby.' But a married man who was living in local authority accommodation thought that housing allocation was more of a lottery than anything else: 'In a few cases they are better off and do have houses. It's only what you hear. It can be just luck.'

Only three of the 24 fathers thought that single teenage mothers did not find it easier to be housed. One cohabiting father living in housing association accommodation thought that one-parent and two-parent families were treated similarly: 'Basically it's just the same (for married couples).' Another man thought that 'married couples come first'.

The third explained that before he had applied for council accommodation he had thought that single mothers were given priority but had since realised that this was not the case. He and his partner had decided to live with their respective parents until they were allocated a property and were surprised to learn that they would have to wait. He described the increasing tension within their relationship: 'It was very difficult because her parents wouldn't have me living there and she (baby's mother) didn't want to live here at my house. Although she did get on with my mum, she doesn't now. They don't speak and no way will her parents let me stay there. We knew I couldn't afford a house so we thought we would try for a council house. We never thought it would take this long (14 months). Single parents are supposed to get priority but it's all gone wrong for me and my girlfriend.'

We found that the fathers interviewed were more likely than their partners to think that single teenage mothers found it easier than married couples to be housed.

Views of the grandparents interviewed

The grandparents, on the other hand, were less likely than the fathers interviewed to think that single teenage mothers found it easier than married couples to get housing. As Table 8.2 shows, just over a third of the grandparents (15) thought they did, just over a fifth (9) did not know whether they did, and 17 thought that they did not.

A few said that while some might find it easier, their daughters had not found it so. The woman with two teenage daughters, both of whom had had babies, said: 'It hasn't happened to none of mine. They've always had to find their own (accommodation), but I do know of one or two; they've got a place from the council.'

Another woman whose daughter was living at home and waiting for council accommodation agreed: 'I know a couple that was told, "If you have a baby, you'd get a home." In (daughter's) case, she just wanted a baby. I don't think she thought about a home.'

Two women said that their daughter had got council accommodation relatively quickly. One was cohabiting: 'It was easy for her but there are some in terrible circumstances.' Another woman whose daughter was single and living in local authority accommodation remarked: 'Yes, I must admit when (daughter) got this flat, I thought she had got a lovely place.'

But not all grandparents agreed that those who had got housing had fared well or any better than married couples: 'My daughter didn't get it that easily. You don't know the ins and outs. Some people know all the ins and outs but I didn't.' Another grandparent whose daughter was single, living at home and waiting for council accommodation remarked: 'I suppose so – but it's not very good housing.'

Some grandparents thought that the isolation and vulnerability of single teenage mothers made it easier for them to get housing. One grandmother whose daughter was single and living at home with her noted: 'Yes, I think possibly it is true. Usually if you are a married couple you've already got somewhere to live so they don't normally get priority. But if there's a single mother who's being chucked out (from her parents' home) she'll get priority.' Another grandparent agreed: 'I think that might be true. It's not fair but it's true. They need more support.'

Three grandparents said that their own daughters had not found it easier to be housed. The daughter of one woman was single and living alone in privately rented accommodation. Her name was on the waiting list for council accommodation but her mother said: 'She hasn't found it easier. She's got no chance of getting a council house for a long time. They've already told her that.'

A grandfather agreed. His daughter was living in privately rented accommodation and on a council housing waiting list. Although his wife who had also been interviewed thought that some young teenage mothers found it easier to be housed, he did not agree and remarked: 'I wouldn't have thought so. Just from the small experience I've had with (daughter). I don't think it's necessarily true.'

Other grandparents felt that single teenage mothers did not find it any easier than married couples: 'It certainly didn't happen to (daughter). Maybe some do but I don't know how they do it. She had to fight tooth and nail... I think council housing is such a nightmare. There aren't enough to go around. They had to fight so hard to get where they are. The stress they went through would split some couples up.' A grandmother who had been a teenage parent herself said that she had not found it easier when she was a single mother: 'Definitely not. I was three years with my mother because I couldn't get anywhere.'

It was clear that some grandparents thought of single mothers as a vulnerable group whose single status would automatically give them priority over two-parent families. A few referred to the lack of council properties which affected all teenage mothers, and thought that their own council was certainly not sympathetic. A woman whose daughter was living with the father of the baby and his mother said: 'No it definitely isn't (easier to be housed). Its very hard for young mothers to get a house, especially with this council.'

Again some grandparents spoke of a lottery system where luck played
a large part in whether people were housed, like this woman whose
daughter was waiting for council housing: 'If you're married you go along
the same lines. It's whether you're lucky enough to get your name picked
out of the hat.' Another woman whose daughter was married also felt that
single teenage mothers did not find it easier and commented: 'I wouldn't
say so. I think if you've got a man at the back of you they take more notice
of you.'

Other grandparents felt that single teenage mothers did not fare well
like this woman who had been a teenage parent herself: 'A lot of teenage
mothers get put in a hostel, and personally I wouldn't like to be put in a
hostel or for a daughter of mine to be put in a hostel.' A woman whose
daughter was single and still living at home commented: 'I don't believe
that. I've seen girls walking the streets with their kids.'

Whether teenage mothers have a baby because they know they will receive extra social security benefits

Views of the women

Just over one third of the women (29) agreed with the statement that
teenage or young mothers had a baby because they knew they would
receive extra social security benefits, as Table 8.3 shows. Women who
were married or cohabiting at the time of interview were rather more
likely than single women to think this was true. However, over half the
women (48) did not think that teenage mothers had a baby to get extra
social security benefits and the rest (7) did not know whether they did or
not.

Table 8.3   Respondents' views on whether teenage women have a
baby because they know they will receive extra social
security benefits

numbers and column percentages

	Women		Fathers interviewed		Grandparents interviewed	
	Nos	%	Nos	%	Nos	%
Yes	9	11	4	17	3	7
Yes some but not all	20	24	7	29	13	32
No	48	57	11	46	20	49
Don't know	7	8	2	8	5	12
Base: women, fathers and grandparents interviewed	*(84)*		*(24)*		*(41)*	

We looked to see whether there were any differences in views between women receiving particular benefits after the birth and those who were not. The only difference we found was that women receiving family credit were more likely than others to think that teenage mothers had a baby in order to receive extra social security benefits. It is perhaps interesting that family credit is claimed by women in paid employment and, in our sample, was more likely to be claimed by married women.

Not surprisingly, most of the women who thought the statement was true (20) said that is was not true of all teenage mothers. A woman who was with a new partner at the time of the interview thought it was wrong: 'I reckon some of them do, but they shouldn't be able to. They shouldn't be allowed to have kids if they think like that.'

A small number said that it was true of other women but not of themselves, such as a cohabiting woman who was still in part-time education at the time of the interview: 'If they don't want to work I suppose they do have a baby in order to receive extra social security benefits. If I wasn't pregnant, I wouldn't do it to get money off the social.' Another cohabiting woman in part-time employment remarked: 'I suppose some do. They've never worked because they're too young. I didn't get pregnant to get benefits, but maybe they did.' Another single woman explained that when she became pregnant her partner was working: 'So it didn't apply (having a baby in order to get extra benefits).'

A few women said that they knew others who had become pregnant to get extra social security benefits. One married woman said: 'I've known people I used to go to school with who've done it. And I know it's because they couldn't be bothered to go to work.'

Several single women said that they would have preferred to be working rather than claiming social security benefits and spoke of what they had missed since becoming pregnant. One woman had been living with her parents when she became pregnant. She was single, unemployed and living with a relative at the time of the interview: 'I'd much rather be earning proper money than the crap they give you to live on. I'd have been living more comfortably at home with my mum. I'd be much better off. Sometimes I regret leaving home.' Another woman who was cohabiting when she became pregnant but was single, unemployed and living alone at the time of the interview remarked: 'If I could live my life over again, I'd be working now and I wouldn't have a kid.'

Another woman who had been cohabiting when she became pregnant, but was single, unemployed and living alone in local authority accommodation at the time of the interview, felt that there was little to gain from becoming pregnant to get extra social security benefits and that women who did so had an unrealistic view of what they would receive: 'I think they probably do (become pregnant to get extra benefits), but they'll have a big shock when they find out what it is. I think teenagers should be made aware of how much it actually is.'

Although some women said that they would prefer to be working than claiming social security benefits, few spoke of plans to seek paid employment. One woman who was single and living alone did: 'I would have worked if I could. That's why I'm trying to get a job now, so I don't have to be on the social all my life.' But another woman who was also single, living alone and unemployed was less optimistic: 'I don't like being on the social, but for me to go out and get a job, I'd have to be earning a lot. I mean the £70 (benefits) doesn't ever last the week. Once I've bought his nappies out of it, it's gone.'

We have seen that well over half (48) of the women interviewed thought that teenage or young mothers did not become pregnant to receive extra social security benefits and the rest (7) did not know whether they did or not. There were certainly strong views shared by over a third of all women (31) that the income from benefits was not enough and that the extra benefits were certainly not an incentive for women to become pregnant. Some women receiving income support emphasised that they were no better off as a result of having a baby because of the added financial burden of looking after the baby.

A woman who was single and had lived with her parents throughout was in full-time education at the time of the interview and did not think that teenage women became pregnant in order to receive extra benefits: 'No. Because that money's going to be spent on the baby, so they won't benefit from it really.' A cohabiting woman expressed a similar view: 'The extra social security benefits never cover what a baby will cost you. I would say that is definitely untrue unless you're mental.'

One woman who was cohabiting when she became pregnant and was single and living with her parents at the time of the interview thought that the motivation to become pregnant was more to do with genuinely wanting a baby rather than wanting extra social security benefits: 'I think that's a load of rubbish! Most mums I know planned their babies because they've always wanted one.'

However, another woman who had planned her pregnancy, and was in full-time employment and living with her partner in an owner-occupied house at the time of the interview, felt that most teenage pregnancies were not even planned, let alone calculated in such detail: 'I think a lot of teenage pregnancies are probably mistakes. They haven't got that in their mind.'

Some women were clear that they had not been motivated to become pregnant to receive extra social security benefits and had known very little about benefits before they became pregnant. One was in part-time education and single at the time of the interview: 'I didn't want to have a baby in the beginning and I didn't know anything about money. A year and a half ago I was so naive.' Another woman who was single and had lived with her parents throughout remarked: 'I didn't know what money I'd get until my dad sat me down and told me. It wasn't something I ever thought about before I was pregnant, or even when I was expecting the baby.' Another woman in full-time employment at the time of the interview explained: 'Benefits were not even thought of. That wasn't my reason. Benefits didn't really come into question. I wasn't begging for anything.'

Views of the fathers interviewed

However, nearly half of the fathers interviewed thought that teenage women became pregnant to get extra social security benefits, while the rest were unable to comment or disagreed, as Table 8.3 shows.

Most of those who thought it was true thought that it was only true of some women. One cohabiting employed father commented: 'Some girls will do that. I don't like any of it. I pay tax.' A married father who was also in full-time employment said that although he did not know whether teenage mothers had a baby in order to get extra benefits: '...some rake in so much from the social it makes me mad'.

An unemployed married man spoke of what he regarded as the easy option chosen by some women: '...who haven't done a day's work in their life. They get the pick of the housing, a lot of them do. They have a lot more upstairs than I've had. They found out that the easy way to get out and leave home and get their freedom is to get pregnant.' Another father in full-time employment also spoke in the same terms: 'If that's all you can do, if you can't get a job and have nowhere to live, it's an easy option.'

There was some disagreement among fathers about whether the social security payments were sufficient to meet the costs of living. One said that single women got generous social security payments: 'They don't seem to have to struggle any more than couples. They must get a lot of help from the social.' But not all fathers thought that women were so fortunate. One father in full-time employment said: 'Maybe some do but I think they'll end up paying out more than they'll receive. It's a big responsibility and if they did that just for the money, they're a bit silly really.'

The fathers were often aware of the costs of childcare, like one who thought that teenage mothers did not have a baby in order to receive extra benefits: 'I can't see how they'll get much more. They get more on paper but they've more to pay out for.' Another man agreed: 'You can't support a baby on what you get. It's nowhere near enough.' An unemployed father felt that he and his partner were less well off after having their baby: 'No. We had more money before the baby was born than we do now.'

One man who had lived with the baby's mother but whose relationship had broken up thought that the split had occurred because the baby's mother wanted to claim benefits as a single parent: 'Yes unfortunately from my own experience. (Partner) said she wanted me out because she'd get extra money.'

Comparing the views of the fathers with those of their partners we found that a slightly higher proportion of the women (more than half) thought that teenage mothers had a baby in order to receive extra social security benefits, even though only one third of the main sample of women thought so. Only 6 couples both felt that it was true and 5 couples both thought that it was not. One woman who was cohabiting and in part-time employment at the time of the interview commented: 'Basically I can't see people going out and getting pregnant to get benefits. Basically you want to go out and work like everyone else.' But her partner who was in full-time employment remarked: 'I suppose some people do. Some will do it.'

A woman in full-time employment said: 'Yes, I've known that to happen. I don't think it's worth it for the amount you get, to be honest. Although some as a single parent are better off doing that than working.' Her partner, also in full-time employment, was not so sure about whether women had a baby in order to get extra benefits but, like his partner, he felt that the income from benefits was not sufficient: 'If that were the case, I don't know how they live. The child benefit doesn't pay for the nappies.'

Views of the grandparents

We found that over a third (16) of the grandparents agreed with the statement that single teenage mothers had a baby in order to receive extra social security benefits, as Table 8.3 shows. Just under half (20) disagreed, and half of these had been teenage parents themselves.

Most grandparents who agreed with the statement said that it only applied to some women. One woman said: 'Some people seem to know what they are entitled to but the benefits aren't enough to live on.' Another woman whose daughter was single commented that she had not been aware of benefits and what her daughter might be entitled to claim: 'Maybe in some cases, but we didn't know what. We're a bit ignorant, I think. When we rang up (the social security office), they just said we weren't entitled. You have to believe what they say, don't you.'

Like the mothers and fathers, the grandparents often remarked that the money received from benefits was not sufficient to meet the expenses of looking after a baby. One grandfather said that women who became pregnant in order to receive benefits might have expected a higher income from benefits than they received: 'If they look after the baby properly they'll be disappointed. I don't think my daughter makes a profit out of the baby.'

A woman who had been a teenage mother herself said: 'I wouldn't have thought so. Because it stands to reason. Those extra benefits are going to be gone before you can blink your eyes.' A woman who had also been a teenage parent agreed: 'It doesn't matter how much – it doesn't cover the cost of having the baby. They might think they're better off but they're not.'

Other grandparents also referred to the costs of bringing up a child and thought that teenage parents did not appreciate how expensive it would be. One woman, whose daughter was single and living alone in local authority accommodation, said: 'The benefits don't give them that much extra for a baby. They don't realise how much a child costs.' Another woman who had been a teenage parent herself made a similar point: 'No. Because it's hard for one parent to live on the social they give now. You only have to look around at these one-parent girls to see how hard it is. And a lot of them do it without thinking. They don't realise how difficult it is looking after a little one.'

Some grandparents thought some young mothers became pregnant repeatedly in order to receive benefits. One woman commented: 'I dare say some would have another one for that (extra benefits), but anyone with common sense would know it's so little, it's hardly enough to feed a baby.' Another woman agreed: 'Yes, I think it's true that some do (have a baby) just to get benefits... I think there should be more help for people having their first baby. I think they should take on some of the ideas of Japan where you get lots of help for your first baby and less and less for subsequent babies. It might stop girls just having baby after baby just to get the benefits.'

A few grandparents thought there was a general perception that this was true of teenage mothers. One woman said: 'I think it's true in a lot of cases. It's what you read in the papers and see on the TV.' Another woman agreed: 'Yes, I think they probably do. It's just what people have said at work.'

Some grandparents commented that their daughter would prefer to be working than receiving social security benefits but said how hard it was to organise and pay for the childcare which would enable them to go out to work. A woman who had been a teenage mother herself did not think that teenage mothers had a baby in order to receive extra social security benefits: 'No. That's rubbish. I know my daughter would rather be working.'

Comparing the views of the grandparents with those of their daughters, we found that a similar proportion thought that teenage mothers had a baby in order to receive benefits. However, some grandparents expressed different views from those of their daughters. One married woman thought that it was true: 'Some people just see kids as money signs.' But her mother did not agree and added: 'It doesn't matter how much – it doesn't cover the cost of having a baby.'

Chapter 9

Case Studies

In this chapter we look in detail at the histories of twelve of the women we interviewed. They were selected to illustrate the diversity we found among teenage mothers in terms of their characteristics, their educational achievements, their employment histories and status, their housing and living arrangements from the time they became pregnant, their knowledge and use of benefits and, not least, their relationships with the baby's father and the different ways in which these developed over the short period between the time that they became pregnant and the time of the interview.

But before we present the case studies we bring together some of the key characteristics of the women. In this report we have drawn attention to the importance of whether the women were still in a relationship with the baby's father at the time of the interview, particularly in terms of their decisions concerning living and housing arrangements. However, we wished to look in more detail at the measurable consequences of the breakdown in relationships. We selected the main characteristics of the women which we considered to be key in assessing the outcome of the pregnancy and drew up Table 9.1 to illustrate the differences and similarities between the 43 women who were still in a relationship with the baby's father and the 41 who were not. Within the groups we indicate the present relationship of the women who were still with the baby's father. These were not necessarily the relationships they were in at the time they became pregnant. In looking at those who were no longer in a relationship with the baby's father and were single and alone, we indicate their relationship with the baby's father at the time that they became pregnant. (The matrix showing the full picture of relationships at the time the women became pregnant and at the time of the interview is given in Table 2.3 in Chapter 2.)

It can be seen from Table 9.1 that women still in a relationship with the baby's father were more likely to have planned their pregnancies and less likely to have considered a termination of pregnancy than those who were no longer in a relationship. It can be seen, however, that the women who had a failed cohabiting relationship were less likely than those in

Table 9.1 Key characteristics of women, by whether still in a relationship with the father of the baby

Number of women	Overall total	Still with the father of the baby				Not with the father of the baby				
		Total	Married	Cohabiting	Non-cohabiting relationship	Total	New partner	Cohabiting to single/ alone	Non-cohabiting to single/ alone	Casual relationship to single/ alone
	(84)	(43)	(15)	(23)	(5)	(41)	(6)	(10)	(21)	(4)
Planned pregnancy	23	18	11	6	1	5	2	1	1	1
Considered a TOP	22	8	1	4	3	14	1	3	10	0
Ethnic minority group	14	10	9	0	1	4	0	2	2	0
Educational qualifications	56	31	12	17	2	25	2	7	14	2
In paid employment	13	8	2	6	0	5	0	1	4	0
In full-time/part-time education	10	6	2	3	1	4	0	0	4	0
Receiving income support when became pregnant	21	8	3	4	1	13	3	7	2	1
Receiving income support after the birth	68	29	6	18	5	39	6	10	19	4
Moved since became pregnant	61	31	9	19	3	30	4	10	13	3
Living with parents at interview	22	8	2	3	3	14	2	3	8	1
Living in local authority accommodation	28	13	5	7	1	15	2	5	7	1
On waiting list for local authority accommodation	28	14	7	4	3	14	2	4	7	1
Baby's father a teenager	18	8	1	5	2	10	1	2	5	2
No contact with baby's father	17	0	0	0	0	17	3	4	7	3

failed non-cohabiting or casual relationships to have considered a termination, frequently because they thought the relationship to be on a firmer footing than it subsequently turned out to be.

Women from ethnic minorities were more likely to be still in a relationship with the baby's father, and, indeed 9 of the 15 married women were from ethnic minority groups. The women still in relationships were rather more likely to have educational qualifications. There was little difference in the proportions of those in paid employment or in education at the time of the interview by whether they were still in a relationship or not.

Only a fifth of the women who were still in a relationship with the baby's father had been on income support when they became pregnant, compared with one third of those no longer in a relationship. Two-thirds of those still in a relationship were on income support at the time of the interview compared with 95 per cent of those no longer in a relationship. It certainly appears that relationship breakdown was a strong indicator of reliance on income support, although it is not insignificant that two-thirds of those still in relationships were also on income support at the time of the interview. This was particularly noteworthy among those in co-habiting relationships, of whom over three-quarters were on income support.

Around three-quarters of both groups of women had moved at least once since they had become pregnant. All the women in failed cohabiting relationships had moved. One third of those no longer in a relationship with the father were currently living with their parents, compared with less than one fifth of those still in a relationship.

Very similar proportions of both groups were living in local authority accommodation or were on a local authority waiting list at the time of the interview.

The baby's father was a teenager in just under one fifth of the cases where the women were still in a relationship with him, compared with a quarter of the cases where she was no longer in a relationship. And perhaps the most striking finding was that in over 40 per cent of the cases where the women's relationship had broken down, they had no contact with the baby's father.

There does appear to be some association between lower educational achievement and receipt of income support at the time the women became pregnant in subsequent relationship breakdown, but it is not particularly strong. However, if the relationship does break down, there is a strong likelihood of subsequent dependence on income support. It is difficult to establish cause and effect, however, and the fact that a relatively high proportion of those still in a relationship with the baby's father were also on income support suggests that the situation is more complex than it initially appears.

This analysis suggests that although relationship breakdown is of considerable importance in the lives of these teenage mothers, the short-term consequences are not immediately measurable in terms of adverse outcomes on most indicators for this group compared with those still in relationships. However, the fact that a relatively high proportion of those no longer in a relationship have no contact at all with the baby's father could well have adverse consequences for the babies, even though some of the grandparents interviewed were very relieved that there was no contact. There are also important questions to be answered about the extent to which these young men can or should abdicate all responsibility for the future of the babies they helped to bring into the world.

We turn now to the stories of the women themselves. Our main classification of the twelve women is according to their relationships with the father of the baby at the time of the interview. These show the wide spectrum of the changing relationships among these teenage mothers, ranging from women who were married throughout the period to women whose relationship with the father had broken down and were single and alone at the time of the interview. Within this broad classification we give details of the women's characteristics, education, employment histories and status, their knowledge and use of benefits, and use these details to illustrate the varied consequences of teenage motherhood. We have selected six case studies illustrating the experience of women who were still in a relationship with the baby's father at the time of the interviews and six who were not, reflecting the proportions found among the women as a whole.

In the first category (case studies 1 and 2) we selected two women who were married at the time of the interview, both of whom were married at the time they became pregnant. The second category (case studies 3, 4 and 5) includes women who were cohabiting with the baby's father at the time of the interview, one of whom was cohabiting at the time she became pregnant. The third category (case study 6) includes a woman who was in a non-cohabiting relationship with the baby's father throughout. The fourth category (case study 7) includes a woman who was in a non-cohabiting relationship with a new partner at the time of the interview. The fifth category (case studies 8 and 9) includes women who were single at the time of the interview but who had cohabited with the baby's father when they became pregnant. The sixth category (case studies 10, 11 and 12) includes women who were single at the time of the interview but who had had a non-cohabiting relationship with the baby's father when they became pregnant.

Case study 1

Background to the pregnancy

Alia was 17 years old and married when she became pregnant. She and her husband had planned the pregnancy. She was still married at the time of the interview when her baby was 12 months old. She had married in Pakistan where her husband was born and was living there when she became pregnant. They had already planned to return to the UK, but Alia moved back to the country before her husband and was advised to work immediately to show that she could support herself and her husband before he also applied to move. She returned to the UK when she was 27 weeks pregnant but her husband was not granted permission to move to the UK until the baby was 9 months old.

Deciding where to live

When Alia returned to the UK she lived with her parents in their owner-occupied house, where she was still living with her husband and baby when we interviewed her. She had worked continuously since the baby was 3 weeks old, initially in a job she did not want, as a packer in a local factory. More recently, she had started working as a library assistant which she preferred. She applied for council accommodation when her baby was born. She had been on the waiting list for 12 months and thought that she would not be housed within the next six months. She was not confident about being housed at all in the foreseeable future because of the points system. She had been awarded very few points on the basis of her initial housing assessment, and said that because she had only 120 points after waiting 12 months, if points were awarded on the basis of 40 each year, she felt that it would be years before she reached 400 points which was the required target to be assured of housing.

Educational and occupational history

Alia completed her full-time education when she was 16 and had 6 GCSEs and an RSA vocational qualification in typing and computing. She was living in Pakistan when she became pregnant and in full-time employment in the UK at the time of the interview.

Social security benefits

She had not claimed any benefits before she was pregnant, and because she was in Pakistan for six and a half months of her pregnancy, she had not claimed any social security benefits until after the baby was born. She received family credit and child benefit after the baby was born. A relative had told her about child benefit and a colleague at work told her about family credit. The couple's main source of income was their earnings from paid employment. Alia had a gross weekly income of £120 per week and her husband earned £90 from his temporary employment. In addition, they received £50.04 from family credit and child benefit.

Case study 2

Background to the pregnancy

Margaret was 18 when the baby was born and her pregnancy was planned. She was married to the baby's father when she became pregnant and was still married at the time of the interview. She suspected her pregnancy early and had confirmed it when she was 6 weeks pregnant. She had not considered the possibility of having a termination of pregnancy. She and her husband had planned the pregnancy together and she had not discussed her pregnancy with her husband, relations, friends or professionals since there was nothing to discuss.

Deciding where to live

Margaret left home when she got married at 17. When she became pregnant she was living alone with her husband in their owner-occupied house. They had not moved and she was very satisfied with the accommodation: 'It's clean, it's not damp. It's all we need and it's ours.' However, they had thought of moving elsewhere within the next few years: 'We'd eventually like something bigger. We'd like a bigger garden for baby. At the moment we have a bank loan for the car so we have to pay that off first and really it's OK here. As everyone says, we've "done all right".'

Educational and occupational history

Margaret finished her full-time education when she was 16 and had obtained 4 GCSEs and a hairdressing qualification – NVQ Level 2. She was not in paid employment at the time of the interview but had been working full-time in a hairdressing salon when she became pregnant and explained: 'I'd given up one job to go and work with a friend who had started a new business (hairdressing). I assured her that I wasn't planning to get pregnant, so we stopped trying. But I didn't realise I was already pregnant.'

Social security benefits

Before becoming pregnant, Margaret was not receiving benefits. While pregnant she tried unsuccessfully to claim maternity allowance and the maternity expenses payment. At the time of the interview she was receiving child benefit only and her only other income source was her husband's earnings from full-time paid employment as an electrician. He too was a teenager when the baby was born.

CATEGORY 2: WOMEN WHO WERE COHABITING WITH THE BABY'S FATHER AT THE TIME OF THE INTERVIEW

Case study 3

Background to the pregnancy

Virginia was 19 when the baby was born. She had not planned the pregnancy, but had suspected it early. She had not considered having a termination of pregnancy. She had had a steady non-cohabiting relationship with her boyfriend when she became pregnant and started living with him after the birth. They were still cohabiting at the time of the interview.

She spoke about the pregnancy, and where she might live, with her boyfriend, mother, sister, another female relative, a friend, her boyfriend's mother and another of his relatives. She also spoke to a midwife and housing officer. She did not discuss having a TOP with her boyfriend or anyone else and remarked: 'We knew we wanted to live together.'

Deciding where to live

Virginia was living with her parents when she became pregnant and her mother suggested that she could continue to live with them until she could get a place of her own with her boyfriend and baby. She moved only once to live in local authority accommodation with her boyfriend when her baby was nine months old. She had been living there for six months at the time of the interview but did not see it as 'permanent' because they were hoping to buy their own house.

Educational and occupational history

Virginia finished her full-time education when she was 16 and then obtained a childcare qualification. She had worked for 2 years as a nursery assistant and left to take maternity leave but had not returned to work after the birth. She was unemployed at the time of the interview.

Social security benefits

She was not receiving any social security benefits before she became pregnant and received maternity allowance during her pregnancy. She received income support and although she also received one parent benefit after the birth, she said that this had subsequently been withdrawn because she was living with the baby's father. At the time of the interview, Virginia was receiving £70 in social security benefits each week, including income support and child benefit. An additional income source was her partner's wage from full-time employment as a painter and decorator. In all, she said that they lived on £270 each week.

Case study 4

Background to the pregnancy

Karen was 19 when the baby was born and had 'come off the pill' and planned the pregnancy with the baby's father with whom she was living throughout. She had not considered the possibility of having a TOP. She suspected she was pregnant just after she had missed a period. She talked about the pregnancy to her boyfriend, mother (who had been a teenage parent herself), aunt, GP and the local authority housing officer. Although the news of the pregnancy came as a shock to her boyfriend they immediately discussed preparing for the arrival of the baby.

Deciding where to live

When she became pregnant, Karen and her partner were already living together in local authority accommodation but had applied for a transfer because it was on the eighth floor and she did not like the flat or the area. She discussed her possible transfer with a housing officer when she was 11 weeks pregnant. Her mother offered her the option of moving back home because of the poor condition of her flat and her asthma. She moved back to live with her mother alone until after the baby was born. She had not been allocated another local authority property by the time the baby was 8 months old, so she and her partner moved together with the baby to housing association accommodation where she had been living for four months at the time of the interview.

Educational and occupational history

Karen completed her full-time education at 16 and had 7 GCSEs. She was unemployed at the time of the interview but before she became pregnant she had worked for six months as a sales coordinator before being made redundant. The pregnancy had changed her study plans because she had hoped to study social work but since the pregnancy she had decided to study part-time.

Social security benefits

When she became pregnant Karen was receiving income support and housing benefit and said that she knew that she could claim extra benefits but did not know how much. During her pregnancy she received maternity allowance and started claiming council tax benefit. While she was in hospital having her baby, she received information about other social security benefits. After the birth she received income support, one parent benefit, a loan from the social fund, council tax and housing benefit and child benefit. She said that she had not reported that she was living with the baby's father. Overall, her net weekly income from benefits was £77 and the baby's father bought things for the baby. He was in full-time employment but she did not state how much their overall income was. She said that although their wedding was planned they were: 'Always falling out.'

Case study 5

Background to the pregnancy

Teresa was 18 when her baby was born and had not planned her pregnancy. She suspected she was pregnant immediately after missing her period but had not considered the possibility of having a TOP. The baby's father was a steady boyfriend when she became pregnant and throughout the pregnancy, but after the birth they moved in together and were still cohabiting at the time of the interview.

Teresa spoke to her boyfriend, her parents and her boyfriend's mother about the pregnancy and where she might live. She discussed termination of pregnancy with her boyfriend and they agreed that they did not want one. They talked about moving in together as soon as they could get a house. In contrast, her father was angry when he heard the news of the pregnancy and his advice was: 'You're still young. If you have an abortion you can wait a few years and try for a baby then.' Her mother also discussed having a termination of pregnancy and Teresa recalled their conversation: 'She said, "You're still young," but I think she wanted me to keep it.'

Deciding where to live

When she discussed with her parents where she would live, her father had initially resisted the suggestion that the baby's father move in with her and her parents but: 'eventually he came round'. They had planned to get a house of their own. She found her boyfriend the most helpful person she spoke to in general, his mother the most sympathetic, and her own mother the most helpful in helping her decide where she would live after the baby was born. Her father was the most unhelpful: 'He more or less just kept out of it really.'

When she became pregnant, Teresa was living at home with her parents as a lodger. She moved when the baby was 11 months old to live with the baby's father. They bought a house which they found very satisfactory and planned to live there 'indefinitely'.

Educational and occupational history

Teresa completed her full-time education when she was 16 and had obtained 9 GCSEs and a diploma in vocational education. At the time of the interview she was in full-time employment as a sales administrator in the same company as when she became pregnant.

Social security benefits

She was not claiming benefits when she became pregnant. She had known that it was possible to claim social security benefits but did not know what. When she went on maternity leave she received statutory maternity pay and after the baby was born she continued to receive this and child benefit. At the time of the interview, she had returned to paid employment and was receiving child benefit only. Her partner was also in full-time employment.

CATEGORY 3: WOMEN IN A NON-COHABITING RELATIONSHIP WITH THE BABY'S FATHER THROUGHOUT

Case study 6

Background to the pregnaancy

Susan was 19 when the baby was born and had not planned to become pregnant. She was in a steady non-cohabiting relationship with the baby's father from the time she became pregnant to the time of the interview. She suspected the pregnancy early and confirmed it by the time she was 6 weeks pregnant. She wanted to have the baby but she considered the possibility of having a TOP after suspecting and confirming her pregnancy.

She spoke only to her boyfriend and mother about her pregnancy and where she might live. Her boyfriend indicated that he would support her in her decision but said that he wanted her to continue with the pregnancy. Susan felt that the issue of where and with whom she was going to live was secondary and in the early weeks of pregnancy their main concern was: 'What the hell are we going to do about the pregnancy?'

Her mother had bought the pregnancy testing kit but said that she must make the decision about having a TOP herself. Her boyfriend and mother influenced her decision to continue with the pregnancy: 'I wasn't on my own. I knew he would support me.'

Deciding where to live

Susan was living at home rent-free with her parents when she became pregnant. She and her boyfriend had agreed that she should stay there during her pregnancy and that she would put her name down for council accommodation just before the baby was born. They had planned to move in together after the birth. She had found her mother and boyfriend helpful, in that her mother bought her the baby's pram and some of the baby clothes and her boyfriend provided the most practical support in preparing for the birth.

Susan was still living with her parents at the time of the interview and had not moved. She found her accommodation very satisfactory but had thought about moving since she wanted to be with her partner and baby as a family. She had been on a council housing waiting list for 16 months and was hoping to be allocated a property in the next six months: 'We wouldn't be able to afford anything but a council house. If the council offered me one, we'd move tomorrow. We thought we would have one by now. The housing manager is coming to see me tomorrow.'

Educational and occupational history

Susan completed her full-time education when she was 18 and had GCSEs and an NVQ Level 1 and 2 in general care practice. She was not in paid employment at the time of the interview but had been working as a health care assistant at a local hospital when she became pregnant. After the birth she decided not to return to work because she did not have anyone to look after the baby and felt that she could not afford to employ a childminder.

Social security benefits

She was not receiving any benefits before she became pregnant and apart from child benefit, she did not know what benefits she could claim after having a baby. She received statutory maternity pay when she took maternity leave and after the birth received income support, statutory maternity pay and child benefit. Her net weekly income from benefits was £80.10 which was her sole source of income. Her boyfriend was not making a contribution because he was unemployed. However, he had started full-time work as a long distance lorry driver three weeks before the interview, but she did not comment on whether he would start to make any contribution to the baby's upkeep.

She saw her boyfriend three times a week and the baby spent 6 hours with him at his own house on a Sunday. She felt that her work plans had changed as a result of becoming pregnant and remarked how little things had changed for her boyfriend: 'His life hasn't changed. He can still go out whenever he wants and that gets me mad. He's good with the baby really, but he's still got his life.'

CATEGORY 4: NON-COHABITING RELATIONSHIP WITH A NEW PARTNER
AT THE TIME OF THE INTERVIEW

Case study 7

Background to the pregnancy

Mandy was 19 when the baby was born and had planned the pregnancy: 'I wanted a baby but my boyfriend didn't.' At the time she became pregnant she was in a steady relationship with the baby's father which broke down before the birth. At the time of the interview, Mandy was engaged to a new partner.

She first suspected she was pregnant when she missed a period and confirmed the pregnancy immediately by visiting a family planning clinic. She had not considered having a TOP because she wanted the baby. She spoke to her boyfriend, her mother, two female friends and a male friend about the pregnancy and where and with whom she might live. In addition she spoke to her GP.

Her boyfriend was shocked to hear of the pregnancy but did not discuss the possibility of having a TOP and did not discuss where she might live because they assumed they would get somewhere to live together. Her mother was pleased and advised her to stay at home until after the baby was born. One friend greeted the news with caution and asked her to consider a TOP, while another friend was pleased and did not discuss a TOP. She spoke to her GP when she was 26 weeks pregnant who helped her fill out a medical form (indicating she had depression) to support her application for council housing. She found her mother was most helpful and appreciated the fact that she could: 'Talk to her about anything.' Her boyfriend was the most unhelpful: 'He was out every night. He was not available. He gave no emotional support and he was sleeping with other women.'

Deciding where to live

When Mandy became pregnant she was living with her parents rent-free. She had already applied for local authority accommodation before she became pregnant but had only had one offer of accommodation on the sixth floor in a high-rise building which she did not consider suitable. She was still living with her parents and three siblings at the time of the interview and found the accommodation unsatisfactory: 'We are short of space for myself and the baby and everyone else. The three other children are all in one small bedroom.' She was hoping to be housed within the next six months and had been waiting for two and a half years: 'I phone the council every day and they are looking for a property. I want my own space and to start a new life with my new boyfriend.'

Educational and occupational history

Mandy had never lived away from home. Her parents had separated when she was 13 but neither had a new partner. She completed her full-time education when she was 14 and had no educational or vocational qualifications. She was not in paid employment at the time of the interview and had never worked. She said that her work study or training plans had not changed as a result of the pregnancy and explained: 'I never really had plans and I have no plans now that I have the baby.'

Social security benefits

Before she became pregnant Mandy was receiving income support and continued to receive it during her pregnancy. She tried unsuccessfully to get a loan from the social fund. After the birth she received income support, lone parent premium, a maternity expenses payment and child benefit. Her net weekly income from benefits was £79 which was her sole income source. She and the baby saw the baby's father once a week but she described an acrimonious relationship between her, the baby's father and his family which had resulted in access problems: 'The rows and physical violence make contact between the baby's father and the baby difficult. The shouting upsets the baby.'

CATEGORY 5: SINGLE WOMEN AT THE TIME OF THE INTERVIEW WHO HAD COHABITED WITH THE BABY'S FATHER

Case study 8

Background to the pregnancy

Geraldine was 17 years old when she had her baby and had not planned the pregnancy. She was living with the baby's father when she became pregnant but their relationship had broken down by the time of the birth and she was single and alone at the time of the interview. She suspected she was pregnant at 8 weeks and had confirmed the pregnancy by the ninth week. She considered having a TOP but did not do anything about it because she did not agree with abortion. She was excited about the pregnancy but knew that the baby's father did not want to have children and he wanted her to have a TOP. In contrast, Geraldine's parents were pleased and did not discuss the possibility of a TOP.

Deciding where to live

Geraldine's boyfriend said that she could continue to live with him only if she had a TOP, but she wanted to continue with the pregnancy. Her parents had both suggested that she return home to live with them. She moved home after the breakdown of her relationship and remained there until the baby was 5 months old when she moved with the baby to local authority accommodation because she wanted to be independent. However she did not like the estate and returned to live with her parents when the baby was 9 months old. She planned to stay there for 4 to 5 years until he started school.

Educational and occupational history

Geraldine left school at 15 and had no educational qualifications. She was working as a cashier when she became pregnant and stopped working when she was 5 months pregnant. She did not return to work after the birth and was unemployed at the time of the interview.

Social security benefits

Before becoming pregnant, Geraldine was not claiming any benefits but received income support and maternity expenses payment during pregnancy. After the birth, she received income support, one parent benefit, housing benefit and child benefit. Her net weekly income from benefits was £78 which was her sole income source.

Neither Geraldine nor the baby ever saw the baby's father and she remarked: 'As far as I know, he hates the baby. He has two others by different mothers. He's the kind that gets girls pregnant and then doesn't want to know.'

Case study 9

Background to the pregnancy

Lynne was 17 when the baby was born and had not planned her pregnancy. She left home when she was 16 because she was not 'getting on' with her mother who had a new partner. She suspected the pregnancy before she was 5 weeks pregnant and confirmed it in her sixth week. She had not considered having a TOP.

She was living with the baby's father when she became pregnant but the relationship had broken down before the pregnancy was confirmed. She was single and alone at the time of the interview and never saw the baby's father. She spoke to her mother, aunt and a friend who was also pregnant, but not to her boyfriend, about the pregnancy or where she might live. There were no discussions about the possibility of a termination of pregnancy.

Deciding where to live

Lynne had moved away from her boyfriend when she was 8 weeks pregnant. Her aunt and mother suggested that she could live with them but she moved first to a friend for 2 months before going to live with her aunt when she was 16 weeks pregnant. She found her aunt the most helpful in advising her about where to live: 'I was offered a terrible house (local authority) in an area I didn't want, but I was so desperate I would have taken it. But my aunt said no.' Lynne moved a third time when her baby was a week old to another local authority property. She found the accommodation very satisfactory but applied for a transfer because she did not like the area and felt isolated. She moved again when the baby was 5 months old to another local authority property nearer to her mother with which she was very satisfied. She had been living there for 8 months when we interviewed her.

Educational and occupational history

Lynne completed her full-time education when she was 15 and had obtained 2 GCSE qualifications. She was unemployed when she became pregnant but had had plans to go to college. She had never been in paid employment and was unemployed at the time of the interview.

Social security benefits

Lynne was receiving income support before becoming pregnant and received income support and the maternity expenses payment during pregnancy. After the birth she received income support, one parent benefit, housing and council tax benefit, disability benefit and child benefit. Her net weekly income from benefits was £120.50 per week which was her sole source of income.

CATEGORY 6: SINGLE WOMEN AT THE TIME OF THE INTERVIEW WHO HAD HAD A NON-COHABITING RELATIONSHIP WITH THE BABY'S FATHER

Case study 10

Background to the pregnancy

Sharon was 17 when her baby was born and had not planned to become pregnant. She had considered the possibility of having a TOP when she first suspected the pregnancy and after it was confirmed but did not do anything about it because she feared: 'I might never get the chance to have a baby again.' At the time she became pregnant the baby's father was a steady boyfriend but by the time of the birth their relationship had broken down and she was single and alone at the time of the interview.

She spoke to her boyfriend about the pregnancy and where she might live but apart from him she spoke only to a key worker at the hostel where she lived during her pregnancy. She suspected she was pregnant at eight weeks and confirmed it within a few days. When she told her boyfriend he said that he would support her and when they discussed a TOP she recalled: 'He just went mad. He didn't want to at all.'

Deciding where to live

When she became pregnant Sharon was living in a hostel. Her parents had separated when she was 13 and her mother was living with a new partner. She did not have contact with her father. She left home at 16 and recalled: 'I couldn't get on with my mother then.' She spoke to the key worker at the hostel about her pregnancy who advised her to move to a mother and baby unit. She moved twice, first when she was 22 weeks pregnant to a mother and baby unit which she was sharing with 13 other women: 'I thought I'd be there for ages because after you've had the baby you have to wait for ages to get a flat, but I got one really quick.' She moved when the baby was 4 months old because: 'My time was up at the hostel... but I was ready within myself to move anyway.' She went to live alone in a local authority flat with her baby and had been there for 7 months when we interviewed her and found the accommodation satisfactory. Although she wanted to move again, she recognised: 'I could be here for years because it's council and they won't move you.'

Educational and occupational history

Sharon left school and home when she was 16 and had GCSE qualifications but did not say how many or what grades. After leaving school she started studying for an NVQ in Health and Social Care but gave up when she became pregnant. She was unemployed at the time of the interview and had no plans to complete her NVQ course.

Social security benefits

She was not claiming benefits before she became pregnant and had not known whether having a baby would allow her to claim social security benefits. During her pregnancy she received income support and later in pregnancy, the maternity grant or maternity expenses payment. She received information about social security benefits from the key workers at the mother and baby hostel. After the birth, she received income support and child benefit. She also received a loan from the social fund but made no reference to the method of repayment. Overall, her net weekly income from benefits was £79, which was her sole source of income. She had little contact with the father of the baby, whom she saw less than once a month.

Case study 11

Background to the pregnancy

Katy was 18 when she had her baby and the pregnancy was unplanned. She first suspected she might be pregnant when she started getting sick at 8 weeks: 'I didn't tell anyone. I didn't know what it was but I thought I could be pregnant.' She confirmed her pregnancy at the GP surgery when she was 10 weeks. She had not considered the possibility of having a TOP.

When she became pregnant she had had a steady non-cohabiting relationship with the baby's father but they had split up before the pregnancy was confirmed and she was single and alone at the time of the interview. She spoke to her boyfriend and parents and two friends about the pregnancy and where to live. In addition, she spoke to her GP, midwife, health visitor and tutor.

Her boyfriend was surprised to hear of the pregnancy because they had already split up but suggested that they 'get back together' which she did not want. They did not discuss the possibility of a termination of pregnancy. Her parents were shocked and suggested that Katy talk to someone who could advise her before she decided whether to continue with the pregnancy. Her mother said she should think about having a TOP but this was not discussed with her father. Both parents suggested that she continue to live at home. Her mother, boyfriend and friends influenced her decision to continue with the pregnancy because she felt supported.

Her GP confirmed the pregnancy and advised her to: 'Consider my options myself and come to my own decision but to realise what I was doing would affect my future.' Her parents were most helpful and she found no-one particularly unhelpful.

Deciding where to live

Katy remained living with her parents throughout. She found the accommodation satisfactory but had thought about moving because she wanted to be 'independent'. She was on a council housing waiting list but had already refused the first offer of a property: 'The council offered me somewhere straight away but it was too far away. Mum is looking after the baby when I'm at college. I couldn't go there and then to college.' She had also thought of renting privately and explained: 'I am looking for a flat to rent privately and claim housing benefit but they are all too expensive. I will have to pay extra myself. Around here the houses are owned so there's no council housing.'

Educational and occupational history

Katy was still in full-time education at the time of the interview. She had 8 GCSEs and was taking an NVQ course in travel studies. The pregnancy had changed her study plans and she decided not to pursue her A-level course because she had missed most of the first year.

Social security benefits

She did not claim benefits before or during the pregnancy. After the birth, she received income support, maternity grant, and child benefit. Her net weekly income from benefits was £80.50 and she said that apart from small infrequent cash contributions, this was her sole income source. She never saw the baby's father but he had weekly contact with the baby through a contact centre.

Case study 12

Background to the pregnancy

Miranda was 18 when the baby was born and had not planned the pregnancy. She had had a steady non-cohabiting relationship with the baby's father when she became pregnant but they had split up by the time the pregnancy was confirmed and she was single and alone at the time of the interview. She suspected she was pregnant at 6 weeks and the pregnancy was confirmed by the eighth week. She explained: 'I told my mum I didn't think I was pregnant, but she did. She wanted me to go for a test but I wouldn't because I didn't really believe it in my own mind.' She wanted to have the baby but had considered having a TOP when she suspected the pregnancy and after it was confirmed. She decided to continue with the pregnancy: 'I wanted to have him but everyone else was saying, "You've got college and everything" and my boyfriend said he'd leave me.'

She talked about the pregnancy, and where and with whom she might live, with her boyfriend, mother, his parents and her GP. Her boyfriend suggested that she should have an abortion: 'He really wanted me to... He'd made up his mind he wanted me to get rid of it and that was all he was interested in.' They did not discuss where and with whom she might live. Her mother was supportive and assured her that she would stand by her whatever decision she made. It was assumed that she would stay at home. Her GP was also supportive and they discussed TOP as an option. Her boyfriend's parents suggested that she have a TOP. Not surprisingly, her mother was identified as the most helpful and her boyfriend as being particularly unhelpful.

Deciding where to live

When Miranda became pregnant she was living at home with her parents and did not move. She thought her accommodation was very satisfactory. She had never thought of moving but added that she would probably stay at home: 'Until baby is old enough to go to school and I can get a proper full-time job and get a house.' She was not on a council housing waiting list.

Educational and occupational history

Miranda completed her full-time education when she was 17, obtaining 8 GCSEs and later an NVQ in business administration. She was not in paid employment at the time of the interview but had worked for 8 months after the baby was born: 'I couldn't afford a baby sitter or to put him in a creche. My grandad was looking after the baby but as he got older it became too much for him and my mother is working full-time.'

Social security benefits

Miranda was not receiving benefits before she became pregnant and received income support and maternity grant in late pregnancy. After the birth, she received income support, one parent benefit, family credit and child benefit. Her net weekly income from benefits was £80.10 which was her sole source of income. She and the baby never saw the baby's father, who was living with a new partner and in full-time employment at the time of the interview.

Chapter 10

Discussion of Findings

This study set out to examine the ways in which teenage mothers make decisions both about their pregnancies and about their housing and living arrangements during the pregnancy and after the birth. The aim of the study was to assess the consequences of teenage motherhood and to examine the decisions and processes which led to different outcomes relating to certain key factors, including housing and living arrangements, relationships with the father of the baby, educational and employment status, and sources of support and income.

The most common perception of teenage mothers is of a group of unmarried women, living alone with their babies on social security benefits in local authority accommodation. This view has, perhaps, been enhanced by much previous research which has tended to concentrate on the experience of single lone mothers, for the legitimate purpose of highlighting the circumstances under which they are living, with far less focus on the broad spectrum of teenage mothers.

We set out to examine the extent to which the common perception was true of the women we interviewed and to follow their histories from the time that they became pregnant to the time of the interview, which took place usually some 21 months later. The strength of this study lies in its examination and analysis of how a cohort of teenage mothers, from different areas, different backgrounds and with different educational and employment histories, came to share the common experience of overwhelming dependence on social security benefits by the time their babies were around a year old.

Our sample of women was drawn from hospital records in three areas, (Hackney, Leeds and Solihull), of women having their first baby when aged 16 to 19. The women were approached when their babies were approximately twelve months old, and we have drawn attention to the fact that our response rate was affected by the probability that many of the women had moved by the time we tried to contact them (see Chapter 1 and Appendix). Difficulties in ensuring a good response from teenage mothers are well recognised (see Speak et al, 1995). However, in spite of the limitations of the sample, which we readily acknowledge, we were able to establish patterns of behaviour and relationship breakdown which reflect those found in other research. Although the current study must be approached mainly as a qualitative study, we have constantly given numerical data in order to highlight the patterns and to show the wide variety of characteristics, relationships and outcomes found among women who are often treated as a homogeneous group, both by the media and policy makers.

The general picture

Perhaps the most important feature of the women's experience was that by the time of the interview, only just over half (43) of the 84 women were still in a relationship with the father of the baby and 41 were not. The vast majority of those still in a relationship with the baby's father (38) were married or cohabiting, while most of the women who were not in a relationship with the baby's father were single and without a steady relationship (35).

The implications of this widespread breakdown in relationships among these young women with small babies were clearly far-reaching, and we traced the patterns of decisions which resulted in increasing dependency on benefits and social housing, in spite of the hopes with which many of those interviewed embarked upon their pregnancies.

One of the main features of the research findings was the constantly changing pattern of relationships. All but six of the women had what they described as a steady relationship with the father of the baby at the time they became pregnant. We found that 35 of the 84 women were married or cohabiting at the time they became pregnant compared with 38 at the time of the interview. But these simple figures conceal considerable movements in relationships, and, apart from the married women, all of whom remained married, we found a changing series of relationship patterns during pregnancy and after the birth, even among those who were still in a relationship with the baby's father at the time of the interview.

We were interested in looking for common characteristics and patterns among these women, all of whom had continued with their pregnancies at a time when over a third of teenage pregnancies end in abortion. The vast majority of them were born in the United Kingdom, were of white ethnic origin and nearly half of them said they had no religion. Nearly half of them said that their own mother had been a teenager at the birth of her first child, reflecting the pattern found in other studies, and a quarter of the sample had a sibling who was a teenage parent. They came from larger than average families, only just over half of them said that their parents were still married to each other, and most of those whose parents had separated had been under five at the time of the separation. This pattern reflects that found by Kaye Wellings in her analysis of teenage pregnancy (Wellings et al, 1996).

Although most had contact with one or both parents, and over a quarter (22) were living with them at the time of the interview, the vast majority had lived away from home at some point, with as many as 10 (12 per cent) having left home by the time they were 16, often, it appeared because of discord within their family.

Nearly one fifth (16) said that they had left school when they were 15 or under, and a further 46 per cent had left school at 16. Two-thirds of the women had educational qualifications, mainly at GCSE level, but not surprisingly, the younger they were when they left school the less likely they were to have any educational qualifications. Over a third of the women had vocational qualifications.

Nearly 40 per cent were in paid employment and 29 per cent in education when they became pregnant, compared with 15 per cent in employment and 13 per cent in education at the time of the interview. 31 per cent were unemployed when they became pregnant, compared with 71 per cent at the time of the interview. But the women had had other expectations. Two-thirds of them said they had changed their work, study or training plans as a result of the pregnancy.

36 per cent were receiving some kind of benefit when they became pregnant, compared with 93 per cent after the birth (excluding child benefit and statutory maternity pay). A quarter were receiving income support when they became pregnant compared with 81 per cent after the birth. The proportion receiving housing benefit also rose from 11 per cent when they became pregnant to nearly 50 per cent after the birth. Over half of them (57 per cent) were totally dependent on benefits as their sole source of income at the time of the interview.

Although over half of the women (45) were living with the baby's father or saw him every day, in other cases contact with fathers was less frequent, and nearly one fifth (16) had no contact at all with the baby's father.

The proportion of women living in local authority accommodation had risen from less than 5 per cent when they became pregnant to 33 per cent by the time of the interview, with a further third of the sample on a local authority waiting list.

But although it was possible to establish some common characteristics, for example, a relatively low level of educational achievement, a relatively high unemployment rate at the time they became pregnant, a higher than average family size and a greater incidence of teenage motherhood among their own mothers, there were still widespread variations among the characteristics of these women.

When we turned to outcomes we found that half of the women were no longer in a relationship with the father of the baby. Those who had planned the pregnancy and those from ethnic minority groups were more likely than others still to be in a relationship, while those with educational qualifications were slightly more likely still to be with the baby's father. More frequent moves were associated with relationship breakdown, but moving in itself was not. There were few differences otherwise between the two groups. Much seemed to depend on the development of the relationship between the woman and the baby's father over the 21 months.

The one common outcome shared by the women was that the overwhelming majority of them were on social security benefits by the time of the interview, with over half of them completely dependent on benefits. Almost all the women who were no longer in a relationship with the baby's father were on income support at the time of the interview, but so were two-thirds of those still in a relationship. There were clear indications that dependence on benefits was an important consequence of teenage motherhood, whether relationships survived or not.

Decisions to continue with the pregnancy

The most important factor in the history of these young women was the decision to continue with the pregnancy. It could be argued that the most important factor was that they became pregnant in the first place, but, as we have seen, only a quarter of them had planned their pregnancies, leaving three-quarters who could hardly be said to have made a decision to become pregnant. Given that a relatively high proportion of teenage pregnancies end in termination of pregnancy, we thought it important to explore the reasons for continuing with the pregnancy.

Although 40 per cent of the women were pleased or delighted to find that they were pregnant, a quarter were shocked and surprised, and a further quarter were scared or horrified. It must be a matter of concern that so many reacted like this when they must have known that they were running the risk of getting pregnant. Their reactions mirror those of women who then seek a termination of pregnancy (Allen, 1985), and underline the complex thinking among women who are fully aware of the risks of pregnancy without contraception and yet take a chance or assume, for no valid reason, that 'it won't happen to me'.

The differences between the women who then decide to have a termination and those who continue with the pregnancy are difficult to determine. Some women were devastated when they found they were pregnant – 'I was gutted. I didn't want to be pregnant...' – but continued with the pregnancy in spite of the fact that they considered termination of pregnancy. It was clear, however, that continuing with the pregnancy was often not so much a decision as an acceptance of what had happened, reflecting a rather fatalistic attitude which characterised much of the behaviour of many of these young women subsequently. It could be argued that those who opt for termination of pregnancy have to make a definite decision, while for an important minority of the women interviewed in the present study, the decision to have a termination was one which they felt they could not make, even though they did not want to be pregnant and knew their relationship might founder.

Among those who had planned the pregnancy, little or no discussion took place with other people on what to do about it, mainly, it appeared, because the pregnancy was wanted, but among the others, there was often extensive discussion with a variety of people about the options. However, it was clear that women were often selective about the people with whom they discussed the pregnancy, and even more selective about what they discussed with whom. Although mothers were found to be the most helpful and supportive, only just over half the women had talked to their mother at all about the pregnancy. Those who had planned their pregnancy clearly saw little point, but others, especially those who might have expected a frosty reception, may well have avoided a conversation in which pressure might have been brought on them to terminate the pregnancy. The parents with whom women discussed their pregnancy were often shocked and disappointed, but most were said to have given total support in the women's decision and to have rarely tried to influence them one way or the other. In our interviews with grandparents, however, it was clear that not all mothers were quite as sanguine as they were described by their daughters, and, it should be stressed, those whom we interviewed were usually grandparents in very close contact with their daughters and their babies.

Women often saw little alternative to discussing their pregnancy with their partners, and it was interesting again to see what a high proportion of partners were shocked or surprised to learn of the pregnancy. Termination of pregnancy was discussed with over a third of the partners with whom any discussion took place. It must be remembered that some partners disappeared before the pregnancy was confirmed while others were overjoyed about the pregnancy so that no discussion was thought necessary. Few partners suggested terminations, although those who did were often reported as reacting in a very brutal manner. However, by the time of the interview, many of the partners with whom discussions took place were no longer in a relationship with the women, in spite of the fact that some of them were described as having a key influence in the decision to continue with the pregnancy. Delight and joy at the thought of becoming a father was very short-lived among some of these young men.

It was apparent that friends and relations were often hand-picked for discussions, and, again, those who suggested termination of pregnancy or pointed out the potential disadvantages of teenage motherhood were not popular among the women interviewed. It was also interesting that professionals were mainly reported as being supportive of the woman's decision to continue with the pregnancy, and few were said to have discussed the option of a termination of pregnancy. There were clear indications that many professionals were following the preferences of the women to continue with the pregnancy, and were offering support in that decision. Those who did not were often reported as being unnecessarily unsympathetic. Professionals who disagree or try to put another point of view to women who want confirmation of their own decision are often thought to be unhelpful or unsympathetic, whatever the situation. It is perhaps significant that women seeking termination of pregnancy also often report lack of sympathy from professionals who do not agree with their decision.

When the women were asked to assess the support offered by the people to whom they spoke, parents, particularly mothers, received a much higher rating than partners in terms of helpfulness, sympathy, practical assistance and financial support. Partners received a low rating on most counts, apart from some financial support. Although it must be remembered that a small proportion of women had not discussed the future of the pregnancy with their husbands or partners, most other partners and husbands were rarely seen as playing a major role in the decision to continue with the pregnancy or in supporting the women throughout the pregnancy. It is perhaps ironic that many of those who clearly did play an important role in dissuading women from termination of pregnancy by promising devoted support were no longer around by the time of the interview.

Our analysis of the ways in which women made their decision to continue with the pregnancy suggests that most of them sought confirmation of their own decision to have the baby through their discussions with other people. If confirmation was not forthcoming, as it certainly was not by some of their partners, the women may have been shocked or upset, but then sought support elsewhere, notably among their parents. It was clear that many of them heard from their parents what they wanted to hear. Some mothers were clearly delighted, but many were not. However, the interviews suggest that their daughters interpreted their parents' unwillingness to be too directive and their offers of support as a sanction for their decision to continue with the pregnancy. Sadly, many of the fears expressed by their parents, particularly their concern that the relationship with the baby's father would founder, had materialised by the time of the interviews.

In their reaction to their pregnancies few women expressed any doubts about their ability to cope with pregnancy or motherhood. Concerns were more likely to be related to fears about what their parents would say, rather than to practical considerations such as how and where and with whom they were going to live and what they were going to live on. It appeared that few of them had given much thought to the future, and that planning for their life as a mother was as remote a concept as planning for pregnancy had been for many of them.

The reluctance to consider termination of pregnancy was striking, especially among some young women whose relationship with the father of the baby was clearly shaky or, in some cases, violent. Many of these realised at a very early stage, often before the pregnancy had been confirmed, that there was no future in their relationship and that they would not be able to rely on the father for any kind of support. We found, like Louie Burghes in her study of single teenage mothers (Burghes and Brown, 1995), a clear anti-abortion feeling among these young women, rarely based on religious grounds, although it was by no means universal.

It was interesting that the women who continued with the pregnancy in the knowledge that their relationship was unlikely to survive were not only those with low educational achievement or with few potential alternatives to motherhood. Some women had plans for further education or careers which they knew would have to be put on hold, if not abandoned, and yet they continued with a pregnancy with little or no potential support from the father of the baby. Again, there was plenty of evidence that planning for the future was relatively unusual and that few of the women reacted to the pregnancy by attempting to take control of the situation. There was a strong sense in many of the interviews of young women being swept along by events over which they were neither willing nor, in many cases, able to exert any influence.

Decisions about living arrangements

One of the aims of the study was to examine how decisions about housing and household change are made by teenage mothers after they have decided to continue with the pregnancy, during the latter stages of their pregnancies and after the birth of their babies. We were particularly interested in the role of other people in these decisions and the extent and nature of their influence on whether the women moved or stayed put.

In the report we have explored in detail the extent to which women moved during pregnancy and after the birth, we have documented the moves made, and we have attempted to establish a pattern of housing careers among these women in the relatively short period of 21 months between becoming pregnant and the time of the interview. We found that 73 per cent of the women moved at least once in this period, while 27 per cent did not move. 35 per cent of women moved once only, 21 per cent moved twice and 17 per cent moved three or more times, with a small proportion of these moving up to 11 times over the period.

Our sample may under-represent the extent to which teenage mothers move during pregnancy and after the birth, in that we were unable to make contact with many of those in our sampling frame simply because they had moved. It is therefore possible that our sample contains a rather higher proportion of women who had not moved at all than might be found in the general population of teenage mothers, although Simms and Smith (1986) found that as many as 45 per cent of the teenage mothers in their sample were still living in their parents' homes 15 months after the birth of their baby, compared with the 26 per cent found in the present study. However, in the current study we found that living at home with parents did not necessarily mean that women had not moved. For example, we found that only half of those who were living their parents at the time of the interview had never moved. We also found that a rather higher proportion of our sample had moved twice or more than was found in the Simms and Smith study, although a similar proportion in both studies had moved once only.

We have already seen the wide variety of advice and support given to the women in their decision to continue with the pregnancy, and the extent to which it appeared that most of them had already arrived at a decision to continue with the pregnancy before embarking on discussions about it. Discussions were therefore often related to seeking agreement with the decision or to receiving confirmation of continuing support and help.

The process of decision-making about where and with whom to live during pregnancy and after the birth was a rather more complicated exercise. First, the range of housing options or future living arrangements was, perhaps not surprisingly, closely related to the status and stability of women's relationship with the baby's father and also, in many cases, to their relationship with their parents. Secondly, the women were living in a variety of places with a variety of people when they became pregnant. Not only did they have to decide where to live but they also had to decide with whom to live. Thirdly, whereas the decision to continue with the pregnancy was really the result of a consideration of two main options – to have the baby or to have an abortion – decisions about housing and living arrangements were considerably more complex, with many more factors to be taken into account. Perhaps the most important of these was often unknown to the women at the beginning of their pregnancy: whether their relationship with the baby's father would survive.

Patterns of moves and living arrangements

As we have seen, the women were starting from different places, which certainly affected their decisions about housing and living arrangements. We sought to establish patterns of living arrangements through following housing histories for all the women. We wanted to see to what extent relationship breakdown was related to certain patterns, even if it was impossible to establish cause and effect.

We first established the broad movements among the sample. From the time they became pregnant to the time of the interview we found that the proportion living with their parents dropped from nearly half to a quarter (some also with partners); the proportion cohabiting with the baby's father (some also with parents or in-laws) remained at just under one third of the sample at both stages, concealing the fact that they were not the same people, since nearly half of the original cohabiting relationships had broken down. We found that 11 per cent were living with a husband at the time they became pregnant, compared with 18 per cent at the time of the interview (again sometimes with parents or in-laws). A few women were living with friends or relatives at the time they became pregnant or at the time of the interview, and four women were cohabiting with a new partner at the time of the interview. However, the most striking change was the increase in the proportion of those living alone, from 7 per cent when they became pregnant to 29 per cent at the time of the interview. Very few of the young women we interviewed had intended to end up as single lone parents, but around half of them had done so, and well over half of these were living alone with their baby.

We have described in Chapter 4 the complicated patterns of movement for those who moved, and we have shown that those who had not moved were made up of two distinct groups of women: those living with husbands or partners throughout the period and those living with their parents, most of whom were no longer in a relationship with the baby's father by the time of the interview.

The women who moved once only were often moving from their parents' home to live with the baby's father, or were already married or cohabiting and moving to other accommodation. Relationship breakdown was relatively uncommon among those who moved once only, in that two-thirds were still with the baby's father, but a group of women had moved out of their parents' home to live alone with their baby.

Women who had moved twice were more likely to be living alone at the time of the interview and less than half were still with the baby's father. More than half of the women who had moved three times or more were living alone and only one in five of them were still with the baby's father.

It can be seen that it was difficult to establish patterns of moves and behaviour. It was clear that there was a link between relationship breakdown and more frequent moves, but there was also a link between relationship breakdown and women who had never left the parental home. There was also a link between more frequent moves and moves to live alone, with all the women living alone at the time of the interview having moved at least once since they became pregnant. Few of the women who had moved were still living with their parents, although a relatively high proportion of those who had moved twice or more had been back to their parents before moving again. Most of those living with their parents at the time of the interview were no longer in a relationship with the baby's father, and most of them had never moved.

Discussions about housing and living arrangements

We looked in detail at the discussions that women had had with other people about where and with whom they would live during the pregnancy and after the birth. It was quite clear that these discussions were far more limited than discussions concerning what to do about the pregnancy, in spite of the fact that such a high proportion of women actually moved during the period.

Among the married and cohabiting women who had not moved, decisions about housing had either been unnecessary in that couples were in satisfactory accommodation together or any move had been postponed until council housing or their own house was available. Discussions had usually been limited to the couple themselves, although there was some evidence of tension among those who were also living with parents or in-laws.

Among the women living alone with their parents, there had often been little or no discussion about housing since they usually had no option but to stay at home, mainly because their relationship had broken down and they were unable to support themselves away from their parents' home. Discussions here were described by both the women and the grandparents interviewed as brief and to the point. These young women were usually very satisfied both with their accommodation and the practical and emotional support received from parents. The desire for security was often uppermost in their minds.

Nevertheless, most of the women who had never moved had thought of moving, either to be alone with their partner, or to find more satisfactory accommodation, or to establish their independence from their parents. There was evidence of some tension within the parental home, particularly if there was overcrowding or the demands of a growing baby were beginning to cause strain within the household. However, some women, particularly a small group living with their mothers only, clearly had very comfortable and happy little households which nobody saw much point in disturbing, including the grandmother who told her daughter she could stay with her until she was fifty if she wished.

Among the women who had moved, there were often reports of conflicting advice from parents and partners about possible living arrangements, with parents often urging caution and partners suggesting plans which often foundered along with the relationship. Partners were rarely reported as the most helpful person to whom women spoke about housing or living arrangements, unless the couple were already living together and were in a stable relationship.

Parents were reported as being much more helpful although there were difficult discussions with some parents who were less than supportive. Most of the most helpful discussions were with parents who wanted their daughters to stay at home, but mothers often played an important role in helping the women to find accommodation, set up home or deal with housing officers.

Discussions with friends and other relatives about housing and living arrangements were often very specific in terms of offers of accommodation or advice on how to get on the housing list. Few women reported discussions with professionals of any kind about housing or living arrangements, although, interestingly, most of those who had spoken to a midwife had received advice. The few housing officers who had been consulted were not found helpful and indeed some were regarded as the most unhelpful people with whom housing had been discussed.

It was clear that decisions on housing and living arrangements were often not the subject of rational discussion, particularly those which involved a move. Moves were often precipitated by relationship breakdown, which was perhaps not the most comfortable situation in which to have reasoned discussions about where and with whom to live, particularly late in pregnancy or with a tiny baby.

There were many indications in the housing histories of the women that they often felt that the moves were out of their control, not only in deciding where to go but also when they would move. It was clear that many of them had expected to stay longer in accommodation than they had, but that other events, including relationship breakdown, had dictated otherwise. Again, there was a strong impression that many of these young women were often following rather than controlling what was happening to them, and that they felt powerless to influence the course their lives were taking. This was compounded by the fact that they had small babies, many of them had little money and few opportunities to earn much. If they had no partner or had an unemployed partner as well, it was perhaps not surprising that they found themselves sucked into a dependency culture which many of them had never contemplated.

It should, however, be remembered that a substantial minority of women had stable married or cohabiting relationships from the beginning, had planned their pregnancies and had planned any moves they had made. Their comments reflected the greater stability of their lives, and the interviews with fathers in this report, most of whom were in married or cohabiting relationships, also reflect this pattern of behaviour and attitudes which was quite different from the majority of the women in the sample. It is important not to assume that teenage motherhood is necessarily accompanied by relationship breakdown, instability in living arrangements and financial dependency, even if there is plenty of evidence to suggest that these are frequent consequences.

Local authority housing

We have seen that one third of the women were in local authority housing by the time of the interview and a further third were on a local authority waiting list. Half of those in local authority housing were lone mothers and over half of those on the waiting list were living alone with their babies. There was a definite move towards social housing among these teenage mothers, although there was little evidence that women had 'played the system' by trying the non-statutory homeless route, or even knew of its existence. There was, in fact, plenty of evidence of lack of knowledge, long waits on local authority housing lists and an inability to understand the system, let alone manipulate it. We found many examples of lonely and isolated women in unsatisfactory and unsuitable local authority and privately rented accommodation.

These teenage mothers had rarely known anything about local authority housing before they had become pregnant and the few who thought they had known something were usually misinformed about whether they would get priority if they had a baby. There was no evidence to suggest that the women had become pregnant in order to get council housing, although when they were asked whether they thought that teenage mothers had a baby in order to get housing, over half of them thought that it was true, at least of some teenagers. There was, however, general agreement among this group that although it might be true of others it was not true of themselves.

But women were often sceptical about the idea that the possibility of council housing might induce teenagers to become pregnant – 'To be honest, I think they're a bit crazy – all that aggravation just for a flat' – and some were sure that housing was not the main reason for teenagers becoming pregnant – 'They make it sound like the council put you in palaces but they don't... Who'd want to get pregnant for the sake of being put in a council flat?'

The fathers interviewed, most of whom were married or cohabiting, were more likely than the women to think that teenagers became pregnant to get council housing, although, again, some thought that this was true of some rather than all teenage mothers. There were views that it was an 'easy option', and that some teenagers might think it would be a good way of getting away from their parents: 'People who are unhappy at home go out and get pregnant and they get a house...'

The grandparents were less likely to think that housing was an important motivation in teenage pregnancy, and were more likely than their daughters or the fathers to comment on the multiplicity of factors involved in teenage pregnancy, including lack of planning and judgement, as well as unrealistic expectations and lack of understanding of the responsibilities of having a baby. As one grandmother commented: 'Ignorance and carelessness possibly but not housing!' And others agreed that teenage pregnancies were often due to mistakes and lack of information: 'They need to use reliable contraception and know where to get it.'

There were mixed views among the women on whether single teenage mothers were more likely than married couples to get council housing. Some married women thought that single women 'got the pick' of the council housing, a view which was not supported by many of the single women – 'Where's my house then? I'm single. I'm a mother...'

It was thought unlikely that women remained single in order to get council housing. It was clear that most of the women interviewed had thought that they would remain in a relationship with the baby's father when they had decided to continue with the pregnancy, whether they were cohabiting or not. We have seen that both cohabiting and non-cohabiting relationships broke down, but there can be little doubt that few, if any, of the women we interviewed became pregnant with the idea that they would end up as single mothers, let alone that they were motivated by the thought of being a single mother in council accommodation.

However, the fathers interviewed were overwhelmingly of the opinion that single mothers did find it easier to be housed than married couples, and most cited examples among friends and acquaintances. Grandparents, on the other hand, were much less likely to agree. There were comments that single mothers had to know 'the ins and outs' or 'fight tooth and nail' and that their own daughters had not found it easy.

Nevertheless, by the time we conducted our interviews many of the women had turned to social housing, often as a key means in their attempts to become independent, whether they were still in a relationship with the baby's father or not. But it could be argued that few of the women living in local authority accommodation were really independent at all, and that increasing dependency on the state was a marked feature of the experience of many of these teenage women over the period since they had become pregnant. We therefore examined the extent to which they had become increasingly dependent on benefits during this time.

Benefits and the dependency culture

This study originally set out to establish how much the teenage women knew about benefits before and after they became pregnant and how they acquired their information. It became clear at an early stage of the research that, in order to make sense of their decisions on living arrangements and housing moves, we also needed to collect data on the extent to which they had received or tried to claim benefits, and we needed broad information on their other sources of income and the amount that they were living on at the time of the interview.

We have already seen that the proportion of women receiving benefits (excluding the universal child benefit) had increased from one third to over 90 per cent, and, perhaps more important, that over 80 per cent were on income support and 57 per cent were totally dependent on benefits as their sole source of income at the time of the interview. Only 15 per cent were in employment of any kind.

It was striking how few of the women spoke of plans to enter or re-enter employment and it was rare for them to envisage a time when they might not be dependent on benefits, even if they were not happy about their present dependency. Again, there seemed to be an acceptance of a fate over which they perceived themselves to have little control. They often bemoaned the fact that their previous work or study plans had changed as a result of the baby, but few appeared to have any idea of how they might change the pattern of their lives by laying the foundations for a return to work or study. As we have noted before, these women were by no means all unqualified or without employment histories, and yet there appeared to be a marked reluctance to reduce their dependence on benefits.

One of the key factors with some was the expense of childcare and the disincentive to work when most or all of their earnings would be taken by payment for childcare. This was a subject which we could not explore in these interviews, but it is clearly an important issue for further investigation. A number of women made it clear that they would rather be working than dependent on social security benefits, a point reinforced in some of the interviews with grandparents, but they felt themselves caught in a situation where they would be working for nothing after they had paid for childcare.

There was some evidence of women receiving one parent benefit when they were cohabiting with the baby's father or a new partner, and evidence of women receiving income support when they were cohabiting with a partner who was in full-time employment, but the extent to which this could all be called genuine benefit fraud was doubtful, given the fluidity of the constantly changing relationships of some of the women. It must also be remembered that our study did not set out with the primary purpose of investigating or measuring benefits.

The level of income reported by most of the women was low, with an average net weekly income from all sources of just over £100 a week. But there was a striking difference between married women who had an average net income almost twice as large as that of single women whose income averaged £76.80 a week. The average net weekly income from benefits (including child benefit) was just under £70. Those who were dependent solely on benefits had the lowest average net weekly income.

It was perhaps little wonder that so few of the women interviewed thought that teenagers became pregnant to get extra social security benefits. The comments of one woman were echoed by many: 'The extra social security benefits never cover what a baby will cost you. I would say that is definitely untrue unless you're mental.' There were a number of bitter asides at the low level of income from benefits that many of these young women were living on, in spite of the wide variety of benefits some of them were receiving.

However, just over a third of the women thought that some teenagers had a baby because they knew that they would receive extra social security benefits. But again married or cohabiting women were more likely to think this than the single women and most of them thought it was only true of some teenagers, who raised strong emotions among a few women – 'They shouldn't be allowed to have kids if they think like that...'

Nearly half the fathers interviewed thought that some teenagers became pregnant to get extra social security benefits and we heard their views of women choosing the 'easy option' of having a baby, 'raking in so much from the social', and 'not having done a day's work in their life'.

But again, many of the fathers and the grandparents interviewed agreed with most women that the amount received in benefits would hardly cover the costs of having a baby. As one grandmother said: 'Those extra benefits are going to be gone before you can blink your eyes.' Grandparents often thought that any teenager embarking on pregnancy in order to get extra benefits would soon be disabused when she realised the costs involved, and were more likely to share the views of the women that the prospect of extra social security benefits was not an incentive to become pregnant.

Fathers

Discussions about teenage pregnancies tend to centre on teenage women. Concern at the high rate of teenage pregnancies in the United Kingdom compared with other European countries (Babb, 1993) often focuses on the need to help teenage women prevent unplanned pregnancies, whether they result in terminations of pregnancy or births. If the teenagers go ahead and have the baby, the discussion then turns to the problems of lone mothers and their dependence on benefits and social housing. As this report and other research has shown, these concerns are justified by much of the evidence. However, an important missing element in much of the debate is the question of the roles and responsibilities of the young men who play such a crucial part in bringing about a teenage pregnancy.

We gathered extensive information from the women we interviewed about the fathers of their babies and we asked all of them whether we could contact the young men with a view to interviewing them. In this discussion of findings we have already drawn attention to our interviews with fathers. It was perhaps not surprising that we were only able to interview 30 per cent of them, since half of the fathers were no longer in a relationship with the women and one fifth had no contact with the women or their babies at all.

We looked in some detail at the characteristics of the fathers as a whole, as reported by the women, since we were interested in building a picture of the men whose partners became teenage mothers. We found that only just over 20 per cent were teenagers themselves at the time of the birth and that the average age was 23. They were less likely than the women to be of white ethnic origin, although 80 per cent were born in the United Kingdom, but like the women, nearly half of them said they had no religion.

They were rather more likely than the women to have left school when they were 16 or over, although 16 per cent of them had left at 15 or under. Just over a third of both men and women had no educational qualifications, but over 10 per cent of the men had A-levels or a degree. The married and cohabiting men were more likely to have educational qualifications than the others. Over 50 per cent were in employment at the time of the interview, some were still in education or their occupation was unknown, but over a third were unemployed.

The views expressed by those we interviewed were undoubtedly different in important respects from those we would have heard if we had been able to contact all fathers, not least because most of those we interviewed were married or cohabiting with the baby's mother. We were able to identify some interesting characteristics among the fathers we interviewed which we were not able to determine for the main sample. They were even more likely than the women to come from a family where their parents were no longer together, and, like the women, they came from larger than average families, although only a quarter of their mothers were teenagers when they had their first babies. They were better educated than the rest of the fathers and more likely to be in employment. Nevertheless, one third of them said that their work or study plans had changed as a result of the baby which had often led to financial pressures or the postponing of opportunities to acquire further qualifications.

They had usually encouraged the women to continue with their pregnancies and only two of them had discussed termination of pregnancy. In this respect they were sometimes more enthusiastic about having the baby than their partners were.

We were able to establish that the majority of the fathers interviewed had shared in the responsibility of having the baby and supporting it. However, this was by no means true of the majority of those we did not interview, a relatively high proportion of whom had no contact at all with the mother and baby. There was little evidence of any attempt to contribute financially to the support of the babies among those who were no longer in a relationship with the women, and, indeed, over a fifth of them were known to be in married or cohabiting relationships with someone else at the time of the interview.

We know very little about the attitudes of the fathers we were not able to interview, other than those reported by the women, but it was clear that few of them appeared to feel much responsibility for the future of either the mother or the baby. The romantic expectations of many of the women we interviewed had clearly been dispelled in less than two years.

Grandparents

We have referred in this discussion to the views of the grandparents we interviewed, whose perspective on the decisions made by the women added an important dimension to the research. We were able to achieve interviews with more grandparents than fathers of the baby, resulting in an interview with a parent or mother-in-law of nearly half the women in our sample. Most of the interviews were with the baby's maternal grandmothers, over half of whom had been teenage mothers themselves. It must be remembered that half of the women's parents were no longer living together.

We were more likely to interview grandparents with whom the mother and baby were living or in daily contact, so that we were not able to represent the views of grandparents who had little to do with the women we interviewed, either at the time they became pregnant or at the time of the interview. It was perhaps not surprising that we interviewed so few of the grandmothers of babies who were living alone with their mothers.

The main theme running through the interviews with grandparents was one of support and acceptance. They may well have had their doubts about the desirability of the pregnancy or the viability of the relationship, but the majority of them had stated time and again that they would support their daughters in whatever they decided to do. It was interesting that some of them stressed that the decision to continue with the pregnancy had to be their daughter's decision and expressed their reluctance to interfere in any way in case it was held against them in the future – 'It had to be her decision, her choice. We didn't want her to blame us later.' As we have seen, the anxieties which some of them had felt had been proved correct, since nearly half of the daughters were no longer in a relationship with the baby's father. The support promised by the women's parents when the future of the pregnancy was discussed had been heavily called upon by the time of the interview in a substantial minority of cases, particularly by the women who had never moved from the parental home.

Grandparents, like the women themselves and the fathers, were often shocked and surprised by the news of the pregnancy, although it could be argued that they had more reason for surprise. But one third of them were disappointed or upset or angry, and it was clear that they often felt that their daughters were too immature or not ready to have a baby and that they had expectations for their daughters which would not be realised: 'I wanted more for her out of life.' But a quarter of the grandparents were pleased or even delighted by the news. Over half of them said that they had wanted their daughters to have the baby, a quarter said that it must be their own decision and only around one in ten wanted them to have a termination of pregnancy, even though others had considered it.

There were strong indications that the grandparents interviewed often felt themselves presented with a *fait accompli* by their daughters and recognised that any attempt to dissuade them from having the baby would be unwelcome. This confirmed the finding from the interviews with women themselves that women tended to discuss the future of the pregnancy only with people who would agree with their decision to continue with the pregnancy and offer support in that decision.

Support was certainly forthcoming from the vast majority of grandparents interviewed and took many forms, including financial help, baby-sitting and indeed childcare. This was not without its toll on the grandparents, and indeed some had changed their work plans, while one third expressed concern at the pressures they were experiencing, especially if both the mother and her baby were living with them. A small baby might have been acceptable, but by the time of the interview the babies were becoming toddlers and bringing additional pressures, particularly if there were other members of the family in the household.

Around half of the grandparents interviewed thought that things had worked out well, but their views were often tempered by their fears of how things might have worked out. There was evidence of considerable relief that their daughters were no longer in relationships they thought were unsuitable or even dangerous. 'Working out well' often meant 'working out better than expected'.

The support and help of their parents was often of crucial importance to the women in our sample, particularly if their relationship with the baby's father had broken down. But this underlined the isolation and loneliness of many of the women who were living alone with their babies at the time of the interview. As we have seen, we were rarely able to interview their parents, and indeed some of them stressed their poor relationship with their mothers and the fact that their fathers had never been part of their lives.

Planning, outcomes and policy implications

The lack of planning and foresight among the teenage mothers in this study has been a constant theme throughout this report. Only a quarter of the pregnancies were said to have been planned, and even among these planners there may well have been a certain amount of post hoc rationalisation by the time of the interview. Two-thirds of the women said their work or study plans had been changed by their pregnancies, but there was little evidence that many of them had had firm long-term plans when they became pregnant. Even when they decided to continue with their pregnancies it was clear that many of them had unrealistic ideas of what was going to happen in their relationship with the baby's father, where and with whom they were going to live and how they were going to support themselves and their babies. The outcomes have been described in detail within this report and suggest that the teenagers had rarely developed plans for their future or any strategy for realising their expectations. In this respect they were probably not unlike most teenagers, but they were different in that they found themselves with the responsibility for a baby.

One of the aims of the study was to examine the common perceptions that teenagers become pregnant to gain access to council housing and to gain extra social security benefits. It was abundantly clear in the interviews that such intentions had not even entered the heads of most of those interviewed. They had not only been ill-informed about housing and benefits before they became pregnant but many of them had never thought that they would be in a position where they would need to know: 'It wasn't something I ever thought about before I was pregnant, or even when I was expecting the baby.'

An underlying theme which ran through the research was the fact that the vast majority of the teenage mothers in this study were not using contraception at the time that they became pregnant. We did not ask specifically about the use of contraception in an interview which was very long and was designed to explore decision-making about the continuation of the pregnancy and housing and living arrangements. Nevertheless it was clear that few of the women had been actively taking steps to prevent pregnancy. But they were not the only participants, and not only were they taking risks but so were the young men.

Three-quarters of these young people may not have been planning to become pregnant, but they were not planning to avoid pregnancy. The extent to which women risk pregnancy has always been apparent, even if the reasons are complex. It has been demonstrated time and again that ignorance of contraception is not an important factor among most women who have unplanned pregnancies (Allen, 1985; Allen, 1991), even though perceptions that family planning services are inaccessible or lack guarantees of confidentiality may be a deterrent to teenagers (Allen, 1991).

Teenage motherhood has been demonstrated to be beset with problems for a substantial proportion of women. This report, among others, has shown the risk that it will often result in negative short-term outcomes for women in terms of relationship breakdown, financial hardship, dependence on social security benefits, lack of a social life, unexpected responsibilities, unsatisfactory housing, not to mention difficulties in forming new relationships if they are no longer in a relationship with the baby's father. Longer-term negative outcomes have been reported as including poor employment prospects, a high divorce rate, larger than average families, higher than average smoking rates and poorer health status in later life (Wellings et al, 1996).

However, the same cannot necessarily be said of the fathers of babies born to teenage women. It appears from this and other research that for the fathers the short-term consequences of the birth are largely determined by whether they remain in a relationship with the mother. It appears that very few of the fathers were supporting the women or their babies if they were no longer in a relationship with them. Although there was plenty of evidence that many of those who were still in a relationship with the women were not contributing much to the support of their partners and babies, there appeared to be a greater commitment on their part to shoulder at least some of the responsibilities for bringing up the baby. It was impossible to gauge how long this would last, and there were disturbing signs of some rocky relationships even among those who were still together.

But teenagers are unlikely to be much influenced by the possibility of adverse longer-term outcomes to teenage motherhood. Young people simply do not look forward to what might be awaiting them in the future and there is little evidence that they modify their behaviour according to what might or might not happen to them, as can be seen by the high levels of teenage smoking, drinking and drug-taking. There is a common belief, as demonstrated so often among women who become pregnant, that they are somehow immune from the possible or probable consequences of their behaviour or actions.

However, short-term consequences may be a different matter, and the results shown in this research of the breakdown of half the relationships with the baby's father by the time the baby was a year old could well be used in an educative way. Virtually none of these young women would have predicted this outcome, and few thought that they would end up as single lone mothers living in local authority accommodation on benefits within two years of getting pregnant. And yet many of them did, and they were by no means happy with their circumstances. The 'rosy' romantic view of love and motherhood had evaporated for many of these young women who had continued with their pregnancies feeling assured of the lasting support of their partners.

It has been demonstrated that sex education programmes at school have an impact on reducing teenage pregnancies, but research has shown that boys receive less adequate sex education than girls (Allen, 1987). It also showed that sex education programmes which concentrate only on the 'mechanics' of reproduction and contraception are not as successful in preventing teenage pregnancies as those which explore personal relationships and allow time for discussion of feelings and emotions. It is also apparent that myths of happiness engendered by early motherhood need to be dispelled among teenagers of both sexes. We found that the young men were often more keen on the continuation of the pregnancy than the women, but many of them then abandoned the responsibility when it became real.

One of the main messages to be drawn from this analysis is that men should share the responsibility for teenage pregnancy and motherhood. However, it is obviously not enough to issue exhortations to young men that they must acknowledge their role and provide support if their partner has a baby. This report has shown that this would often fall on deaf ears, even if the women concerned were willing or able to pursue claims against them.

There is clearly a need for better and more coordinated programmes of education in sex and personal relationships, which are geared much more to exploring emotions and feelings as well as the roles and responsibilities of both men and women. But these should be laced with robust information about likely short-term outcomes of teenage pregnancies and of the reduced opportunities available to teenage parents, particularly teenage mothers, to lead an independent life and to have fun. Educational programmes must be related to the lives teenagers lead and want to lead. The comments of one single non-working mother who was living alone with her baby summarised the views of an important minority and could be the starting point of any educational programme: 'If I could live my life over again, I'd be working now and I wouldn't have a kid.'

But there are many factors, apart from the romantic view of love and motherhood, to be overcome if educational programmes are to be successful. The belief that some teenagers become pregnant to get away from home and live on social security benefits because they cannot get a job was still prevalent, even among the women interviewed. It is well demonstrated that the longer a woman remains in education and the more qualifications she has the less likely she is to be a teenage mother. But cause and effect should not be confused and a woman is clearly likely to stay longer in education and acquire more qualifications if she does not have a baby at an early age. There is a need not only to help lone parents return to work, but also to help all teenage mothers to improve their educational and vocational qualifications so that they are more able to become independent. As one of the grandmothers interviewed pointed out: 'If the mothers are blamed or victimised, then the children suffer and become our damaged adults of the future.'

Conclusion

A positive approach to reducing the adverse effects of teenage motherhood, while at the same time concentrating resources on reducing teenage pregnancy rates, is clearly essential. But there must be a change in the culture that accepts that young men can abandon all responsibility for their babies in spite of having taken no steps to prevent pregnancies and having encouraged their partners to continue with their pregnancies because they think abortion is wrong. Perhaps it is not surprising that men feel increasingly marginalised in our society today when they put themselves so deliberately outside the frame. But there are many dangers in sustaining a culture in which an important minority of young men have no role or responsibility in either work or family. This has been a recurrent theme in this research.

In this report we have looked in depth at less than two years in the lives of a wide variety of teenage mothers and presented a complex picture of their characteristics and the factors affecting their decisions about the pregnancy and their living and housing arrangements. The results have made depressing reading at times, but we end on the positive note that half of the relationships had not broken down, and that among these teenage mothers were many who were happy with their babies, in stable relationships with young men who shared their responsibilities and maintained the delight so many of them had shown when their partners became pregnant. Not everyone was on social security benefits, some of the young women were working or studying for further qualifications and some were living in their own homes. The future was undoubtedly not all gloomy for many of the others, some of whom were redesigning their lives with the help and support of their parents or new partners while others were determined to make a new life for themselves and their babies.

Appendix

Methods

(a) The study population

The main evidence collected in this study came from semi-structured interviews conducted in 1996 with 84 women who had had a baby in 1995 when aged between 16 and 19 in three areas: Hackney, Leeds and Solihull. Interviews took place with 27 women in Hackney, 34 in Leeds and 23 in Solihull. Our aim had been to interview 100 women – approximately 33 in each area, but we experienced difficulty in achieving sufficient responses within a reasonable time from the available sampling frames in Solihull and Hackney, although we achieved our target in Leeds (see below).

We also interviewed 24 fathers of the babies: 20 in Leeds, 2 in Hackney and 2 in Solihull. We interviewed 41 grandparents of 39 babies (both maternal grandparents were interviewed in two cases): 8 grandparents in Hackney, 13 in Solihull and 20 in Leeds. Most of the grandparents interviewed were maternal grandmothers (35), but we also interviewed 2 paternal grandmothers in Solihull and 4 maternal grandfathers (one in Hackney, one in Leeds and two in Solihull).

(b) Sampling frame and design

The sample was generated from lists of all women who had had a first baby when aged between 16 and 19 in hospitals in the three areas: Hackney, Leeds and Solihull. Access was negotiated through the consultant obstetricians in the three hospitals which cooperated in the study. The records of all 16–19 year old mothers over a period of three to six months in 1995 were identified by hospital staff and scrutinised to ensure that the baby had not died or been adopted and that it was a first baby. (The period varied according to the number of births identified in each area.) This constituted a complete series of first births to 16–19 year old mothers and no sampling took place. The aim was to interview women when the babies were approximately 12 months old, but it was recognised that there would be a spread of ages of the babies at the time of the interview because of the relatively low numbers of births to teenage mothers, particularly in Solihull.

It was vital to ensure complete patient confidentiality, and it was agreed that the approach to the women should be made by the hospital. Two letters inviting the woman to take part in the study were sent out from the relevant hospital: one from a consultant obstetrician at the hospital and one from Policy Studies Institute. The pack also included a sheet for women to complete with details of (up-to-date) address and telephone number where they could be contacted (and change of name if appropriate) together with a reply-paid envelope to be returned to PSI. PSI needed this information to be able to contact the women at all, since we did not have their details. Reminder letters were sent by the hospital approximately three weeks after the first letter and a final reminder letter three weeks after this. It should be noted that PSI could not follow up non-respondents by any other means. Women were offered a £10 voucher if they participated in the survey.

Access to the fathers and the grandparents was achieved through asking the women interviewed whether we could approach them.

(c)   Response

The babies were born between March and November 1995 and interviewing took place between June and November 1996 when the babies were on average 13 months old. The interviewing took place in Hackney first, followed by Solihull and then Leeds.

We were aware that other researchers had encountered great difficulty in ensuring a good response from teenage mothers, for a variety of reasons, not least their lack of motivation and reliability in keeping appointments (see Speak et al, 1995), as well as the fact that at least half of them are known to have moved after the birth. The only addresses which were available to this research were those of the women at the time of the birth.

We therefore agreed with the hospitals that the numbers of teenage mothers to be identified from their records should exceed those we aimed to interview by one third. In the event we had to draw a fresh sampling frame in both Leeds and Hackney. We were unable to do this in Solihull since we had already covered most of the relevant 1995 births in our original list.

We had only one or two refusals to participate although a small number of respondents did not keep appointments. The relatively low response rate was mainly attributable to non-response to the letter. The reasons for this were beyond the control of the investigators: (i) we had no means of knowing to what extent the women had moved without leaving a forwarding address or without being forwarded letters which were sent to their original address; (ii) we had no other means of following up non-respondents since we did not have access to their names and addresses and could not breach their confidentiality with the hospital; (iii) although the letters were clear about the intentions of the survey, it is possible that women might have been suspicious about the reasons for the research; (iv) it is probable that the inertia or lack of interest among teenage mothers identified by other researchers played a part.

Our impression from conversations with the teenage mothers whom we succeeded in interviewing was that the lack of response from their counterparts was due mainly to the fact that they had moved. This impression was confirmed by professionals working in the hospitals, particularly in Hackney where there was said to be considerable movement of population, particularly in this age-group.

Perhaps the main reason for the relatively low response from the fathers of the babies (29 per cent) was that only half of the women were still in a relationship with the father of the baby at the time of the interview, and a relatively high proportion of those no longer in a relationship with the father had no contact with him at all. In other cases the women were reluctant for us to approach the fathers, while in other cases the fathers were reluctant to be approached. We interviewed grandparents of nearly half (46 per cent) of the babies. Women did not always have close relationships with the grandparents of the baby, and, in addition, we were unable to interview those who lived some distance away.

There was a clear over-representation of fathers in Leeds and some over-representation of grandparents in Leeds. The fathers interviewed were mostly married or cohabiting with the women interviewed, which was more common in Leeds than in the other areas. The greater closeness of family ties in Leeds could well have resulted in easier access to grandparents.

(d)   Questionnaires and interviewers

The questionnaires were developed drawing on previous work funded by the Department of Health conducted by one of the authors (Allen, 1985) on counselling services for women seeking a termination of pregnancy. Many similar issues arose in the present study, including information on conversations with key people involved in the decisions made by the young women about their pregnancies. We also drew on other studies conducted by the same author which interviewed teenagers about sexual health and fertility issues (Allen, 1987; Allen, 1991).

The questionnaires were fully structured, in that the exact wording of each question was specified and the questions were in a predetermined sequence. The questionnaires for the grandparents and fathers contained many of the same questions as those in the questionnaires for the women. A fairly high proportion of questions allowed for an open ended response and the interviewers were expected to record the answers verbatim. The interviews were carried out by a team of experienced interviewers and PSI staff.

(e) Data analysis

The analysis of the type of data generated in a study of this kind is multifaceted using both quantitative and qualitative methods. The questionnaires were analysed using the predetermined codes on the questionnaires, as well as coding frames developed from detailed textual analysis of the open-ended questions. The use of the software package Quantum enabled us to analyse the hierarchical data structure. Verbatim quotes were extracted from the questionnaires and selected for inclusion in the report in a rigorous manner in proportion to the numbers making such comments.

The responses of the women were related, as appropriate, to the responses of the fathers and grandparents of the babies who were interviewed (see especially Chapter 8 of the report).

The study was essentially qualitative in design, but we considered it important to establish a firm quantitative framework for the analysis. The main report draws on the quantitative data to illustrate the wide variety of characteristics and experience of the teenage mothers from the time that they became pregnant to the time of the interview. The extent to which the quantitative data can be regarded as a basis for generalisation to a wider population must be treated with some caution, but it is fair to say that the data are much in line with other recent research and provide a firm basis for the qualitative analysis presented in the report.

References

Allen I (1985) *Counselling Services for Sterilisation, Vasectomy and Termination of Pregnancy.* London: Policy Studies Institute

Allen I (1987) *Education in Sex and Personal Relationships.* London: Policy Studies Institute

Allen I (1991) *Family Planning and Pregnancy Counselling Projects for Young People.* London: Policy Studies Institute

Babb P (1993) 'Teenage conceptions and fertility in England and Wales, 1971–91'. *Population Trends.* No 74. HMSO

Burghes L (1993) *One Parent Families, Policy Options for the 1990s.* Joseph Rowntree Foundation

Burt M R (1986) 'Estimating the public costs of teenage childbearing.' *Family Planning Perspect.* 18: 221–226

Bury J (1984) *Teenage Pregnancy in Britain.* London: Birth Control Trust

Clark E (1989) *Young Single Mothers Today: a qualitative study of housing and support needs.* National Council for One Parent Families

Clark E and Coleman J (1991) *Growing up Fast: a follow up study of teenage mothers in adult life.* Trust for the Study of Adolescence

Ford R, Marsh A and McKay S (1995) *Changes in Lone Parenthood.* Social Security Research Report No 40. London: HMSO

Ermisch J (1996) *Household Formation and Housing Tenure Decisions of Young People.* ESRC Research Centre, University of Essex

Hopkinson A (1976) *Single Mothers: The First Year.* Scottish Council for Single Parents

Hudson F and Ineichen B (1991) *Taking it Lying Down: Sexuality and Teenage Motherhood.* London: Macmillan

Institute of Housing (1993) *One Parent Families – are they jumping the housing queue?* Briefing paper

Joshi H (1990) 'The cash opportunity costs of child bearing – an approach to estimation using British data'. *Population Studies.* Vol. XLIV: 41–60

Kiernan K (1995) *Transition to Parenthood: young mothers, young fathers – associated factors and life experiences.* Welfare State Programme Discussion Paper 113. London School of Economics

Marsh A, Ford R and Finlayson L (1997) *Lone Parents, Work and Benefits.* Social Security Research Report No 61. London: HMSO

McGuire A and Hughes D (1995) *The Economics of Family Planning Services.* A report prepared for the Contraception Alliance. London: Family Planning Association

McRae S (1993) *Cohabiting Mothers.* London: Policy Studies Institute

NHS Centre for Reviews and Dissemination (1997) *Effective Health Care: Preventing and reducing the adverse effects of unintended pregnancies.* Volume 3, Number 1. Churchill Livingstone

OPCS (1986) *Birth Statistics for England and Wales, 1985* FM1 No 12. London: HMSO

OPCS (1988) *Birth Statistics for England and Wales, 1986* FM1 No 15. London: HMSO

ONS (1996) *Population Trends.* Winter

ONS (1997a) *Birth Statistics for England and Wales, 1995* FM1 No 24. London: HMSO

ONS (1997b) *Conceptions in England and Wales, 1995* Monitor Population and Health, FM1 97/2. London: HMSO

Phoenix A (1991) *Young Mothers?* Oxford: Blackwell

Russell J K (1988) 'Early teenage pregnancy'. *Maternal and Child Health.* 13 (2) 43–46

Simms M and Smith C (1986) *Teenage Mothers and their Partners.* London: HMSO

Smith T (1993) 'Influence of socioeconomic factors on attaining targets for reducing teenage pregnancies'. *British Medical Journal.* 306: 1232–5

Speak S, Cameron S, Woods R and Gilroy R (1995) *Young Single Mothers: barriers to independent living.* London: Family Policy Studies Centre

Wilson F (1980) 'Antecedents of adolescent pregnancy'. *Journal of Biosocial Science.* 12: 141–152

Wilson S H, Brown T P and Richards R G (1992) 'Teenage conception and contraception in English regions'. *Journal of Public Health Medicine.* 14: 17–25

Wellings K, Wadsworth J, Johnson A, Field J, Field B, Petruckevick A et al (1996) *Teenage Sexuality, Fertility and Life Chances.* A report for the Department of Health using data from the National Survey of Sexual Attitudes and Lifestyles. London School of Hygiene and Tropical Medicine